OCEAN NOMAD

The Complete Atlantic Sailing Crew Guide

~

*How to Catch a Ride, &
Contribute to a Healthier Ocean*

© 2017 Suzanne van der Veeken
Oceanpreneur Publishing
Photographs: © 2017 Suzanne van der Veeken
Map illustrations: © 2017 Rafał Zatwarnicki

Editors: Jessica McCarthy, Jose van der Veeken, Dirk Aardsma, Ludo Lévêque
Interior book design: Paul Uhl
Cover design: Miladinka Milic
Front cover photo: Jean-François Tricot
Author photo: Marcel Verheggen

First Edition September 2017
ISBN 978-90-827454-2-9

Ocean Nomad is available at www.oceannomad.co
For special book requests contact ahoy@oceannomad.co

By Suzanne van der Veeken
oceanpreneur.co

TESTIMONIALS

"A must read for everyone who loves the ocean. Suzanne hands you the guidelines for sailing adventures, and she clears the path for all your 'but what ifs' and the 'yes but' . . . . Yes, the book is about hitch-sailing and loving the ocean, but most of all she encourages you to take the step to pursue the dream instead of postponing it. So read the book, explore what works for you and create your adventure!"
— **LONNEKE RENTINCK** (NETHERLANDS)

"After meeting Suzanne in January 2014, I followed her adventures closely via social media. When she started her first hitch-sail adventure I was absolutely amazed: is it really possible to cross an ocean if you don't have sailing experience!? Inspired by Suzanne's adventures and her very well-provided details and information on the subject, I felt totally ready to throw off the bowlines myself. And I did! To me, Suzanne is THE example of 'if you put your mind to it, you can do it'. This book will inspire and inform many more adventurous souls around the world. Thanks, Suus for being such an inspiration and friend!"
— **JANNEKE DIJKHUIS** (NETHERLANDS)

"Suzanne was the last of twelve hitchhikers (barnacles, as we decided to call this 'breed') I picked up between Grenada and Dominican Republic. What a pleasure! She's turned hitching rides on boats from a sketchy endeavor to graceful art. Do as she says. She is the doyenne of sailboat hitchhikers!"
— **CLIFF LYON** (CAPTAIN)

"I loved reading about the boat hitchhiking adventures and how Suzanne does sensitisation work about our oceans. So much that she inspired me to try the boat hitchhiking thing as well. From the first moment I read her writing, I knew that I wanted to do the same! I just loved reading with how much passion she realises her dream step by step. When we were full of doubts if it was the right thing to do, I returned to what she wrote and re-convinced myself that it was all for the best. And it worked out! We sailed from the Canary Islands to Cape Verde. There we spent one month looking for a boat to cross the Atlantic Ocean. We finally found one and went from Cape Verde to Barbados. Suzanne has been a major source of inspiration!"

— **PAULINA** (LUXEMBOURG)

"Having sailed with Suzanne from France to the Canary Islands, Cape Verde and St Lucia I have seen how enthusiastic and committed to her mission she is. Having read her book now, I can sense the enthusiasm coming out at me from the pages and feel that her book is an inspiration and fantastic guide on hitch sailing and ocean preservation. It should be on every yacht out there at sea."

— **STEVE GREEN** (YACHT MASTER INSTRUCTOR AND OCEAN MASTER)

"Suzanne's book is a two-part guide book. The first half guides you into the nomadic world of sailors. Once you have arrived, the second half implores your vital participation and duty to become an ocean advocate. This ambitious guide book is the spark that will ignite your sense of adventure and provoke your compassion to create a better world."

— **MONIQUE MILLS** (CANADA—CAPTAIN AND OCEAN CITIZEN)

"I hadn't even gone further than Mediterranean and seen the ocean even once in my life. I found out about Suzanne who stood out there with her stories across the Atlantic. The positive vibe she was sparkling in our correspondence encouraged me, and has always made me sure that I could do whatever I dream of. Thank you, Suzanne for helping me opening up a new path, a new mindset of life, not only with the way you hit the oceans but also with you being so sensitive about the future of our world and the oceans and making efforts for it."

— **BARBAROS** (TURKEY)

DEDICATION

My little nephew Hugo and niece Mathilde
My wish is for you to experience the beauty of ocean

My Parents
Thank you for providing a playful outdoorsy childhood. And for the
eternal mental support, no matter how crazy the adventure.

The Ocean
Thank you for giving adventure, play and life. This book
is one way to give back.

And to all the Adventure Seekers!
On the ocean, you'll find it.

FOREWORD

By Edwin Butter & Marjo Boertien
Las Palmas de Gran Canaria, June 2017
Sailing Research Vessel 'Grace of Aberdeen'
Founders of *OceanConservation.org.uk*

"Are you crossing the Atlantic?"

"Are you also looking for a boat?"

You will likely hear these questions dozens of times a day when in the *'Muelle Deportivo of Las Palmas de Gran Canaria'* (the harbour) between November and February each year. The Canary Islands, and Las Palmas, in particular, are a very logical and convenient place to prepare for an Atlantic Ocean crossing, so it is no surprise that many sailing yachts and (aspiring) sailors gather here every year.

Captains and crew come from all walks of life and with all kinds of ambitions and expectations. For some, crossing an ocean on a sailing boat is a once in a lifetime adventure long dreamed of, for others, it is the start of many ocean crossings. For some, it is already a way of life, and for others, it is 'just' a means to get the boat and themselves to the Caribbean as soon as possible.

Whatever the reason for crossing, it is not something to be taken lightly. Besides technical issues, sailing experience, food, and safety (just to name a few of the issues) it is super important to get along with each other on board. After all, there is no choice but to do this together, 24 hours a day over the course of three weeks. It's wise to be picky, both as captain and as crew!

We, as boat owners and liveaboards, are picky indeed when it comes to taking on crew. The most important thing for us is 'the personal click', sailing experience is not essential for us (so don't let a lack of sailing experience hold you back!). Having a good spirit on board is vital when embarking on an adventure like an ocean crossing.

Some crew thinks the selection easy. A befriended captain took on two inexperienced sailors as crew, who arrived on board with huge bags of food supplies and drinks. They figured that they would not have to pay for the passage ("You are going anyway") if they brought their own food and cook their own meals in their cabin on a small camping gas cooker! Needless to say, they did not pass the test. It doesn't work like this. And it does make sense to prepare yourself.

There are many stories, both about crew and about captains. Good stories as well as bad stories. More often than not, the crossing is a great experience for both. And sometimes it is not. For both parties, it would be very nice to find out if things work out before departure.

This is how we got to know Suzanne. We remember very well meeting her and her fellow crew members. All of them, people with lots of dreams and a drive to make their dreams come true. Some things the aspiring sailors told about the state of the boat and the (large) number of crew did not make sense to us though. Especially the fact that the captain/owner seemed to change crew as quickly as he would change his underwear because he didn't like the fellow, we found very peculiar. As things got even weirder, the whole crew decided to leave. And rightly so!

There they were, on the terrace of the *Sailor's Bay*, a group of more than ten people, seeing their dream dissolve into thin air. They were sharing their experience and picking up their pieces. It was a touching sight how they helped each other through this time.

Suzanne surely was one of the first to pick up her pieces and move on. Back to the adventure, she had started, but in a different way: the way that would suit her best. She kept on believing that she was going to sail the ocean; not crossing was not an option!

And of course, she managed. Not only did she cross enjoying it fully, but she also developed a great interest and knowledge in 'ocean issues'.

This is how Suzanne stands out for us: her never ending enthusiasm and eagerness to learn and discover more possibilities in life, and actually go on and just do it. She is not just making her dreams come true, but she is also caring for the planet she discovers. Even more so, with this book, she is giving you all it takes to do the same!

When we talk to people about why we dedicate our lives to raising awareness about the oceans and the actions people can take to preserve them, we often get the question "Is it really that bad?" Yes, ladies and gentlemen, it is that bad. The oceans reflect the state of our planet as a whole: the depletion of the waters due to overfishing, the effect of land based agriculture, plastic pollution, climate change messing up ecosystems and so on, show us that we are at a tipping point in human history. The coming decades will be crucial, and the good news is that there is a lot that can be done to change our direction. If there is one way to see and feel this for yourself, it is by doing an ocean crossing.

In this Suzanne also stands out as a leading example: she shows that you can enjoy life to the max *and* take care of the planet at the same time. So it is absolutely great that she took the time and effort to create a reference book that has it all: extensive information about how to hitchhike the Atlantic and how to prepare for it as (aspiring) crew, with a consciousness about what you can do for the oceans. A holistic approach so to speak, to make a dream come true.

So, go ahead, dig in, read, explore! Preferably with at least one toe in the sea, a lake or a river, just to get a touch of the feeling how everything is connected through water.

Guaranteed you will be inspired by Suzanne's writing!

PREFACE

n 2014, I decided to take the dream to sail around the world to the next level and see if I could somehow do an ocean passage. I figured if I can successfully cross an ocean, I can continue chasing the dream to sail around the world. I was curious what it would be like to be on a boat for a longer period of time. Are the waves really as high as in the movies? What would it feel like to see land after weeks on the water? Is the Caribbean really like I imagine it to be? There was only one way to find out: to go for it! There were no excuses: my studies were finished, I had no housing commitments, no boyfriend, no best friends' wedding and the cold winter was approaching. The timing for a big first ocean adventure was perfect!

There were just a few challenges to tackle. I had no boat, I had no idea about sailing, and the adventure funds were pretty low. And as ambitious as I am, I didn't just want to sail; I wanted the whole package. I wanted to learn about all the aspects of seamanship, technical aspects of the boats, navigation, energy management, weather, the stars and I wanted to learn more about the ocean itself. I wanted to learn from the sailors.

As a nature lover and advocate, I felt the need to contribute, to attach a mission, an exploration, and meaningfulness to the adventure. I wanted to see what was going on with our oceans, marine life, and find ways to make a positive change for the good. I wanted to learn all this by being out there and exploring the sailing lifestyle. I wanted a lot. I was not the only one looking for this. I was curious, determined and naïve. Did I actually know what I was getting myself into by catching a ride across the Atlantic?

No. I did not. Fast forward two years later . . , I do. I have figured it all out! I hitched a ride across the Atlantic three times now. I threw myself into the whole sailing scene to learn whatever there is to learn when crossing the Atlantic Ocean as crew. I've experienced high seas, low seas, good times, bad times. I have learned loads about sailing, seamanship, and people.

Almost every day someone asks me: "How do you find a boat?" This can't be summarised in one sentence. Finding a boat is one thing, finding the *right* boat is what makes all the difference.

Figuring out how to tackle this Atlantic Ocean adventure can be a maze for a newbie. There wasn't a go-to resource on how to catch a ride across the Atlantic. Loads of research, experimentation, lessons learned, and three ocean crossings later, I have realised that now I am the resource. I decided to put it all down and help you make this happen: happily, safely and meaningfully. With this book, I aim to help you navigate the wild wild west of figuring out the Atlantic Ocean crossing as a newbie. This is the book I wish was out there when I naively started the 'Let's catch a ride across the Atlantic' adventure.

I discovered so much as a result from crossing oceans. What has struck me most when going across is what I learned about the ocean itself, how important it is for us, and the serious state of decline it is in. As ocean nomads, we can 'just' cross an ocean and have a memorable adventure, but we can do more! We can make the experience truly rewarding, for ourselves, the ocean and for the places we visit. The ocean brings us so much. As fanatic users, we are responsible for bringing life back into the ocean.

I hope this book inspires, encourages and motivates you to make your ocean-crossing dreams happen. In addition to practical tips, information and stories, I've included some actionable takeaways on how sailors can make a positive difference for the ocean. This book provides the bearings. It's up to you to gather the courage, take action and make the most out of it. NOW is the time, because 'later' may never arrive. I wish you a safe, happy and adventurous journey.

—Suzanne

TABLE OF CONTENTS

INTRODUCTION

CATCHING A RIDE ACROSS THE ATLANTIC

No boat, no budget and no sailing experience, but a dream to cross the Atlantic Ocean on a sailboat. How can you make this ocean travel adventure happen?

Every year thousands of sailboats cross the Atlantic Ocean. It's a thing. Many of them like to have crew to make the trip more relaxed, more fun, and sometimes more affordable. Then, there are people out there, like you and I, aspiring to sail the Atlantic Ocean passage but don't have a boat.

So, on the dock, do you just put your thumb out, hold a sign saying 'Caribbean' or 'Europe' and wait for a sailing boat to pass by? If it were that easy, then I would not have had to write this book. It is not a straightforward endeavour. There are a few aspects you have to be mindful of to make an Atlantic ocean crossing a happy and safe ride.

When I first started exploring this adventure, after a few weeks of searching on the internet, I thought I had found the coolest boat, captain, and crew in the world. It sounded too good to be true. It was. I had no idea what I was getting myself into. I should have done more research. I learned how not to pursue this adventure. My determination though has also taught me how to do it. I have sailed across the Atlantic Ocean three times on strangers' sailboats: twice from Europe to the Caribbean, and once from the Caribbean to Europe. All these experiences were unique—

different routes, different weather, different boats, different people, different everything! I wouldn't change a thing—I would do every one of the crossings again in a heartbeat.

I have written this guide based on the lessons learned from my Atlantic Ocean boat hitchhiking adventures, and insights from ten years of solo slow travelling around the world. But the book is more than just a compilation of my tips, lessons learned during the crossings and stories from the four boat's which I've crewed on. To give a sense of what it's like on both sides of the wheel, I surveyed 90 Atlantic Ocean crossers: 58 persons who have sailed across as crew, and 32 captains who crossed the Atlantic with crew. I asked them questions about their Atlantic sailing journey.

The comprehensiveness of this book has made the guide not only useful for crew members, but captains can also get ideas on where to find crew, how to prepare them and how to handle crew related tasks. Also, enjoy the read about what an Atlantic Ocean passage is like from a hitch-hiker's perspective.

In this book, you will find an ocean of information that will help turn your Atlantic Ocean sailing dream into reality. It has been designed to guide you from the idea of "someday I would like to sail across the Atlantic, but, but, but. . . ," to freeing up the time to do it and sail across to the other side. Discover whether ocean sailing is for you, where to find a boat, how to assess the safety, what to pack, and how to make a positive impact along the way. It's a useful guide for sailing newbies as well as those with some sailing experience who want to know where to start looking for a boat to cross the Atlantic, what to do to prepare, or who just want to read more about what it's like. Whether you find a boat in advance online, or locally in the harbour, whether you contribute money for the trip or not, here's the information you need as a first-time ocean crosser to prepare yourself and jump happily and safely on board. Become excited, be a well-prepared crew member, have a happy journey of searching and sailing the Atlantic Ocean, and be hooked to this life-style forever! Become inspired for ocean adventure, make your dream come true, and who knows—you might even become an ocean ambassador. "Someday' I would like to make a big sailing trip!" starts TODAY!

HOW TO NAVIGATE THIS BOOK?

The book has four sections: On shore, On the Ocean, On the Other Side, and Ocean Love & Conservation. Each section includes a number of chapters containing an abundance of stories, ideas, actionable tips and related internet resources.

You can take the guide with you to use as a handbook while you're on the journey. Each section and chapter stand on its own. You can use the Table of Contents or to navigate directly to the topic of your interest. I have tried to describe the most logical order of the preparations and the actions to take when living the 'hitch a ride across the Atlantic' adventure. Chronologically the book helps you to go from dream state into action state. If you're not sure whether ocean travel is for you or not, read the first chapter: The Adventure! Hopefully, this will ignite a spark for you to set out on your own adventure. The 'On Shore' section talks about the boat search and preparation. It covers what you need to bear in mind while still on shore. If you are curious to find out what the adventure is like, navigate to the 'On The Ocean' section. After that, you probably can't wait to get started and should start reading again from the beginning of this book. The 'On the Other Side' section provides the bearings for leaving the boat and moving on. If you want to learn about the ocean and contribute to a healthier ocean, set course to the Ocean Love & Conservation section. You can start making a difference: today.

The parts in which I talk about my personal experiences are high-lighted in blue (my favourite colour). You'll be reading quotes of the surveyed people when it says Hitch-sailor: " . . . " or Captain " . . . ". Out of respect to a captain, and the new owner, I refer to the boat I did not cross the Atlantic with, with an alias name 'The Bounty'. Sailors speak a different language. Words that used to be foreign to me and I think may be new to you, I have put in **bold.** You can check the meaning in the Glossary at the end of the book. Navigate to the Appendix for *measurement conversions.*

WHAT'S IN THE BOOK?

In short . . .

SECTION 1: ON SHORE

1. **The Adventure**
   What's the adventure all about? Should you do it or not.

2. **Atlantic Ocean Passage: The Bearings**
   Learn about the sailing routes and seasons across the North Atlantic. From where and when do boats cross? How much time and money does it cost? What weather can I expect?

3. **The Search For a Ride**
   How, where and when can you find a boat? This chapter includes a thorough analysis of relevant crew websites.

4. **Atlantic-Passage Harbours**
   Practical destination and boat search information on the main ports of departure and arrival.

5. **Safety & Happiness Check**
   Go through the safety and happiness checklist to find out if it's a reliable, safe, and happy captain, crew, and boat match. Learn what captains expect from you as a crew member. What agreements should you make.

6. **Take-Aways For The Captain**
   The focus of the book is on crew. But for a safe and happy passage, collaboration, communication, and expectation management between the captain and crew is key. This chapter provides some useful info for captains considering taking on crew.

7. **Preparation: On Land**
   Good preparation can make or break the experience. How to prepare as crew? What should you think of before stepping on board? From telling your mum, the packing challenge, and preparation for seasickness, it is all here.

8. **Preparation: On Board**
   You're on board! Before throwing off the bowlines, there are preparations to be made. Learn about provisioning, crew safety measures, and how to be ready the day you leave.

SECTION 2: ON THE OCEAN

9. **Stories from the Ocean**
   What is it like to be on the ocean? Read ocean travelogues from the different boats I've been on.

10. **Life at Sea, Happenings & Situations**
    "We have a situation" is a phrase you'll hear on every boat, multiple times, if not daily. What happens at sea? And how do you tackle various situations as a crew member? Learn about being on 'Watch', and how to deal with aspects like cooking, washing, sleep, boredom, limited resources, waste, and fellow crew.

SECTION 3: ON THE OTHER SIDE

11. **Landing And Leaving**
    Can you just leave the boat? How to dispose of waste? Is it easy to find another boat or job once you arrive?

12. **Back On Land**
    What's it like in the Caribbean? What's it like in Europe? How to go around on a budget? Where to find a coconut?

SECTION 4: OCEAN LOVE & CONSERVATION

13. **Why is the Ocean So Important?**
    By experiencing the ocean first hand on a boat, you will be amazed by its beauty, gain a deep respect for its power, and also see its decline. Why is the ocean so important in the first place?

14. **What is Happening To The Oceans?**
    We hear about climate change, plastic pollution, overfishing and many other challenges! But what is actually happening to the oceans?

15. **What is Being Done to Save it?**
    Read about a selection of ocean organisations that inspire, provide good data, and that can help you learn more about the ocean. They are all eager for you to get involved!

16. **What Can You Do as Crew?**
    What can we do as a crew member to make a difference for the ocean? How can you minimise your impact? How can you contribute? What can we do at the frontline, as sailors, with our special connection to the sea?

On Shore

1

THE ADVENTURE

*"Twenty years from now you will be
more disappointed by the things that you didn't
do than by the ones you did do. So throw off the
bowlines. Sail away from the safe harbour.
Catch the trade winds in your sails.
Explore. Dream. Discover."*

– H. JACKSON BROWN'S MOTHER
(Mother of Writer)

SHOULD YOU DO IT OR NOT? HOW TO START? Why is it such a magical adventure? In this chapter, you read why you should take the plunge to cross the Atlantic Ocean on a sailing boat. And, when you should maybe not! What does crewing involve? Read a little sneak peak of what it's like: the exciting parts, and the tough parts. Get the mindset of Walt Disney's "if it can be dreamt, it can be done." Excuses like "I don't have money" or "I don't have time" will be thrown overboard for good.

1.1 WHY SAIL ACROSS THE ATLANTIC OCEAN?

If two-thirds of our world is ocean, why do we spend most our lives on land? There's a whole watery world to be explored out there. Exploring by boat gives the ultimate freedom feeling. You just go where the wind blows. It's a sustainable and adventurous way to travel long distances.

A sailboat can bring you to places where no one else goes, while being entirely surrounded by nature. You don't have to imagine how Columbus felt when he saw land after weeks on the open water—you can experience it for yourself! Here are some reasons you should take the plunge and cross the Atlantic Ocean.

It's an adventure

Life on land is pretty comfortable, isn't it? For life on a boat that isn't always the case.

It's a big step out of the comfort zone without the luxuries you are familiar with on land. To take on the challenge of an Atlantic crossing will guarantee an adventure. With only the power of nature, you can travel all the way to another continent. Isn't that incredible in itself?! It's how it was done back in the days before airplanes and cargo ships. Yes, you can prepare, plan and plot but you still have to hop on the boat and just do it. And there is no way back! Be prepared to be in an adventurous state of mind. It's a new situation that you put yourself into, and it won't all go as planned. There will be many situations to tackle that are beyond your current knowledge or experience. You'll need to be inventive. You will become more self-reliant and expand your skills and abilities. Crossing the Atlantic Ocean is an expedition, though not the most challenging ocean **passage** out there. It's an 'easy' one, and a fantastic starting point to motivate you to conquer more oceans.

It's simple and sustainable

Air travel pollutes the environment and is expensive. Cruise ships and cargo ships are even worse. Not only for the amount of fuel they burn, and the waste they create, but also for disturbing marine life with the noise they make. A sailing boat impacts the environment but it's minor, and we can make it minimal (more about that in Chapter 16). A sailboat moves forward, powered by the wind. Electronics can be powered by the sun and by the wind. Travelling by sailboat is simple and sustainable.

Escape the winter

The Atlantic sailing routes and weather patterns fall perfectly to escape winter or hotness in the Caribbean. The **trade winds** pick up just in time to carry you away from Europe when the cold sets in. Every day at sea it gets a little warmer as you get closer to your final destination: the tropics! Then, as the Caribbean weather gets super-hot and hurricane season approaches, it's a perfect time to head back to Europe to enjoy springtime flowers, greenery and fresh summer fruits.

Digital detox

Almost everywhere we go, at any time of day or night, we are connected. With the internet just one click away, and an overload of interesting stuff to check, it takes willpower to resist the urge to connect. An ocean passage eliminates the temptation altogether! You're away from everything, long enough to disconnect from everything but nature and your shipmates. Being in nature allows you to just be. It's a major disconnection from society, long enough to rethink life and rewire yourself for the way forward. There is no WiFi*. No media. No stress. No deadlines. No pressure. No people wanting something from you, except for the captain expecting you to take part in duties on board. That's (in most cases) fun stuff. It may take a couple of days of restlessness to adjust to the peace of the sea. But the rewards are worth it. Being offline allows you to have the most beautiful and deep conversations without anyone being half-present because the phone is distracting you. Being offline means realising what you love the most. You will create space in your mind and in your life to ponder what truly matters. You will master the art of being present, which I believe is the most happiness generating skill you can have.

A way to reach paradise

The ocean is the real destination of this trip. But let's be honest, the Caribbean islands are pure paradise! Imagine arriving in the tropics after a long time at sea and having left winter. Imagine jumping into warm Caribbean waters ten seconds after you wake up. Life with coconuts, fresh tropical fruits, and 'dancing barefoot in the sand opportunities everywhere' is another dream becoming a reality. If you go the other way, to Europe, it's another kind of paradise. Life will be cheaper (depending on where you go!), you'll experience the beauty and scents of springtime flowers, a glass of wine on a terrace, and high-speed WiFi.

* If you *really* need the internet, it is possible at a price.

Arriving in paradise. St. Vincent & the Grenadines

Gratefulness

"At sea, I learned how little a person needs,
not how much.

— ROBIN GRAHAM
(Sailor & Writer)

As sailors, we are intricately connected to the ocean on a daily basis. Crossing an ocean provides a deep and lasting respect for nature. You're dependent on it to make it safely to the other side. You will experience the power of the wind and the waves, and realise how precious our resources are, such as water, fresh air, power, and fresh vegetables. You will become aware that what might be considered normal 'back home', is not so normal on a boat.

The luxuries of living on land: sitting up straight in your bed in the morning, taking a shower lasting more than ten seconds, pouring a coffee of that doesn't spill, flushing a toilet, a fresh apple in a fruit bowl, sleeping on a bed that doesn't move, food that stays on the stove, power plugs, getting through your morning routine without four new bruises, doing dishes with warm water, walking more than ten metres, friends to talk to, WiFi, and so much more. All the things we take for granted on land become priceless when you have experienced life without them. For the rest of your life, you'll be grateful having realised what it's like not to have all these land luxuries.

Sailing makes you a conscious consumer and a more grateful person for every little luxury thing. With limited storage and cooling, food sharing, and adaptation, you have to think about every item you bring on board and why. After an ocean crossing, you will appreciate every drop of water, fresh fruit or vegetable and a good night of sleep even more. Back on land you appreciate and notice fresh food, flavours and senses of a place because you probably have eaten a lot of the same foods for weeks and finished the good stuff after a week or two, *if* you provisioned well.

The Atlantic Ocean Salty pups. All met during the adventure!

Meeting like-minded people

When searching for a ride, preparing the boat, and arriving on the other side, you will meet so many interesting people. Everyone has his or her story and reasons why they are or want to be on a sailboat. It's a great community. I used to have an image in my head that sailing is only for rich people, that it's about showing off boats and boat toys, and that as crew you're just meant to scrub the **deck.** My image of this changed completely after I hung out in Las Palmas for a while. Sailors are free spirits and ocean-minded people. Most of them share the same dream to live a simple life on a sailboat, set off to explore the world, and live life on their own terms. You'll meet those that have made this dream happen! And you'll be one of them. You connect with fellow aspiring sailors that are on the same mission. Who knows who you may meet during these adventures and what opportunities may come from it.

A learning experience

Crossing an ocean is more about **seamanship** than sailing. The extent to which you will learn to sail depends a great deal on the captain, boat, weather and your attitude. If you want to learn how to sail, taking a course, and gaining coastal sailing experience, will teach you more about just *sailing*. The smaller the boat, the more you'll understand how sailing works. Seamanship is the most interesting and challenging part of an ocean adventure. You may have the biggest bank account but once you're at sea nothing can be googled or bought. And no person can be hired to fix something. You have to be inventive as situations arise and you'll learn from experiences along the way. You'll learn to work with your hands. You learn about the wind, the weather, geography, stars, navigation, sea life, boats, yourself, people, and much more. You'll also be able to finish a couple of books, podcasts, movies and arrive a wiser man or woman. When else do you take the time to observe, read and learn? Socially, mentally and physically, you will grow.

You'll also learn a great deal about the ocean. It's only since my first crossing that I learned how bad the situation in our ocean *really* is, and how dependent we are on it for our own survival. When you see what's happening with your own eyes, talk face-to-face with people living on and for the ocean, and experience its value, it makes you eager to learn more. And it gives rise to an urge to do *something*. On this journey, you will also see fishing fleets, trash in harbours, in the ocean and on the beaches, endangered species on the menu, and damaged corals. These are just a few situations that make us pause for a moment. In reality though, that 'moment' is a constant. We are at the forefront of what's happening. And we can do a lot to make a positive impact.

Connect to nature

> *"In nature's economy the currency is not money.*
> *It is life.*

— VANDANA SHIVA

Most of us spend more time indoors than outdoors. It's easy to forget the natural world we're coming from and living in. On the ocean, you face the wind and water elements and find that connection to nature. Imagine a scene with no traffic, no news, no pollution, no civilisation. Just wind and water—plenty of that! A scene where you can gaze for hours to the millions of stars above you; enjoy the dozens of dolphins sliding through the water at the **bow** of the boat; admire the pink-orange-red sunrises and sunsets, without any airplane trails changing the fluffy and cauli-flower-like cloud patterns. You'll become very aware of the natural world around you. This inspires. And it's eye-opening. You come to realise how disconnected from nature we are in our daily lives. In the middle of nature, far away from civilisation, you will see a plastic bottle floating by. A human made thing that doesn't belong there. Witnessing that makes you think about the impact that we are making as people. And as individuals. When I saw that bottle, I could not even guarantee it wasn't mine! I have thrown 'away' dozens of bottles in my life. Now I have learned, there is no 'away.' You may have seen it on social media or in the news: plastic parades, straws in turtles, disappearing islands, whales washed ashore. . . . Usually we're far away it's hard to make it tangible. It doesn't really affect us. Or so we think. But by being out there, you literally broaden your horizon. You will see for yourself what impact we are making and what's going on with the ocean. The trashed and fishless waters you will see, will make you think, gain fresh perspectives, and may inspire you to act to turn the tide of the ocean challenges. More about that in the Ocean love & Conservation section of this book.

Fresh perspectives

"The future is in the hands of those who explore . . .
and from all the beauty they discover while crossing
perpetually receding frontiers, they develop for
nature and for humankind
an infinite love."

– JACQUES YVES COUSTEAU
(Ocean explorer and documenter)

Imagine looking up into the sky every night and seeing galaxies. It makes you feel small and on top of the world at the same time. It will make you rethink your place in the world. An ocean passage allows philosophising about life and your purpose in it. Did you know that an average person makes 2,800 choices in a day? I heard that on the radio the other day. Whether it's true or not I don't know, but I believe we're close to that. Oats or pancakes for breakfast? Green tea or mint tea? Red pants or blue pants? Check Facebook or Pinterest? Just stroll through the super-market, and you're already 100 decisions further. Isn't that IN-SANE? Realise how much of our energy that takes. You will realise this in the provisioning part of the adventure. That's an adventure in itself. By having to provision for weeks, you will look at food and waste from a different point of view.

Finally, on the ocean, you can just *be*. Imagine you cut a number of decisions you make from 1,000 down to ten per day—like, shall I drink tea or coffee, read this book or that one, wearing shorts or long pants, sit on the front **deck** or in the cockpit? That's it really. And it's great! Imagine how much extra energy you have for being, enjoying, living and thinking!

On the ocean you can rediscover your values, and what really matters. On land, we often want a constant stimulus. We keep ourselves busy. On a boat, you get trained for what the Caribbean will bring: slowed down island style living. By being 'out of the system', away from depressive

Loads of time for deep blue thinking.

media headlines, advertisement on stuff we don't need, social media feeds with cat videos and other people's cool lives, noisy traffic, stinky air, is when you connect to your true self. You'll take a break from the rollercoaster that's all about being busy, productive and convenient. It's a reset. You will have time to just simply let your mind wander. When does that still happen? It will clear your head, enhance your creativity and the most brilliant ideas will come up! With fresh perspectives, you'll start to look at your life differently. It's experiences like seeing a bottle in the middle of nowhere that makes you pause and think. You will think a lot about your life, what you're doing, and why you're doing what you're doing. And perhaps, having gained a fresh point of view, you might realise that it's time to adjust the course in some areas of your life. With all the space created in your head, you'll feel accomplished and ready to take over the world once you've arrived!

> *"The real voyage of discovery consists not in seeking new landscapes, but in having new eyes."*
>
> **— MARCEL PROUST**
> *(French Novelist)*

It's healthy

*"The ocean stirs the heart, inspires the imagination
and brings eternal joy to the soul"*

— ROBERT WYLAND
(Ocean Artist)

The ocean doesn't only work for healing mentally; it keeps us sane physically! Day in day out, you can breathe the fresh ocean air. Imagine what energy, oxygen, and aliveness that brings to your well-being. When else will you have three weeks of pure fresh ocean air? Pure air is a luxury these days! You'll also stock up with vitamin D from the sunshine (but be careful with too much sunshine!). Another ingredient for optimal health.

Making memories

*"It's the possibility of having a dream come true that
makes life interesting.*

— PAULO COELHO
(Writer)

It's an experience you will remember the rest of your life. You'll look back one day and say 'Hell YEAH! I crossed the Atlantic Ocean on a sailboat! **Why did crew want to cross the Atlantic Ocean?**

"It was a lifetime dream to sail the oceans, this way I'm able to do it without owning a boat."

"To experience the solitude of being surrounded by the sea, and to experience what an ocean crossing was like. As part of a trip that was meant to be undertaken without airplanes, to experience the real distances of the world."

"It's a bucket list thing."

"To discover a new way of travelling."

"A long-standing wish."

"To go to the other side. I don't like planes."

"I love the ocean, and I love to try out new things. And I enjoy travelling slowly."

"I love sailing, and a transatlantic has been a dream for a while."

"I figured crossing the Atlantic would be a great adventure, I would be able to visit Cape Verde and some Caribbean Islands that otherwise would be difficult to visit, and I would gain sailing experience which could come handy during future trips in the Pacific."

"I wanted to slow down time, appreciate it. Understand the distances that we make to cross oceans."

"Sailing around the world is more sustainable than flying. Also it's quite the adventure being stuck on boat for 2–4 weeks."

"I wanted offshore experience and adventure. It was part of my quest to circumnavigate the world without using any airplanes."

"I wanted to go to South America and didn't have the funds for a flight."

"I want to become a skipper."

"Everybody advised me that it was impossible. But it was my dream, and I wanted to do it."

"It's one of these crazy things to do in your life."

"Getting sea miles for my yacht-master."

"I wanted to have the experience of sailing and being in the middle of nature, of the ocean, respecting and understanding it."

"I was always dreaming to cross the Atlantic, reach the other side of the ocean, spend time in the tropics, with a lot of time for myself, to think, watch the stars, take a deep breath with fresh ocean air. Keep calm."

"Ireland is cold in the winter."

"To regenerate and renew my motivation for my studies and future plans."

"Take my coastal sailing experience to the next level, experience being on the ocean, learn a few more things about sailing and get to know more about myself."

All sorts of reasons. All kinds of dreams. You're next!

1.2 SNEAK PEEK: WHAT'S IT LIKE?

"The sea, once it casts its spell, holds one in its net of wonder forever.

– JACQUES YVES COUSTEAU

A few of my favourite moments

It's hard to pick a favourite moment out of all the memorable experiences I have had on the Atlantic crossings. Here are a few:

- The moment we set sail out of Las Palmas. New friends were making noise and waving goodbye. After weeks of dreaming, searching, preparing, it's finally happening!
- The moment we saw lights when we were approaching Cape Verde after six days on the open sea. It was the first time I ever sailed into a country.

- Shooting stars, fluorescent plankton discos in the waves, the sound of breathing dolphins followed by the splash from a jump.
- Being on watch, just me, a pod of dolphins, and the sunrise.
- Celebrating my birthday in the middle of the Atlantic. My fellow crew even arranged jumping dolphins on the horizon. . . . And chocolate cake!
- The moment I set foot in Tobago, sipped a fresh coconut, and ate fresh vegetables.
- The moments behind the wheel with 18 knots of wind, no autopilot, all sails up, feeling the boat and just steering course by that bright start I picked from the sky.
- The moment I woke up with the smell of pine trees, after days and days of only ocean breeze. Land Ahoy!
- Both times I crossed the Strait of Gibraltar. It's a spectacular passage, seeing where and how the different seas and continents come together.
- The moment I woke up on land and realised that I had disembarked "The Bounty [1] "

The highlights of the hitch-sailors:

"There were two whales with us for four days, we jumped in and swam with them hanging on a rope at the back of the boat!"

"The crossing of the Atlantic as a whole. The sunrises and sunsets. Same for the moon. The starry nights and the Milky Way. The company. And most of all: the ocean!"

"Sailing **downwind** *at night with a spinnaker on. Being alone on the* **deck** *together with the dolphins."*

"Appreciating the mid-Atlantic high seas and the earth's perspective from the 18m high foremast top during 17 knots wind and 4m high waves."

"During my first crossing: when they called me (I was sleeping after night watch), and they showed me the Surinam coast. I had fulfilled my dream."

---

1   In respect to the captain and new owner, I refer to this boat under alias name "The Bounty."

"I swam right in the middle of the Atlantic, 4,000 metres deep, nothing around—no wind at all, swam around our little boat without securing rope, for like 20 minutes. . . . An extraordinary experience!"

"Waking up every day surrounded by the ocean. Seeing stars I never saw before. Fantastic sunsets. The captain's cat. Making a French Galette des Rois on board. There are too many!"

"When we found the boat after two weeks of searching, and we saw that it was going to be true. We were going to across the Atlantic.

"Solo shift, 3:00 am, day eight. Simply amazing."

"The stars, the isolation, yet freedom, the simplicity of life aboard. Maybe the silence of no wind or the loudness of storms. To be scared and overcoming that."

"Just the feeling to cross the Atlantic."

"Three days of whales 'pacing us' under the boat. The underwater camera was great!"

"Sleeping outside in the hammock and waking up to see a dolphin light show. They were jumping around in the middle of the night in the fluorescent water."

"A sunrise when a crew mate kindly brought me breakfast while I was steering. The sky lit by a deep purple light. A few minutes later big blue Atlantic dolphins went to play with the **bow** and sang."

"Visiting the different islands and meeting great people."

"The amazing food onboard!"

"The night watches alone; I loved feeling the breeze, seeing the stars and hearing the waves."

"Each night watch with the amazing views of the stars in the sky."

"Being at sea, out of sight of land just enjoying the freedom and peace of the ocean."

"Leaving the Strait of Gibraltar was the moment I knew it finally started. Arriving at Cape Verde and being happy to survive the trip there. Crossing the equator, and swimming next to the boat in the middle of the ocean."

"Sunshine!"

1.3 REALITY CHECK & OCEAN CREWING BASICS

A few basics about the trip and terminology that will help you navigate this journey.

All sorts of terminology are used to describe 'us,' the aspiring ocean passage maker, hoping to find a ride: Sailboat hitchhikers, wannabe crew, freeloaders, pickup crew, hitch-sailors, and barnacles as a captain and I came up with during my last 'hitch-sailing' trip. It all comes down to the same thing: spontaneous crew on a strangers' sailboat. Since we're not actually hiking and freeloading should not be the intention, in this book I sometimes refer to 'us' as *hitch-sailors*. Whether you have sailing experience or not, whether you contribute money or not, or whether you found the boat in advance online or locally in the harbour. A hitch-sailor is usually only on board for a passage. In this case, the Atlantic.

Crew is a more general term, which is basically everyone on the boat except for the captain. Crew can be short-term but also be on board for years. In charter, when it's a business to take people on board, you also have 'passengers' that pay and are not always expected to work. As crew you help with whatever needs to be done to operate the boat.

Who are you dealing with? You hear about yachties/yotties, sailors, live-aboard sailors, cruisers, captains, skippers, and boat owners. What's the difference?

Yachties/yotties, cruisers, and live-aboard sailors basically mean the same thing. These are in general people that have made a boat their home, cruise around, and often become comfortable in places, stick around, change plans, or don't make plans at all.

Sailors are the people who are actually out at sea, sailing. They are moving. These can be yachties, cruisers, or live-aboard sailors. Though sailors are often not the opposite. Those who mostly want to sail often choose to not own a boat. A boat means ongoing work and maintenance. Some live-aboard sailors have not sailed for years but simply live aboard their boat.

Captain and Skipper means the same. This is the person who is in charge of navigating the boat. For yachties, cruisers and live aboard sailors, this usually means it's also the owner. Some boats though, have owners that are not able to or don't desire to be in charge of sailing the boat. They have someone else to captain the boat. As a crew member boarding a boat, most important is that you feel happy and safe with the captain, since that's the person in command.

You have to adjust your travel plans to the boat; you can't have boats adapt to your travel plans. Sailboats don't work like ferries going from A to B on a schedule. Sailboats deal with seasons, routes, weather, break-age, and all sorts of variables. You can't 'just' find a boat going from Spain to Mexico in August. It's not a common route, *and* August is in the midst of hurricane season! You can't find a boat going from Canada to Africa, arriving on date x. It's a huge passage with so many variables along the way. You have to be flexible with time and destination if you're looking to sail across.

Why would captains (or boat owners) spontaneously take a stranger on their sailboat? Many boat owners have been preparing and paying for months or even years to do this. With the technological advances in nav-igation and communication that exist today, they often don't *need* you. Boats take on crew because they like help, they like more fun, they like more sleep, or like to cover costs. If they can't source crew members from their own network, you might get lucky.

It's not always sunshine, wildlife and happy days. If they take you, you should be ready to adapt and work. Sailing across the Atlantic is not a holiday. There is always work to do, especially while preparing, and you share the responsibility to keep the boat going safely. The captain is in command, and you must follow their orders, whether you agree or not.

Therefore, it's so important that you don't just hop on any boat but research the boat, captain, and crew carefully. Realise that anyone can buy a boat without experience or license. It's not just a day trip. For weeks at time, you will live, work, eat, cook and maybe even share a bed together. Non-stop. You don't stop on the Atlantic (if you're lucky only for a swim). You're sailing day and night. Sailing across the Atlantic is like camping in the wild with a bunch of strangers. Only you can't walk away. . . . Many personalities come together in one small space. The tiniest habits and behaviours can become an annoyance. You have to adapt and deal with it. An ocean crossing can be challenging, and it will be challenging.

Jill, a 'yottie' who sails around the world with her family on Yacht Mollymawk, has taken strangers on board for the Atlantic crossing, and also has had many aspiring sailors 'knocking on her boat' to ask for a ride. On her blog she explains it perfectly to the first time crosser:

> "We LOVE taking people sailing, but the risks entailed in this undertaking are real, and they're something to bear in mind. Yotties need to bear them in mind, and hitch-hikers need to understand them and be aware of what they are asking us to do."

She explains . . .

> "Many hitch-hikers seem to look upon a yacht as if it were a means of transport. This is understandable, because a yacht is a means of transport. However, that is not the way that we yotties think of our boats. When we are using them to race around the cans or to make a little excursion at the weekend, then we think of them as a marvellous invention and a source of great pleasure; and when we live aboard them, we think of them as Home Sweet Home. Now, why the heck would anyone want to invite a complete stranger straight off the pavement and into his home (1)? How many families do you know who would be happy to share their communal living space—the space where they cook, eat, sleep, and shower, and the space where they are accustomed to wandering naked all day—with a total stranger? And not just for a weekend but for a whole month!
>
> When you hitch a ride aboard a sailing boat you're committing yourself to living in absolute intimacy with your fellow sailors for the time it takes to get from one side of the pond to the other, and your hosts are making the same commitment (2)."

Be clear on *why* you want to do this. And be 100% happy and confident on with *whom* you're jumping on board.

That said, within the challenge, there will be days that come close to perfection! Sunrises, sunsets, pods of dolphins around the boat, gazing far into the galaxies, having deep conversations, and getting closer to yourself and nature for an extended period of time. It's a ticket to paradise with the adventure of a life time. It's an experience you will never forget, and will make a good story to tell your grandkids.

1.4   WHEN IS IT MAYBE NOT FOR YOU?

Why do *you* want to sail across the Atlantic Ocean? It may not be the right adventure, if you just want a free ride to save on airfare.

- You just want to go from A to B, arriving date x.
- You can't commit to at least a month.
- You want an easy and cheap way to learn to sail.
- You want to learn to sail in general.
- You're not excited about sailing and all that comes with it.
- You need to be alone often. You will hardly ever be!
- You can't adapt to a new situation with new people.
- You want to sit back and relax.
- You're emotionally unstable or depressed.

If any of these are true for you, then you might want to pass on an adventure like this for now. But any other doubts can be taken away! There's only one way to find out; make the decision and go for it! The seemingly impossible is not the path of the least resistance, but definitely the most rewarding one. Believe that it's going to happen and tell everyone it's going happen. Then it *will* happen. It's called the law of attraction. You just need willpower, determination and a smile on your face.

Where to start? With research! Which you're doing right now by reading this book! Let's keep going!

1.5 HOW TO START: GET THE RIGHT MINDSET

"We have to continually be jumping off cliffs and developing our wings on the way down.

– KURT VONNEGUT
(Writer)

You have the dream, but somehow you keep watching Youtube videos of people that sail around the world, 'like' Facebook updates more than you create, and watch Instagram videos of others that are actually living your dream. You want more! But you're stuck. Because you tell yourself. . . .

"I'm too young. I'm too old. I don't have time. I get seasick. I'm afraid I will get seasick. I don't have any sailing experience. I don't have money. I like the idea, but I don't know if sailing is for me. I need WiFi. The adventure seems too big. I need to pay my rent/mortgage. I should study, find a job, get serious and settle down. My job won't let me go. I have a wedding to go to. I have to work. My family might need me. . . ."

Really? I mean, REALLY? The biggest reasons for people not pursuing the dream of crossing the Atlantic is time and money. Or maybe it's fear. Fear that the world, your job, or family will fall apart when you're 'out' for a month. Money should not be a problem. There's no shop in the middle of the Atlantic. If you follow the suggestions in this book €1,000 is likely to keep you more than covered for a whole month of ocean adventure including food, stay, and transport. A doable amount to save up and it can be cheaper with more creativity and luck.

But you've got bills to pay? Which bills are you actually paying in the first place? Stop the phone plan; sub-rent your house, work harder the months before if you need to. Get a side hustle. And another one. And another one. Ditch the stuff you don't need. Do what you have to do to free up funds. In general, we are so busy working on things that don't matter so we have money to buy things we don't need and then eventually throw 'away.' In the end, does this contribute to individual happiness or a happy and healthy planet? Maybe in the short term. But in the long run? Imagine the freedom feeling brought by a life less centred about money and stuff. And the feeling of having made your ocean crossing dream happen!

What you really *do* need for an Atlantic Ocean crossing is *time*, the most valuable thing in the world. The Atlantic crossing takes time. But I promise you it's a good investment that will bring you more valuable time in the future. Unless you join a rally, **charter** or a strictly organised boat, you'll need at least a month. Chances are you don't have a month. You may have commitments to a job, house, partner, sports team, pet, or family. . . . Or maybe it's the expectation of having to be there for the holidays, your friend's bachelor party, your newborn cousin. If you live for other people's lives, you will never have the time for yourself. There's always something going on. I'm sure the world will keep turning if you're not around for one month. But how to make that happen? Where to start?

I didn't have sailing experience, and I didn't have much money. I had no idea if I would get seasick (I do! But that's OK). I had no idea about sailing. I had no funds. I had no idea how this whole boat thing worked. I was worried about what Mum and Dad would think. They invested in my studies. I should do something with that, right? I had no idea how to tackle this adventure. What I did have was willpower, determination, and time. How did that happen in the first place?

Let me give you a bit of background. How did I phase into this life-style of endless adventure travel?

You know the feeling of super excitement, that make your eyes sparkle, that makes you channel all your energy towards it, that makes you lose all sense of time and any other nonsense occupying our days? For me that comes from exploration. In the broadest sense. I developed an extreme curiosity for discovering new cultures, places, adventure sports, and par-ticularly, the ocean. For ten years I've been slow travelling the world, one adventure at a time.

My first big achievement during an outdoor adventure abroad occurred when I was eight years old. In a wild river, somewhere in the Belgian Ardennes, there was this BIG Rock, just sitting there (read: small stone in a river). It just had to be 'climbed'. So, with my little pink rubber boots on my feet, I hopped into the water and climbed that rock. I felt on TOP of the world and screamed loud out to my parents: "I'm standing on a rock!" They still put this in the postcard every time I take off for a new adventure. Nothing has changed.

I followed the path you're 'supposed' to take. I was 17 when I finished

high school. A year younger than everyone else. I skipped a class in primary school. Still not sure why that happened. I guess I was bored or too
smart. Anyway, after high school I wanted to go travelling, but everyone
told me not to. Like most of us in the western world, I grew up in this 'funnel'
of going from one educational institution to another. That's our system
for getting you 'ready' for the big world out there. When you finish high
school, you are supposed to go to the next educational building. I fully
realise it's a dream for many and I am fortunate to even be able to choose
and study. But at age 16, when you have to decide on this, I was still way
too playful to sit down and study. I wanted to learn through experience and
go travelling. But everyone told me not to. "You should study something!"
(everyone, 2003). Young, privileged and full of assumptions, I listened and
I went to university. I just picked 'something.' I decided on 'Leisure Studies.'
I figured if I couldn't actually do leisure, maybe studying it would make
this all a bit more exciting. I had no idea what else to study because I had
no idea about what was happening in the world. What could I dedicate
myself to with passion, and what would really matter? For two years, I
didn't feel like I was learning something useful. Is this it? What am I learning
this for? I want to explore! To really get a broader view of the world, we
have to go out there and experience. Now that I have done that, I would
actually love to go back and study, to enrich myself with knowledge of the
world that I have explored. I have no regrets about anything but I did take
some detours and wasted energy worrying about what others would think.

> *"To myself I am only a child playing*
> *on the beach, while vast oceans of truth lie*
> *undiscovered before me."*

– ISAAC NEWTON
(Natural philosopher)

One day . . . . "Shouldn't you maybe quit your study?", said Mum
(yes, mum!). She noticed I wasn't enjoying any of it. I didn't even consider
quitting as an option. I was doing what I thought I was supposed to do.
Around that same time Sabine, one of my best friends, convinced me to
go on my first snowboard holiday to France. Wow! Now that excited me.
It was ciao to my studies and hello to a five-month snowboard season! I
found a job with a tour operator and bar in the French Alps. I could snowboard during the day, every day! This adventure opened my world and
mind. I was in a flow state for five months. After playing in the snow in the
Alps, I spent another few months tasting salt by working in a surf camp
on the French Atlantic Coast. These experiences made me curious about

a long-term ocean adventure. I did go back to studying but it had to be something international so I could somehow stay in this adventure flow.

Now, I roll from one adventure to the another. But this doesn't come from luck. In essence, it's willpower, determination and setting clear priorities that get me out there. Step by step, I have created a lifestyle around my curiosity for the world. The last ten years have brought me to every continent except Antarctica. I don't see myself as a traveller, per se. Rather, I go on long-term adventures with many small adventures included along the way. It's a nomadic lifestyle. I usually stay in a place for a few months, if not ten. But no day goes by without doing something outdoors. The most important rule to live by: no day without play!

Wherever I went, I tried to do fulfilling work and contribute to the local scene as best I could. That is the most important lesson I learned after all these years of slow travelling: Whatever adventure I'm on, it should help someone else, to make it rewarding. The more I found out about what's going on in this world, the more I became driven to not just have fun, but to do more. I've realised that it's not at all about me. It's about having a purpose.

The world is facing many challenges. I'm fortunate, healthy and wealthy with time. I'm lucky to have been born in The Netherlands, to have a passport and a family that has raised me to be a healthy and educated kid. I don't only aim to be part of the solution; I have to create solutions! In Peru, I helped Andean communities develop small scale tourism experiences; In Tonga (a South Pacific island nation), I researched tourism and adaptation to climate change; I helped the island of Saba to become more sustainable; In Indonesia, I worked with locals to help them get the word out about their small tourism business. All these travels made me want to help other travellers to experience such rewarding interactions. I started blogging to share my thoughts and wisdom from my slow travels to help other travellers make the most of their journeys—not just for themselves but for the people and places they're visiting.

My travels have always been around the ocean. Diving, snorkelling, surfing, kitesurfing—I've done it all and could never get enough. Ocean activities do magic for the body and soul! A few years ago, I started getting into freediving and sailing. These water sports have brought me to new territories, have made me see the serious problems facing our ocean. It's nasty and needs attention. I've become a voice for an ocean that can't speak but is screaming louder than ever. We need time to find and create solutions so that we, our kids and the rest of the animal kingdom will be able to live. The one thing we can't buy is a new planet and we're currently using the one we have like we've got a spare. I've dedicated my time to saving it, while being in and on the ocean as much as I can. It keeps me energised, and I would love for you and the children of our future to experience its magic as well.

"Does your money grow on trees?"

It sure looks like it, right? This is the number one question I am asked: how do I finance all this? I fund life with time, love, and dedication. It doesn't cost much money. My lifestyle costs considerably less than the average person who asks me this question. I choose to live with little in order to have more freedom to explore. I don't own stuff and I find this incredibly liberating. No house, no car, no furniture. Just some freedive gear, and a computer so I can share the fun and make an impact. I've been writing this book while couch surfing, **hitch-sailing**, house-sitting, and boat-sitting: win-win situations with no money and lots of excitement (and adaptation!). I don't book hotels. I do some research, join the local community and ask the locals for advice. If they can live on US$300/ month, so can I. And so I did! I've lived for months on less than that. I've lived until I only had one peso left for one more **coconut** left. Though I don't recommend it, I do know that there's always a way. Did you know you can live off coconuts for an entire week, if not more? Plenty of time to find a solution to raise the adventure fund! I help people; they help me. Exchanging skills and services is what has got me far. And I'm Dutch, being frugal is a skill that's in my blood ;). But really, what do we need? I'd rather invest in memories than in things. I wish I could live for 500 years, just to experience all the things I would like to experience. It's unlikely that I will hit that age (though reading about longevity a lot I do believe we can vitally age to an extraordinary number if we raise our standards and live up to it). It's better I use time wisely now, do what I can to conserve the ocean for those to come, and have a blast while doing it. At the end of the day our system is based on money and I need some of it too. I've been able to facilitate the adventures through various avenues—my blog, consultancy work in sustainable tourism, organising sailing trips, teaching freediving, video and photo creations, and now also sailing! There is always a way. Sometimes I earn a few pesos, other times simply the experience. This ocean nomad does need to save up now for my own sailboat so I can take you hitch-sailing as well as my family, that has never sailed before! So thank you for buying this book!

I realise I'm not the average case. I ditched the 'conventional life' a while ago. Actually—I never 'arrived' there in the first place. I have never understood the concept of sitting in an office day after day on pre-defined times that may not be your mental peak hours. Surely the numbers in your bank account every month are a benefit and a necessity in a world that's centred around money. But there's a different way. To maximise the number of memorable days, I've set different priorities. I created a lifestyle of freedom so I can decide when I use my creative brain and when it's time to simply play. This takes huge sacrifices too. I can't just buy the latest mermaid fin. Okay, maybe that's not that huge. But I also miss out on friends' and families' milestones like weddings, babies and birthday parties. I can't just book a flight or pause my mission for every event. But the lifestyle I designed does allow me to continuously be out there in the happy zone, the ocean, and pursue my mission of saving it. I'm lucky to have a happy and healthy family. I'm a fortunate fool. That said, over the years, I've worked super hard towards the dream. I work on the strangest hours creating content, like this book, when others are out partying. That cool photo in the top of the mast isn't taken by itself. I have to climb the mast first.

This 'make it happen' mentality became stronger through freediving. It's a sport that explores limits of the body and mind. Freediving has taught me that by just staying calm, chilled-out, and intensely in the moment, our body's capabilities go far beyond what I thought was possible. Unleash the inner mermaid/merman in you! The more you're in a flow state, the better you'll perform.

It's the same above the surface. I was fascinated by boats. But besides navigating the inflatable rubber boat we took out on camping holidays, I didn't know anything about boats or sailing. It seemed quite a distant reality for me to sail across an ocean. I didn't grow up near the sea. But I've always been drawn to it. During my ten years of slow travelling around the world on all continents but Antarctica, there has been one constant in my life: the call of the ocean. In, at or near the sea I'm the best version of myself.

I've always been a water person. It's my star sign. It's my Chinese sign. Being in, near or underneath the surface just feels great. I've made many water sports my hobby: surfing, kitesurfing, diving and freediving. But I never really got into sailing. It was during an internship in Mauritius a few years ago, that I saw the inside of a sailing boat for the first time. I remember me thinking 'wow how cool if I could actually sleep on a boat one day.' That thought did not leave my mind. My first overnight stay on a boat was in Australia. Despite seasickness, I fell in love with this way of life. A dream to "One day, sail around the world" was born. Ever since that first sailing trip, I have had my antenna out for sailing opportunities. I've become very eager to learn everything about sailing, **seamanship** and the ocean. On my way to fulfilling that big dream, I've done a few day sails, by just going to harbours and meeting sailors. I learned some basic skills but over all my sailing experience was still negligible. However, the enthusiasm about it grew. I was so curious about the real nomadic sailing lifestyle! The nomads that actually cross oceans and go around the world. Hitch-sailing an ocean seemed like a good starting point for me to get a step closer to making the 'sailing around the world' dream happen. I 'just' (what was I thinking?) had to throw myself into a situation where I could learn all about it. Now, dozens of adventurous hitch-sail experiences later, and with many lessons learned, I feel ready to be a captain. The less realistic a dream might seem, the more I can be driven to do whatever it takes to make it happen. When we explore beyond what we think we are capable of, nothing is impossible.

"The most dangerous risk of all: the risk of not doing what you want on the bet you can buy yourself the freedom to do it later.

— RANDY KOMISAR
(Entrepreneur)

How did my parents react?

"Mum, Dad, I am going to try to hop on a boat with strangers to cross the Atlantic Ocean.

I can hear Mum thinking, "Oh dear, why don't you just settle down, find a man, make babies and live a normal life?.

Although my parents sometimes wish that things were different, they support me in everything I do. They know that I don't just chill and play on the beach all day. This wasn't the first time I announced a crazy adventure, but this one was a less tangible. Our family has no experience with boats, sailing and how this all works, so for them, it seemed like a risky thing to do. When I was on my way to boat number one, I found a postcard in my duffel bag: "Dear daughter, we won't be surprised if the next thing is going to be limbo-dancing with penguins on Antarctica." Even if they didn't like it, my parents said: "If that's what you want to do, do it." I'm lucky to have liberal parents like this. And to still even have my parents around. That's not that common anymore.

What does Mum actually think about it? I asked her: "The first time she announced an Atlantic crossing by sailing boat, with strangers, I was not amused. Thankfully, she left boat number one and she ended up travelling with a captain from our own home village. That made it a bit less scary. The second trip was a west–east crossing, for me meaning "coming back home", so that was okay. The third time was the ARC+. There was a good website about the event, enough information and as it seemed, a good boat and crew waiting for her. But still, I wondered, what was so special about doing this for the third time? So what did Mum do? I went to Las Palmas to see it for myself. And I must say: that was overwhelming. I was welcomed like a VIP by the owner, got to meet the captain and fellow crew members and was allowed to look around the Eau Too. That was very reassuring. I was proud of my girl and happy for her.

I asked mum. So I also asked my Dad. What did he think about me setting off for a big sailing trip? "The love for sailing didn't come from me. I never did that. But I do have a special place in my heart for water, lakes, cascades, seas and oceans, just like her. From birth she watched me, and later also her mum, disappear under water and come back up an hour or so later. I am a scuba diver. Suzanne also got her divers license. I made some amazing dives with my daughter, in the Mediterranean, the Red Sea and around Mauritius where we visited her. That is also the place where she picked up the new hobby of kite-surfing. We kept on keeping track of her as she travelled around the globe. She went away again to support the women of in a community in Peru. She then had her home in Tarifa for a few years, where I saw her almost turning her newest hobby into a profession, being a kite surf instructor. But the ocean called. And she went for a bigger challenge: crossing the Atlantic by sailing boat. As her father, I more than once thought: Wow, my little girl is a real dare devil. How does she do it? I admire her for her passion for the beauty of our oceans, for her incredible efforts to try and save our waters. And I want to thank her for showing us, her parents, around the planet and make us meet new friends all over the globe. In them, I recognise the open minds and attitude, which we taught our daughter when raising her into the most wonderful person she is now."

～～～～～～～～～～～～～～～～～～～～～～～

Get the mindset right: determination and proactivity

If you really want something, you have to gather courage and take action. Step by step you can move closer to make the dream happen. The journey is worthwhile.

We make excuses, procrastinate, or just react to whatever situation appears. It keeps us in our comfort zones. It keeps us warm and we know we are okay. That's the thing. It makes us feel okay, not *alive*! In today's world I see too many people who are not enjoying the ride of life. Always facing some sort of "problem." And when that problem is solved, there's always a new problem around the corner. They are constantly in a survival mode. The years go by without actually remembering what you've done. If you react to every situation that crosses your path, then your life is lived by others instead of by you. You will grow old without big stories to tell to your grandchildren. The thing is, there is always something going on that is immediately important but not helping us to realise our dreams. What's more important in the long run? We are wired by the expectations of society, the constant need to earn money, and the urge to be productive for the sake of others peoples' judgement. And for what?

To buy stuff we then put in the trash, and then are trashed back onto our plate? To suffer burnout before age 30? To save money for 'later' and start living the dream the day your body doesn't let you anymore? Time is much more valuable than money. We can always make more money but never more time. It requires some creativity, proactivity, adaptation, and shift in thinking, but it makes life exciting and rewarding. You must pro-actively pursue your dreams to make them happen. Set your standards and live the way you want to live. Happiness is worth more than any bank account. Choose time over money. The best investment you can make.

How to set your mind to it?

Drive, passion, and purpose bring us everywhere. If you're clear *why* you want to go, only take those actions that bring you closer to your dream and mission. Say *no* to everything and everyone that prevents you from going where you want to go. Don't spend your time with people you don't really like. Don't waste time on a job you hate. Don't lose hours scrolling down your Facebook feed and looking at how awesome other people's lives are. Step one: Spend time with those awesome people instead! The internet makes it easier than ever before to connect with like-minded people. Find your tribe. Sign up for *Meetup.com, Couchsurfing.org,* or a Facebook group where you can find people passionate about the same things. Find out which globetrotters are maybe simply around the corner looking to meet a fellow adventure seeker. Spend time with people who make you happy, bring out the best in you and share the same dreams. This will give you tremendous energy and encouragement to go out there and do it. This will make step two a breeze.

> *"You are the average of the five people*
> *you spend the most time with.*
>
> **— JIM RHONE**
> *(Motivational speaker)*

By telling you all this, I hope to shake and wake you up a bit to realise that the time to make your dreams happen is *now.* Be your authentic you and to do what excites you, at any stage in your life. Be who *you* would like to be. Follow your own path and don't let anything or anyone hold you back. Be present and act in the now. Dreams are meant to be pursued, not postponed. Who knows if tomorrow will even arrive? If you are happy, you are your best you, and your surroundings will be happy as well. Happiness is contagious. Make your life a good one! Not only for yourself but for those in need and those to come.

You don't have to make it a massive years-long adventure. You could take one month off from work. If you do want to sail across the Atlantic, you have to start working towards that. Tell your family, tell your boss, block your agenda and make 'crossing the Atlantic' your priority. This is what you will remember when you're old, not the time your boss didn't approve your leave because an 'important' work problem had to be solved. The most difficult step is stepping out of the door! Once you've done that, the rest is easy.

> *"Because in the end, you won't remember the time you spent working in the office or mowing your lawn. Climb that goddamn mountain."*
>
> **– JACK KEROUAC**
> *(Writer) Or sail that vast ocean!*

Of the 58 hitch-sailors surveyed, only two didn't want to do it again. Other responses to the question: 'Would you do it again?' were:

"Yes! I'm heading for the Pacific in the coming 18 months."

"If you want to do this, there's a way. Time to gather courage to take action!"

"Yes, definitely. Sailing is always an adventure; but with another crew, boat, and captain, and in a better month."

"Yes, in a heartbeat—I want to do the Caribbean/Bermuda/Azores and maybe stay in the Azores for a month or so!"

"Absolutely. I have done two trans-ats [transatlantic] and one trans-pac [transpacific], along with numerous Newport to Caribbean and back. I just simply love offshore sailing."

"Yes, because I loved every second of it."

"Yes, because it is such a nice feeling to be in the complete sailing mode. Instead of the small trips like 300 nautical miles (NM) where you are always busy, with the finish on 2000nm, it is too far away and you are just busy sailing."

"Absolutely yes!!!"

1.6 COASTAL HITCH-SAILING

"The journey of a thousand miles
begins with a single step."

— LAO TZU
(Chinese Philosopher and writer)

If you want to move into sailing, you don't have to cross an ocean right away. As a matter of fact, if you have never sailed before or if you want to learn *how* to sail, start near the coast. Coastal cruising is where most sailing action happens. A trip near shore or a short passage can be a way to figure out if an ocean passage is for you.

I recommend starting with mini hitch-sailing trips. In the beginning, I found sleeping on a boat to be a huge experience in itself. Go for a short hitch-sailing trip, like island hopping in Greece, Canary Islands, Cape Verde, the Caribbean or the Azores. This is the leisurely way to sail. It's fun, relaxing, and involves lots of jumping in the sea. It brings you to harbours and bays, which the crowd doesn't reach. You'll be hooked. And in the unlikely event you're not, or it doesn't match with the captain, you can hop off on the next island! As opposed to the Atlantic, where the next island is thousands of nautical miles away. You owe it to yourself, captain, and fellow crew to be confident you're ready for an ocean passage.

A few years ago, I was in Australia and I 'hitch-sailed' on a boat for the first time. First, I went to all yacht clubs along the coast of Queensland to see if I could join a boat for a day sail. Many harbours organise "join a yacht on Sundays" events, where anyone can join boats for an afternoon leisure sail. This was great! But I was 'oh so curious' to experience what it would be like to actually sleep on a boat. I dreamt of visiting the Whitsundays (Island Archipelago in Queensland, Australia) but I could not spend hundreds of dollars on a three-day hammock tourist trip. Besides, for real excitement, I needed to go beyond the tourist trail and explore places not in the guidebook. I found a boat on the internet and a few days later I was island hopping around the Whitsundays. The 'easy' thing with coastal sailing is that you can just hop off at the next port. On the ocean you can't!

Are you ready to go for the ocean-crossing? Even so, I recommend going sailing with the crew and captain first. Preferably for a few days at least. See how you get along and what condition the boat is in. I (thankfully!) did that on the first boat I was going to cross the ocean on. The test sail made me realise this was not the right boat for me to cross an ocean with. An ocean crossing is an adventure where there is no way back and no way to hop off. Sailing is slow. The ride is going to take a while, so you *really* need to be sure that you get along with the people. It's a big time invest-ment! You want to be able to share the fun, not just the ride.

1.7 SNAPSHOT OF MY HITCH-SAIL EXPERIENCES

Here is a snapshot of my Atlantic Ocean experiences.

Boat 1: *The Bounty*
Hopped on: La Gomera, Canary Islands, Spain. November 14, 2014.
Hopped off: Las Palmas, Canary Islands, Spain. December 7, 2014.
   Ocean life is unpredictable, and for reasons I will explain later, I did not feel comfortable crossing an ocean on The Bounty.
Boat & Crew: The Bounty is a 44ft Beneteau. We had an amazing crew team of six different nationalities, all young people with big dreams.
The route: We sailed 400 NM (Nautical Miles) around the Canary Islands (La Gomera, Tenerife, Isla Graciosa, Fuerteventura, Gran Canaria) in 21 days.
Costs: Sharing food and fuel costs (+/– €5/day). My task was document-ing the journey and helping the captain find crew.

Boat 2: *Sea Ya*

Hopped on: Las Palmas, Gran Canaria, Spain. Mid December, 2014.

Hopped off: Tobago, Trinidad & Tobago (South East Caribbean). March 1, 2015.

Boat & Crew: Sea Ya is a 44ft ketch captained by Rudy, a cool young dude who just happened to be from my hometown, Bavel. Along with me, there were two lovely Belgian ladies on board. We set sail on January 15th for Trinidad/Tobago, via Cape Verde. One crew member left in Cape Verde.

The route: Leg one: Gran Canaria (Canary Islands)—São Vicente (Cape Verde): 850 NM in 5.5 days. **Leg two:** Cape Verde—Tobago: 2,262 NM in 18 days.

Costs: €10 /sailing day (€240 total) + sharing food & fuel (+/– €600 with 3 crew). Total individual costs: €440.

Boat 3: *Cyclos II*

Hopped on: Antigua, Antigua & Barbuda, Caribbean. April 20, 2015.

Hopped off: Palma, Mallorca, Spain. May 25, 2015.

Boat & Crew: *Cyclos II* is a 90ft ketch, a superyacht. This was a delivery passage. We were a crew of seven, which included four permanent crew, two professional hired sailors, and I. We hand steered the whole passage since we didn't have an autopilot. With seven of us, this was no problem! Although I started out as "Suzy zigzag", I'm now an experienced compass steerer!

The route: Leg one: Antigua—Faial, Azores, Portugal: 2,900 NM in 12 days.

Leg two: Faial, Azores, Portugal—Palma, Mallorca, Spain: 1,100 NM in 11 days.

Costs: €0! Flights and expenses were covered by the captain, as well as a few days' pay for helping to clean the boat.

Boat 4: *Eau Too*

Hopped on: Fréjus, France. October 9, 2016.

Hopped off: St. Lucia, Caribbean. December 6, 2016.

Boat & Crew: Eau Too is a 57ft Black Sea yacht built in 2007 and refitted by the current owner over the last few years. Eau Too set sail for a circumnavigation around the world. We had seven people on board, representing six nationalities: Lebanon, Poland, France, Australia, UK, and me from The Netherlands. As part of the ARC+ rally, we left Las Palmas with 74 other sailboats, bound for the Atlantic Ocean via Cape Verde.

The route: Leg one: Fréjus (an attempted stop in Morocco—no place in the harbour)—Lanzarote—Gran Canaria: 1,522 NM in 12 days. One crew member left in Gran Canaria, but we found a replacement in Las Palmas.

Leg two: Gran Canaria—São Vicente (Cape Verde): 850 NM in seven days.

Leg three: São Vicente–Saint Lucia (Caribbean) 2,200 NM in 17.5 days.

Costs: €0! Fuel, ARC+ contribution and food was paid for by the owner (who was not the captain), and all crew also received €700 euro 'pocket money' per month.

2

ATLANTIC OCEAN PASSAGE: THE BEARINGS

*"One does not discover new lands without consenting
to lose sight of the shore for a very long time."*

—ANDRE GIDE
[Writer]

WHAT TO EXPECT FROM AN ATLANTIC SAILING ADVENTURE? Learn about the passage routes from Europe to the Caribbean, and from the Caribbean to Europe. When do boats cross the Atlantic? Where do they sail? What's the weather like? What kind of boats make this passage? How much time and money does it cost? Which rallies take place?

2.1 SAILING THE ATLANTIC OCEAN

The word "Atlantic" comes from the Greek "Atlantikos," meaning the "Sea of Atlas." The Atlantic Ocean is the second largest ocean in the world (after the Pacific), covering about 20% of Earth's surface. Christopher Columbus is often said to have been the first to cross the Atlantic and discover the Americas on a voyage to find a trade route to Asia. He did indeed discover land, but believed until his death that he was in Asia. Actually, Columbus was not the first European to reach what is now known as American land. As written in the 13th century Icelandic legends called

Sagas, the Viking explorer Leif Erikson landed on the North American Atlantic coast around the year 1,000 while on an expedition from Iceland, nearly five centuries before Columbus arrived in 1492.

During the second half of the 19th century, more and more leisurely Atlantic crossings started to take place, especially with larger and more luxurious sailing yachts. Over the last century sailing has become more popular, and more accessible. What used to be an imposingly vast ocean has turned into an increasingly popular passage for ocean adventure travellers. With modern well-equipped boats, it has become a safer and more feasible undertaking than it was back in the day. Now more than ever, the adventure of the ocean passage is available to anyone who is willing to take the plunge.

2.2 THE ATLANTIC SAILING ROUTES

Hundreds of sailing yachts make the Atlantic Ocean crossing each year. These undertakings don't happen all year round. Boats are dependent on the weather and seasons. Although the weather can't be guaranteed, boats avoid risk by simply being in the right place at the right time. Most boats travel the North Atlantic starting from Europe to the Caribbean or South America. Some boats make the passage from Africa to the other side. From the Americas, boats mostly go to Europe. Several different routes exist. The most popular route is the North Atlantic circle, driven by the season and **trade winds:** the Southern route goes from east to west and the Northern route from west to east. A small but increasing number of yachts also make a high **latitude** voyage like the North West passage or cross the South Atlantic from Africa to Brazil. I'll discuss the popular routes in more detail.

Southern route (east-to-west): Europe—Caribbean/Americas

Main route: Western Europe (mainland Spain and Portugal) or Mediterranean → sometimes Madeira → Canary Islands → sometimes Cape Verde or West Africa (Senegal or Gambia) → Caribbean/ South America.

High season: November, early December, January, and February.

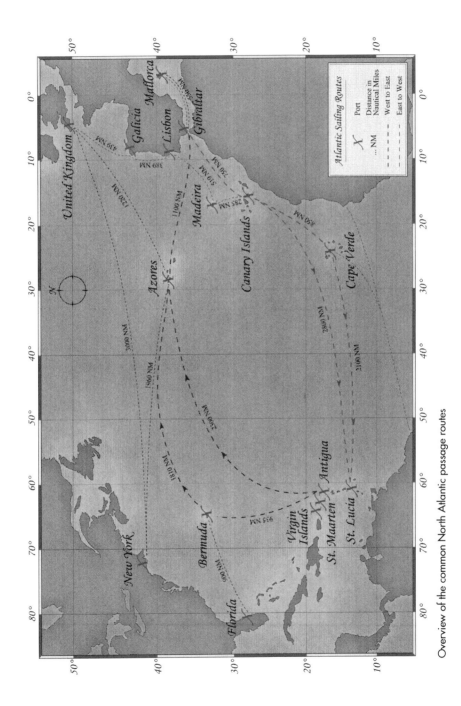

Overview of the common North Atlantic passage routes

The East to West route is the 'easy' route to sail. Around 1,500 sailboats make this crossing every year (this is a rough estimate, as there is no overall administration). Most of them go to the Caribbean. Few boats go to South America.

Sailing vessels in Europe start to make their way south during the **Northern hemisphere** summer season. Boats coming from northern Europe aim to cross the Bay of Biscay by latest September. Sometimes they stop in mainland Spain and Portugal to explore, provision, and get ready for the next passage. Boats coming from the Mediterranean mostly leave in September or October before autumn kicks in. Sometimes boats stop in the Portuguese island of Madeira. Almost all boats head south to the Canary Islands, an island group belonging to Spain, located West of Africa.

The Canary Islands are often the last port of call before the big journey begins. Las Palmas, on the island of Gran Canaria, is the most popular harbour, and the capital of the island group. Here is where the sailors find their spare parts, tools, charts, and provisions that are needed to set off well prepared. The islands of Tenerife and Lanzarote are also often chosen as the last stop before heading out to the ocean.

When departing the Canaries, boats often sail south until 'the butter melts,' to a **latitude** where they can find the most reliable **trade winds**. 20 degrees north is said to be the safest zone to head west.

Since Cape Verde is practically on the route, some boats choose to break up the passage and make a stop here. About a third of passage makers make a stop in this 10-island country, generally on the island of São Vicente. The Cape Verde island archipelago lies about 850 nautical miles south of the Canary Islands and 350 nautical miles west of the African coast. A stop in Cape Verde makes the Canary Islands—Cape Verde leg a nice appetiser before crossing the ocean. If you or any other crew member has never done offshore sailing before, it's a good test. You could leave the boat in Cape Verde may the journey did not work out as expected.

Few boats head to Brazil, French Guiana or Suriname. Boats going to Brazil sometimes choose to stop in Senegal or Gambia, instead of Cape Verde, before sailing into the ocean.

Due to the favourable trade winds and ocean **currents,** turning around is not an option, unless it's within the first day or two. One-day sailing west can take a few days to get back east. With the wind coming from the Sahara and the boat sailing in warm **currents,** it becomes nice and warm. As you go a bit further south every day, the temperatures get higher and higher. Goodbye winter, hello summer!

Northern route (west-to-east): Caribbean/ Americas—Europe

> **Main route: United States/Caribbean → sometimes Bermuda → Azores (most times) → Europe mainland, UK or Mediterranean.**
>
> **Route far north: US/Canada → sometimes Canada → Northern Europe.**
>
> **High season: End of April—July.**

The route from the Americas to Europe is the more adventurous passage. The weather is less predictable than from east-to-west. This journey is not 'just' a **down winder** like the east-to-west passage. There is likely to be more sailing action on this route.

An estimated 1,000 boats sail the passage from the Americas to Europe every year. The number of crossers is lower than the east-to-west passage as boats either continue their journey to the Pacific, leave their boats in the Caribbean for another season, sell them, or have them transported back to Europe on a cargo ship. There may be less boats making this passage; there are also less people for looking to crew.

Boats start to make their way to Europe as of April, to leave the Caribbean before the **hurricane** season starts. During the Caribbean 'generally **hurricane** free' season (December—May) boats that plan to sail across to Europe, often start south in the Caribbean and make their way north where they will leave for Europe or the USA. Those heading for Europe mostly set sail from one of the islands in the northern Caribbean, especially from the more popular sailing islands: Antigua, St. Maarten, or BVI. Some boats leave from the USA and Canada.

The West to East route often includes island stops in Bermuda and the Azores. By taking this route, it's likely to have the most reliable wind. A few boats take the route far north, along Nova Scotia, if they choose to go to Northern Europe. This route far north skirts the iceberg area. Though unlikely these days, icebergs have even been seen south of the Azores. Bigger yachts with decent fuel capacity often take the less predictable wind route directly from St. Maarten or Antigua. They take the risk (of mostly facing light winds in 'the Azores high') and go straight to the Azores. Aside from boats bound for Northern Europe and sailing more north, only a few yachts skip the Azores.

2.3 WHEN TO HITCH A RIDE?

Southern route (East to West)

OCTOBER This is when boats start to leave for the Atlantic. The weather is still tricky and inconsistent at this time of year. It's a risky month to set sail. It's still officially **hurricane** 'season' until the first of November. **Charter** boats which need relocation to the other side, often leave early to experience the full Caribbean season. It's a good time to start searching for a boat. You'll be one of the first. There is less crew competition. Due to a higher chance of hurricane development, think twice if you want to leave in this month.

NOVEMBER The Caribbean season begins the end of November. More boats start to cross the Atlantic. It's a good month to search for a ride locally. It's a competitive month too. More aspiring crew members are present in the harbours of the Canary Islands, predominantly Las Palmas. November is also the month when the Atlantic Rally for Cruisers (ARC) takes place. This is a fun but popular event to join. Looking for a ride in the **ARC** is competitive, and may be more expensive.

DECEMBER Boats leave during the first week of December. Then the numbers drop until the end of the month as many prefer to celebrate Christmas and New Year's Eve on shore.

JANUARY This is when the **trade winds** really start to kick in. Winds are usually more consistent. With winter setting in around (southern) Europe, it is a nice time to leave, and there's a good chance of finding a boat. It's quieter on the dock than in November, and many adventure seekers have already found a boat or gave up the search before Christmas.

FEBRUARY Since most boats prefer to take advantage of the full Caribbean season, which ends in May, fewer boats leave later in the season. Around February there are fewer boats, but also fewer boat seekers around. This gives you a reasonable chance to find a spot.

MARCH–MAY Boats are crossing, but not many. There won't be many hitch-sailors around since most of them aim for a winter escape and leave earlier.

JUNE Hurricanes generally start to develop in June. They build up on the southern route of the Northern Atlantic Ocean. Very few boats leave. It's a tricky month to go to the Caribbean. It's less risky for boats going to Brazil, since South of Cape Verde is out of the hurricane zone.

JULY–SEPTEMBER Hurricane season. Hardly any boat will cross the Atlantic to the Caribbean during this time. If one does, it's super risky. Passages to Brazil can still be made, though very few boats do.

Northern route (West to East)

APRIL Boats generally head east towards Europe starting April when the chance of facing a bad winter depression has dropped. The Antigua Sailing Week and Antigua Classics also takes place in April. These are spectacular events to attend, after which many boats leave for Europe, making Antigua a good place to find a ride. Weather can still be rough in April. In April 2017 tropical storm Arlene passed between Bermuda and the Azores. This was the second tropical storm ever measured in April.

MAY Most boats set off in May. Most sailing events have finished, **hurricane** season is approaching, and so is summer in Europe. Hurricane season officially starts on June 1st (at least for most insurance policies), so boats want to leave the Caribbean from mid-May since the weather is safer.

JUNE–JULY The weather will be a little bit warmer. Boats do leave during this month, though fewer than in May. Since in the late months of winter and early spring, depressions move in a northerly direction, it's safest for boats to have passed the Azores by then, which is June/July. In June–July it's more likely to find a boat higher north, in the USA, than in the Caribbean.

AUGUST–DECEMBER August and September are the months when hurricanes are most likely to develop, creating dangerous and challenging conditions across the western Atlantic. Hurricane season lasts until November, and very few boats cross the Atlantic during this time. When it's autumn in the **Northern hemisphere,** October and November, weather between the Azores and northern Europe can be rough. It's not a favourable time to be out on the ocean.

JANUARY, FEBRUARY, MARCH Avoid. Due to winter, not a safe time of the year to sail this route.

2.4   HOW LONG DOES IT TAKE?

The duration of the journey depends on different criteria such as weather, the boat (weight, size, shape), sailing skills on board, whether or not the boat stops along the way in any of the islands, and if an engine will be used on non-windy days. Some boats cross in two weeks; for others, it takes a month. It's better to talk in distance (**Nautical Miles/ NM)** than in time. You never know what will happen.

Before boats arrive at the last port of departure before sailing the Atlantic, which is most often an island, a passage, or two, need to be undertaken (For example mainland Europe to the Canary Islands—as you can see on the map). On stops 'along the way' there are preparations and explorations to be done. Boats will only set sail if there's a good weather window. Which sometimes means, waiting for weeks. Crewing on a shorter multi-day passages is a great way to figure out if offshore sailing is for you.

Boats make a longer distance than a 'direct line' due to wind direction, wind shifts, **currents,** and steering inaccuracies. The general rule of thumb is to add 15–20% distance on top of the plotted route to calculate the 'real' distance that you will be covering from port to port.

The Southern (east-to-west) passage is the 'easier' one, but also the longer one, depending on where you leave from. First, boats have to reach the Canary Islands from wherever they are in Europe. From the Mediterranean and the South West point of mainland Europe, it's about 750 NM to the Canary Islands (5–7 days—once there is a good weather window). From the Canary Islands to Cape Verde it's 850 NM (5–8 days). The Canary Islands to the **Windward Islands** in the Caribbean is roughly 2,700 NM distance (16–21 days).

On the Northern (west-to-east) route, boats go via Bermuda for the best winds. From the British Virgin Islands (BVI) to Bermuda it's 854 NM (5–9 days sailing). From Bermuda to the Azores it's 1,900 NM (14–17 days sailing). From Antigua to the Azores it's 2,300 NM (12–20 days sailing). Depending on where you're going to when leaving the Azores it's about 700 NM (4–8 days sailing) to the west coast of Portugal. It will take an additional 3–10 days if you're going to the UK, or to the Balearic Islands in the Mediterranean Sea.

It can also happen that you face days of hardly any wind. On my last crossing from Cape Verde to St. Lucia we had ten days with hardly any wind. We had the luxury of a **cruising chute** and an engine. But our boat was heavy and therefore safe, but slow. A hitch-sailor mentioned in the survey that "it took 40 days from the Caribbean to England due to no wind!" This is almost double the days for an average West to East crossing. Be prepared for a long ride. It can happen.

Pre-departure, you should allow yourself *at least* a week in the harbour to find your ride. Super lucky people find a boat within a few days, others after three months. This is all part of the fun.

How fast do boats go?

- The bigger the boat, the faster it goes. The heavier the boat, the slower it goes. Hull and keel shape, sails, and sailing skills, make a big difference too.
- Catamarans go faster than most monohulls (less displacement).
- A **monohull** of between 30–40 **feet** (10–13 metres) covers an average distance of 100 Nautical Miles a day.
- A 50+ feet monohull or catamaran averages 150–200 **Nautical Miles** a day.
- In general, there *is* no general; every voyage is different.

Learn about knots and miles so you can calculate duration based on distance and average boat speed.

DO: spend time in the Canary Islands, Cape Verde, and The Azores. These island archipelagos are beautiful places—I didn't want to leave!

CHAPTER 2 – ATLANTIC OCEAN PASSAGE: THE BEARINGS

DON'T: have a strict timeline. Ocean passages are dependent on weather, so trips can turn out longer or even shorter than scheduled. Be flexible! The plan might change as well.

How long did it take me?

EAST-TO-WEST

On *Sea Ya* (January–February 2015, 44ft ketch), it took us 5.5 days from Las Palmas to Cape Verde (850NM), and 18 days from Cape Verde to Tobago. We stayed one week in Cape Verde (too short!).

On *Eau Too* (November–December 2016, 57ft monohull), it took us seven days from Las Palmas to Cape Verde (850NM), and 18 days from Cape Verde to Saint Lucia. With the ARC+ we stayed five days in Cape Verde. On this trip, we had about ten days of hardly any wind. Since the boat was heavy, we were slow on light wind days. We used the engine to keep up with our daily calculated average of 120 miles per day.

WEST-TO-EAST

On *Cyclos II* (April–May 2015, 90ft ketch), it took us 12 days from Antigua to the Azores and ten days from the Azores to Mallorca. We stayed one week in the Azores. Again, I wish I could have stayed longer. All crossings (including the stopovers, but not including the preparation and on-shore fun before and after) took about one month.

2.5   HOW MUCH DOES IT COST?

You can either pay, or if you're lucky earn to cross as crew. These are the five most common scenarios (further explained below):
1. Daily Contribution.
2. Shared Expenses.
3. Expenses Covered.
4. Paid Passage. Captains pay you for your work.
5. Pay your Passage.

It depends on what kind of experience you want, what skills you can contribute, your funds, and the owner. Unless you are a highly experienced sailor, it will probably cost you some money. Like on land, housing, food, and transport cost money even when you are at sea. Contrary to what many may think (and I used to think), most cruisers are not money rich people. They often invest all their money and time into making the big sailing dream a reality. What are you willing to contribute to making yours happen?

Daily Contribution

Since massive boat investments are made to cross the Atlantic, many captains ask for a daily or passage contribution. An average of €10/day—€20/day is asked which helps to cover boat expenses. This amount doesn't come close to the total costs an average boat owner spends to cross the Atlantic safely.

During a **rally**, like the Atlantic Rally for Cruisers (ARC), some boats ask up to €50/day. Yacht entrance fees for the **ARC** are high, and for many cruisers, this rally is a 'bucket list' event to attend. If the captain does not have a commercial chartering insurance, they shouldn't ask for a contribution fee higher than the costs of the passage.

Shared Expenses

Some captains ask to share journey expenses like food. On an average sailing yacht crossing the Atlantic, you will pay your share for food (+/– euro/day— varies greatly on how you provision) and other personal costs (like travel and visas). On many boats, fuel and marinas fees (those costs vary widely depending on preferences and location—research and ask!) are also shared.

Usually, customs and immigration charges (in most countries this includes a charge for the boat and a small fee per crew member), and occasional Marine Park fees are covered by the captain. Customs and immigration fees can range from a few dollars to hundreds of dollars, so *if* you're sharing these costs, research the destination(s) you're going to, to know what this might cost you.

The crew team can choose to exempt the captain for chipping in for food. He or she has invested seriously in making the boat ocean worthy. It's a polite gesture, and you can show your appreciation for having been welcomed on board.

Expenses Covered

Some captains cover food, fuel, and harbour/mooring fees. Sometimes even transport costs to and from the boat are covered. So if you're lucky, an ocean sailing adventure might not cost you a cent. It's rare to find a ride entirely free of charge. I've met several boat seekers who crossed for free in exchange for a helping hand. With a free ride it's probable you're expected to work more than average. Free rides are the exception, and saving money should not be your main reason to sail across an ocean. It will cost you time, which you could spend more efficiently working to earn money for a flight ticket or two.

Bigger yachts often have more funds, but they also have more work to be done. Your ride may be a mix of leisure and a job. Larger yachts often take one or two crew in addition to their permanent and/or hired professional crew. For them, you're a cheap helping hand, so this can be a nice win-win.

Paid Passage

If you're super lucky or highly experienced, you could find a ride and get paid too. Sometimes owners/captains don't just want, but *need* crew, and some of them will pay if you have the right skills to contribute.

Pay to be passenger

If money is not an issue, you can also choose to pay a few thousand euros to be crew on a commercial **charter** trip.

Extra costs to take into account

- Costs of getting to and from the boat.
- Accommodation, food, and drinks in pre-departure and arrival harbour towns.
- Gear you might want to have, like a good jacket, duffel bag, cap, or a camera to capture the fun. Check if there's an ocean-worthy life jacket for you on board, or you have to provide your own.
- Travel/health insurance.
- Backup funds for when it does not go as planned.
- Visa.

WHAT DID CREW PAY?

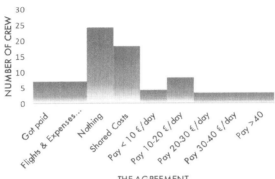

THE AGREEMENT
*shared costs: food, fuel, and marina fees.

To get a better idea of what everyone is paying and charging, I asked the hitch-sailors and captains in the survey what they paid and charged. More than half of the respondents shared the costs of food, fuel, and the marina, and often contributed a daily fee.

HOW MUCH DID IT COST ME?

	The Bounty	Sea Ya	Cyclos	Eau Too
Transport to and from boat	€125	-	-	€400
Accommodation prior/after crossing	€200	-	€100	€35
Food (on board only)	€100	€300	-	-
Fuel	-	€100	-	-
Marina Fees	-	-	-	-
Customs/ Immigration	-	-	-	-
Daily Contribution	-	€300	-	-
Payment	-	-	-	€1,000
Total Costs	**€525**	**€700**	**€100**	**No costs**

1. **THE BOUNTY:** I paid transport expenses to and from the boat (€90 one-way flight The Netherlands–Tenerife, €35 ferry from Tenerife to La Gomera), accommodation on shore since the boat was delayed (€100), and when I left this boat (€100). We shared costs of food and fuel (€5/day). I didn't pay any extra daily charge as I struck a deal to help out with photos, story-writing and finding crew. The rest of the

crew paid €35/day, on top of the shared costs. This is above average. Eventually, I did not cross with this boat.

2. **SEA YA:** All crew (including me) paid €10/day, on sailing days only, and we shared fuel and food costs (approximately €10/day). The captain paid for marina and immigration fees. Travel expenses to and from the boat were also up to the crew to cover themselves. I was already in Las Palmas, so I didn't have transport costs here.

3. **CYCLOS II:** The captain paid for flights to and from the boat, covered all food, harbour and fuel expenses, and even paid me for a few days of cleaning the boat afterwards. On land, expenses were on me except for a few crew dinners. The rest of the crew on board were either per-manent crew or hired professionals. This was a **delivery**.

4. **EAU TOO:** The owner, who was not the captain, gave all crew 'pocket money'. We received €700/month for crewing on the boat. All on board expenses were covered by the owner as well. I also received €100 contribution for transport to the boat, which cost me €500 in total.

   NOTE. I did not include personal costs on shore like bicycle rental, a beer in the bar, going out for dinner, and own foods I brought on board. This is all personal but *do* take these costs into account. You mostly likely will go out at some point.

All sorts of arrangements exist to cover the costs and charge for an ocean passage. Because I did not research the first crossing well enough, left 'The Bounty,' and had to find another boat, I lost a few hundred euro's in the process. The journey of *Sea Ya* reflects the average costs for an Atlantic Passage. I was incredibly lucky with *Cyclos* and *Eau Too* that contributed to my expenses. With the second and third crossing, it helped that I already had gained some experience. It's not common to catch a ride for free or to get paid.

The captains propose the arrangement. Understand that it's their boat, it's up to them. You take it or leave it. Realise that contributions asked, go towards increasing safety and comfort on the boat. This is in your own interest. You will thank the captain for buying that spare part, so you can fix it or the trip isn't delayed for a week because a spare had to be flown in. That can cost you. With smart provisioning, you can reduce your costs (and environmental impact!). That said, while you may have a budget, the amount you pay is not as important as being on a boat where you *feel* happy and safe, and that is safe! For any ride, but especially a 'free' ride, make sure the intentions, expectations, and safety situation are acceptable. Dynamics and workload will be different as opposed to a situation where everyone chips in. More on assessing happiness and safety in Chapter 5. Overall, if you take the average cost per day, the expenses are not more than when living or travelling on land.

DO: expect to chip in. Be clear and make agreements in advance about which costs will be shared.

DON'T: pay in advance (unless for a registered charter). Be super sure you want to cross with this boat before handing over your cash. I know people who left boats for valid reasons and are still trying to get their money back (up to thousands of euros!). When you are sure, I think it's acceptable to pay 50% on departure and 50% on arrival.

2.6 NORTH ATLANTIC WEATHER

The basics on the weather in the North Atlantic.

Weather System

Air naturally moves from high-pressure to low-pressure areas to balance the pressure difference. This causes winds. An **anti-cyclone** is a high-pressure weather system around which air slowly circulates clockwise while at the same time air moves towards a low-pressure centre. In the north Atlantic the anti-cyclone (also referred to as subtropical high) is known as the 'Azores High.' This anti-cyclone changes in size and can move north or south, but it is usually situated about at 30 degrees' **latitude,** where the Azores are. The weather patterns in the North Atlantic, and accordingly the sailing routes, are mostly influenced by the Azores high. As opposed to cyclones, anti-cyclones are linked to calm and nice weather.

Wind

As sailors, we're after wind. South of the Azores High the clockwise system have a favourable wind direction bringing boats from Europe to the Caribbean. Trade winds are the prevailing pattern in lower **latitudes** of 20 degrees north of the Equator (when the butter melts). The trade winds cover a broad belt from West Africa to the Caribbean. They are called 'trade winds' because back in the days, these winds made it possible to bring goods to other places for trading.

Since the wind generally comes from the north-east and boats head direction south west, the wind comes mostly straight from behind. It makes the journey a **down winder** and a rocking ride. The boat swings from left to right. . . . All. The. Time. Don't worry; you'll get used to it. For most of the year, the trade winds blow on the southern side of the Azores High.

During a typical crossing, the trade winds are 3 to 5 Beaufort. There can be days with light wind, days with no wind and periods where the wind speed reaches up to 6 or even 7 **Beaufort.** Winds are generally more consistent and stronger between January and March, making that a good time to sail across. The winds are lighter in summer, which is also the hurricane season.

From the Caribbean to Europe the wind is less consistent, and the crossing is usually more intense. The main consideration is to not get stuck in the Azores High, where there are areas of very little wind. This is why boats often choose to go via Bermuda (instead of straight to the Azores from the Caribbean) since it's a more reliable wind route.

Temperature

Air temperatures vary with **latitude, current,** and month of the year. When you go from Europe to the Caribbean, the temperature will become more pleasant every day. Roughly every three degrees' latitude you move south, you can add up one degree Celsius to the mean air temperature. Whereas in the Canary Islands the average air temperature is 19 degrees Celsius, in Cape Verde you already have brought yourself to 23 degrees Celsius. From mainland Europe to about midway between the Canary Islands and Cape Verde, the water temperatures are relatively cold, and so is the air temperature. From where the trade winds kick in, you'll start to sail over warm waters. Warmer sea water comes with warmer air temperatures. Add warmth directly brought by the sun, and from half way point, you may wish for a few degrees colder. The sun is intense and shines almost every day. With the reflection of the water you have to be careful to not get sunburnt. Be prepared for the sunshine.

On the route from the America to Europe, you will have colder waters and therefore more frigid winds but not extreme cold, unless you leave before April which is not recommended. At night and during squalls you will thank yourself for having a good jacket.

Since you can and will have all sorts of weather, pack layers of clothes so you can adapt to the situation.

Navigational Hazard! Various measurements are used at sea, and different measurements are used by different nationalities: Celsius, Fahrenheit, feet, metres, miles, nautical miles. It can be confusing! See the Appendix for measurement conversions to make sure you're on the right page.

Currents

The north-east trade winds also generate a **current,** a flow of water that gives a favourable average one-knot push towards the Caribbean. This North Atlantic current is also part of a big clockwise moving system, which covers the entire ocean south of **latitude** 40 degrees north. When going east, the current can be minor up to the Azores. From the Azores, you are likely to pick up favourable current originating from the Gulf Stream.

Waves

You can be surfing the waves or looking over flat water like a lake. Waves in the ocean are referred to as **swell.** When the wind blows for a duration of time, it moves water, resulting in swell. Swell continuously moves, and it can continue to travel when there's no wind. Since swell is generated by distant weather systems, the ocean can still be rough when there is no local wind. When the wind is strong, swell is likely to be higher, since strong winds also are related to distant weather systems. Swell is hardly affected by the wind you have locally.

The angle of the swell as opposed to the direction to which the boat is going determines a large part of the comfort. When going with the swell, which is common between for example the Canary Islands and Cape Verde, you'll be surfing the waves with the boat, resulting in top boat speeds and excitement. When the swell comes from a side direction, you may occasionally receive a splashy 'hello' from **Neptune.**

Atlantic swell generally means big long waves as opposed to short, small waves in the Mediterranean, Caribbean Sea, or large lakes. You'll notice the difference if you sail into the Atlantic from the Mediterranean. Atlantic swell is more comfortable. Swell is generally expressed in **feet** (ft.), and in the 5–10 ft. range during the Atlantic passage. You can have days with no swell, which can allow for a swim! You may also have a day with swell reaching heights of 15–20 ft. or even more. This is rare but spectacular! Another reason to do your research on the seaworthiness of the boat.

When having a consistent swell, coming out of a particular direction for an extended period, it can be a good reference to check if you (or a fellow crew member) is steering well on course.

Squalls

On the ocean, you will also witness and experience **squalls**. A squall is a sudden, local **gust** or storm, and something to look out for, and antic-ipate on, during **watch.** They are common. They travel 20–25 **knots** and usually in the same direction as the wind. They normally come with rain and sometimes thunder and lightning. When you're in a squall, the wind suddenly picks up to around 25–30 knots and you might get a few buckets of rain. They usually only last about half an hour.

Tropical Storms and Hurricanes

As the water in the Atlantic becomes warmer, the region becomes more prone to the development of **tropical storms** and **hurricanes.** To minimise risk, avoid the **hurricane** season. The official Atlantic hurri-cane season, as defined by **NOAA,** falls between June 1 and November 30. In this period 97% of the hurricanes have occurred up to 2017 (3). The highest hurricane frequency is from August to October. When the winds in a tropical depression reach 35 **knots** (9 Beaufort), it is called a tropical storm, and given a name. When the wind speed reaches over 64

Squalls on the horizon

knots (12 Beaufort), it becomes a hurricane. Hurricanes often originate between five to 15 degrees' **latitude** north and south of the equator. They form on the ocean, sometimes as far east as the Cape Verdean islands, and travel westward towards the Caribbean. Both the frequency and intensity of hurricanes varies considerably each year. In April 2017, tropical storm Arlene was located between Bermuda and the Azores. This is very unusual early and north in the year. Hurricanes in the South Atlantic are extremely rare.

Navigational Hazard! If the word 'knots' is new to you, navigate to 'knots: speed & tying' first, and learn what it means, before you go nuts on knots.

Learn more about weather reading and forecast resources in 7.2 'skills to work on.'

What was the weather like on my crossings?

I have completed two crossings from Europe to the Caribbean: one in November, and one in January. In January, we had much better winds, which made the sailing more exciting!

EAST TO WEST

Mid-January (2015) we set sail with *Sea Ya* from Las Palmas to Cape Verde. Around the Canary Islands and Cape Verde acceleration zones can speed up the wind by ten to 20 knots. On this leg, we couldn't have had better conditions. 850 miles took us 5.5 days, even making 185 miles in a single day. We surfed the waves and averaged seven knots. That's seven miles we covered per hour. We had an average of 20 knots of wind. With the exception of a few days of eastern wind, most days we had north-east wind. The first half from Cape Verde to Tobago went smooth and quick. For the second leg, we had less wind but always some breeze.

The nice thing about leaving for the ocean crossing in January is that you've had a taste of winter in Europe. From there it only becomes warmer. The water temperature started with 23 degrees Celsius in the Canary Islands, 25 in Cape Verde, halfway across the ocean we measured 31 degrees Celsius! In the Canary Islands air temperatures were between 12 and 20 degrees Celsius in December and January. The journey from the Canary Islands to Cape Verde was chilly. Especially at night, we needed a jacket, sweater, and hat. After a few days, though, we could ditch the jacket, socks and every day we took off another piece of clothing. During the day shorts were okay. The air temperature in Mindelo (Cape Verde) was a pleasant 20–25 degrees in January. When we set off from there for Trinidad & Tobago, we still needed our long pants and jacket. Then every day it got a little bit warmer. Halfway we began to feel our presence in the tropical zone. The rest of the journey we could wear shorts and didn't need to bother with layers, socks, hats and scarfs anymore. This saves precious snoozing minutes with less time getting ready for watch.

Mid-November (2016) we leave for Las Palmas–Cape Verde with *Eau Too*. In November, average air temperature is pleasant in the Canary Islands. You can generally walk around in shorts. Between the Canary Islands and Cape Verde the air temperature was between 20–25 degrees during the day and a little chillier at night. We didn't need the wet weather outfit. It took us six days. Conditions on this leg were good with an average of 16 knots of northeast wind. From Cape Verde to Saint Lucia we had little wind. The first ten days the wind was between five and ten knots. I was hardly wearing long pants after Cape Verde.

WEST TO EAST

In April (2015) the lines are thrown off *Cyclos II* to navigate from Antigua to the Azores. Westerly winds dominate on this route. The winds on the northern route are less consistent. But on average we had 20 knots of wind. Not bad! Since you're going to higher **latitudes,** it gets colder every day. But that's also nice after a few months of tropical weather, and you certainly won't be freezing. Summer is approaching in Europe. About 70% percent of days were sunny. We had two days of almost non-stop rain since we chose to go straight to the Azores from Antigua and not via the recommended Bermuda route. An extra set of dry clothes was welcome! The water was colder, getting down to 17 degrees Celsius in the Azores.

2.7 TYPES OF BOATS CROSSING

What kind of boats can you expect to find crossing the Atlantic Ocean?

Small sailing vessels

Many privately-owned sailing vessels cross the Atlantic, to spend a sunny sailing season either in the Mediterranean or Caribbean, or as part of their around the world voyage. It is a big thing for them, and attracts all sorts of seamen and women: young 'pirate' dudes who have escaped the rat race, adventure couples, retirees, families, groups of friends, and single older sailors. The largest share of the captains is between 50—65 years old. It's the group that has the time and money resources to sail.

All sorts of nationalities make the crossing, with the French and Swedish seeming to dominate the fleet. By crewing on a small sailing yacht, you'll be involved with every aspect of **seamanship** and sailing. You will learn a lot for sure. Many boats choose to stop in Cape Verde or the Azores and often don't have tight schedules.

Boats come in all sorts of shapes and materials. Hulls are made from steel, wood, aluminium, and today mostly of fibreglass (plastic). 90% of the boats crossing the ocean is bigger than 36ft, with most of them measuring around 44ft. (14m). A smaller yacht could also be perfectly ocean worthy. I've seen boats of 26 ft. crossing the pond. Some adventure people row across the Atlantic. In 2017 someone even Stand Up Paddled (SUP) across the Atlantic. Being on any boat is a luxury compared to that. Six surveyees crossed the Atlantic on a boat smaller than 36ft. and all of them would like to do it again.

Both **monohulls** and **catamarans** cross the Atlantic. Catamarans are generally faster, more spacious, and rock less. On the flip side: they can flip! If they do, it's a major challenge to come up again. Don't worry, this is extremely unlikely. Having seen hundreds of boats planning, preparing and making the crossing, I estimate that roughly 70% of the boats that cross are monohulls.

Big yachts/Superyachts

Many larger yachts cross the Atlantic as a '**delivery**', where a boat needs to be taken from point A to B. Boats have to be moved across the ocean for a new **charter** season, for the private owner who will hop on board again on the other side, or because someone bought it on the other continent.

Usually paid and professional crew do these types of deliveries. Hitch-sailors can be a cheap extra set of hands.

A yacht is a 'superyacht' when it is over 24 metres (79ft.). These are *big* yachts. They often have generators running every day to keep fridges and freezers going. They load up thousands of litres of fuel and water, and are less dependent on the wind. As such, there is less risk and generally more comfort. These trips often run on a tight schedule, so there won't be much flexibility for stops along the way (like in Cape Verde or the Azores). In most cases there will also be more people on board (five-eight people compared to three-five on smaller vessels).

Crossing on a big boat like this is faster, less adventurous, and more comfortable. The crew are often younger, and some live and work permanently on the boat. Many of them have crossed the Atlantic Ocean numerous times and are therefore less excited about it than the average 'yachtie'. Timelines are tight and there's often not time for island exploration. Usually, you are expected to work hard.

Charter yachts

If you would rather not have the pre-crossing adventure or spend time searching for a boat, and/or if money is not an issue, you can book a **charter** ocean passage. Charter trips are organised on all sorts of boats: small, big, monohulls, catamaran, and racing boats.

Numerous racing yachts cross the ocean reaching boat speeds up to 35 knots! In addition to professional crew, spots are sold and you can sign up for a wet and speedy adventure guaranteed.

A charter trip costs between €2,000 and €10,000. An organized trip like this could be advantageous if you're on a tight schedule. It's more likely to leave on the planned date. At the same time, the time schedule could be a disadvantage. What if the weather window is not ideal to leave? In many cases, though not always, everything is taken care of such as provisioning and cooking, so you wouldn't have to figure out much yourself.

Another consideration of booking this type of passage is that you won't know your shipmates. When you search the adventurous way, you have the opportunity to meet the other sailors before you commit to joining the crew. On a chartered passage you're stuck with whoever else has booked the trip, even if you don't like them.

Tall ships

Every year numerous tall ships cross the Atlantic, like the Stad Amsterdam or Oosterschelde. I haven't experienced this (yet!) but sailing across on a large traditional boat must be spectacular. Many young people work on the tall ships. You could either try that or simply buy yourself a passage.

Tall Ship Stad Amsterdam in Horta (Azores)

Ferries

There are no sailing ferries (yet), although boats are being built for this purpose. At the time of writing, Voyagevert is conducting feasibility studies to construct the fastest and largest sailing catamaran for a ferry service as a sustainable alternative to flight for transatlantic travel.

Cruise ships

Another kind of ferry are the cruise ships. More and more cruise ships cross the Atlantic to do the season on the other side. They need relocation and spots on board are sold as 'repositioning cruises.' It's often cheaper than airfare and your house rent combined. One option that is cool, is 'Nomadcruise,' an Atlantic crossing for entrepreneurs and digital nomads.

These floating cities are not an environmentally friendly way to cross. It takes around eight days and a lot of noise to cross with a cruise ship. Data on emissions is remarkably difficult to find. Some sources state that an average cruise ship at sea emits more, and less filtered, smoke than one million cars combined each day. In a one week trip, a large cruise ship generates ten backyard swimming pools of **blackwater** (raw sewage), and 40 more swimming pools of **greywater** (water from sinks, baths, showers, laundry and galleys). They also generate large volumes of oily **bilge** water, sewage sludge, garbage and noise (4).

Cargo ships

More cargo ships cross the Atlantic than sailboats. This is a non-sailing ship option that can take you across. Cargo ships usually rent out a few cabins to passengers. This costs a few thousand euros. Travelling with a cargo vessel can be a good alternative if you want to cross the ocean, don't like sailing, and do not want to fly. Prepare to be surrounded by engine noise. Crossing on a cargo would take one to two weeks. Depending on weather, cargo and size, cargo vessels run between 15–25 **knots.**

There are also *sailing* cargo Atlantic crossing possibilities out there. 'Tres Hombres' is a 32 metres **Schooner** transporting traditional goods like rum and chocolate between the Caribbean and Europe. Timbercoast is a 1920 built 43.5m Schooner that transports goods like coffee and gin. Both ships welcome crew on board helping out with this sustainable way of transporting goods.

My preference

"What kind of boat are you joining?" This was the first question most people asked me when I told them I was going to cross the Atlantic Ocean. I knew nothing about boats, and thought "Does it matter? I just want to make the passage!" Having sailed across on three completely different boats, I know now that the type of boat determines large part of the experience. Not just because of the boat, but because of the tasks and people involved with that type of boat.

Of all the options, my preference is to crew on a smaller **monohull** sailboat of 40–44ft—basic, but adventurous and on these boats I've met the coolest captains. Monohulls are more fun to sail. It's easier to 'feel' the boat as opposed to a catamaran. It's kind of like a scooter versus a quadbike. Smaller boats generally allow for more exploring and socialising time around the harbour—since there's usually less work to be done.

Above all, getting along with fellow crew and captain is most important!

2.8 RALLIES

You can also try to crew on a boat in a **rally**. A rally is a group of sailboats making the same passage at the same time. This can be more fun, social, safer (because of regulations and more helping hands around), and leaves on a schedule. It can also be costlier and more competitive to find a crew spot.

The ARC (Atlantic Rally for Cruisers)

The Atlantic Rally for Cruisers (ARC) is the biggest rally across the Atlantic, taking place in November every year. Around 200 boats set sail together for the Caribbean, departing from Las Palmas and arriving in St. Lucia. Another 75 boats sail away with the ARC+, also from Las Palmas, just before the main ARC starts. The ARC+, which I joined on my third crossing with *Eau Too,* includes a stop in Cape Verde. ARC Europe is a smaller rally that leaves from the British Virgin Islands (BVI) via the Azores, to Lagos in Portugal. The ARC1500 goes from the USA to the BVI.

Many gatherings, workshops and parties are organised around the ARC, which gives the whole adventure an extra dimension of fun and community. Safety of participants is taken seriously. The ARC organization has set a minimum standard for safety and communications equipment. Boats joining will be inspected by the ARC organization (always, also do your own research on the boat, captain, and crew).

When the ARC happens it's busy and hectic in the harbour of Las Palmas. With many other aspiring crew members looking for a boat to cross with. Unless you are well experienced, or willing to pay extra to join the crew, it will be a challenge to find a boat. As one hitch-sailor said: *"There were like 50 people looking for a boat. Just too much competition."* I was offered a spot on board the *Eau Too* for the ARC+ because of the experience I had gained on my previous two crossings.

If you are determined to join a boat for the ARC, start your search months in advance to increase chances of success. ARC boat captains tend to look for crew much earlier than others. Last minute crew changes happen often so if you're after the ARC but late with searching try to arrive in Las Palmas at least two weeks beforehand. You'll be there when boats start to sail in to make their preparations. You can also try discounted marinas for ARC participants on the route to Las Palmas (for example Rubicon Lanzarote), to investigate for potential ARC crew spots. ARC participants are allocated a harbour spot one week before sailing out so that's when you want to be in Las Palmas. Or why not lend a hand with the ARC organisation? Last ARC there was a smart Italian guy that nailed himself a job as the shuttle bus driver. This gave him many opportunities to chat with the ARC participants, and he found himself a spot. So did a few other determined aspiring crew members I met in Las Palmas.

The city of Las Palmas itself acknowledges that the ARC is a big event for them. Many restaurants and local entrepreneurs have special offers for ARC participants.

If you are a sailing newbie, or prefer peace and quiet, I would avoid Las Palmas in the run-up to the ARC, and concentrate your search around non-ARC participants in other harbours in the Canary Islands. Other boats who are not part of the ARC are making their preparations elsewhere while they wait for space to free up in the harbour. Chances are higher that you will find a boat.

Learn more about the ARC and event dates on *worldcruising.com/arc*.

Other Rallies

- **ODYSSEY RALLIES** Jimmy Cornell, who with numerous circumnavigations and published sailing books, is a big name in the cruising world, organises four different Atlantic Ralleys: Atlantic or Caribbean directly, and Atlantic & Caribbean via Cape Verde. With the theme *'Our Ocean-Our Future',* you can participate in events and seminars prior to departure and learn all about sailing and ocean conservation. This event has a maximum of 50 participants, which keeps the vibe like a little family. It departs in November (optional via Cape Verde) and January from Tenerife (optional via Cape Verde) and arrives in Barbados. Learn more on *CornellSailing.com*

- **ILE DU SOLEIL (ISLANDS OF THE SUN)** This French organization runs two rallies: one following the route Madeira–Morocco–Senegal–Brazil and a separate rally going from Madeira–Canary Islands–Cape Verde–Caribbean. Learn more on *rallye-ilesdusoleil.com*
- **THE ROYAL OCEAN RACING CLUB** (RORC) organises a transatlantic race from Lanzarote to Grenada. Learn more on *rorcTransAtlantic. rorc.org*
- One of the amazing races that involve an Atlantic crossing is the Clipper round the world race. It's not easy to board one of these as crew if you don't have experience or are on a budget, but it's still worth checking out, if only for the photos. Learn more on *clipperroundtheworld.com*

3

THE SEARCH FOR A RIDE

"The will must be stronger than the skills."

— MUHAMMAD ALI
(Sports figure)

YOU'VE DECIDED TO GO FOR THE CROSSING. Great! The decision alone is already exciting. Now, how and where can you find a boat? Where to look on the internet? In which harbours can you find a ride? How to profile yourself? What to watch out for if you are a girl doing this alone? How likely is it to find a ride as a couple? This chapter discusses the aspects of the boat search.

3.1 WHERE TO FIND A BOAT?

"Luck is what happens when
preparation meets opportunity."

- SENECA
(Roman writer & philosopher)

The most common three methods to find a boat are through connection via internet platforms, personal contact at the harbour, or referrals from your network. There is no fixed "best" approach. It depends on what kind of experience you want. It depends on luck. And it depends on your efforts. In general, to increase the chances of finding a boat, throw out as many lines as possible to give yourself a better chance of catching something. Try different approaches. Do be careful not to get tangled up, by committing to multiple boats.

PRO AND CONS

	Pros	Cons
Your Network	• Crew with personal references is preferred over complete strangers	• Smaller chance of finding a boat via reference if you're a newbie in the sailing world
The Internet	• You can connect with captains all over the world • You can search far in advance • You can carefully craft your first introduction, profile, and questions	• Hard to find out if you will get along • Difficult to assess if experience and boat state is as claimed • Scamming ground • Crew websites ask for a contribution
Harbours	• Quicker to find a boat last-minut. • Easier to 'feel' if it's a possible match • Easier to identify state of the boat • Fun!	• Last-minute gives you less time to do proper investigation • You find few boats that make the crossing • Cost and time intense

Your network

Boats usually look for crew in their network first. If they can't find the skills or availability from people they know, they look further on the internet or in the harbour. You might already know some seafarers, or maybe some of your friends have sailors in their network. Spread the word about your mission. Use the power of social media connections. Ask your friends if they have any tips, links or connections. They may or may not, but they will keep you in mind if they hear or read about any possibilities. Everyone is willing to help.

Before I started the sailing journey, I had only met a handful of sailors. I contacted those I knew with a personal message to ask if they might know anyone who would be crossing the Atlantic any time soon. My network didn't give me any leads for the first crossing, but for the second it did, leading me to *Cyclos II*.

The Internet

Today's technology allows us to find out about crew positions and connect with captains all over the world. The internet has connected us more than ever. In this section you'll learn more about crew websites, sailing forums, and social media communities that can be helpful in your boat search.

If you are a complete newbie like I was, spend some time on the internet first. Read blogs of sailors, captains, crew, and explore crew websites. It gives you a better idea of what **passage making** is all about, who's looking for crew, what kind of boats are out there, and what they are searching for.

> *Navigational Hazard! These platforms are set up with the right intentions. Though be aware that there are people out there misusing the platforms for other purposes than finding crew to help sail the boat. The internet is also a place for scams. You must be wary how, where, and with whom you connect and exchange personal details. Be especially cautious when:*
> * *No profile photo of the captain is present*
> * *Little information is given*
> * *Only female crew is considered*
> * *Captains immediately ask your email addres.*
> * *Your questions are not being answered*
>
> *Read more on assessing the happiness and safety in* Chapter 5

Let's explore the platform possibilities of the world wide web.

Crew websites

Some entrepreneurs have set up a website with the specific purpose to facilitate the matching of boats with potential crew and vice versa. There are numerous crew websites out there. They all have search engines and selection criteria to find a match, in both ways.

I've reached out to the crew websites' management and reviewed noteworthy ones relevant to an Atlantic crossing. There is no 'best' crew website. Each one has their unique edge and differs in other aspects. Choose your favourite(s) and sign up!

> **NOTE.** The internet is a fast changing landscape. The information presented here is a status impression dated August 2017. Findings are found through analysis of the websites, and responses from website management of whom most replied to me on questions asked about their platform. I have not taken into account future plans of any website since plans often change, especially in anything related to sailing.

FindAcrew

Findacrew.net

ABOUT

Find a Crew, founded in 2004, is one the first online crew and boat networks. This global matchmaking platform has consistently been growing ever since, and states to be the world's largest online crew and boat network. On the platform, you can check for sailing opportunities, paid and unpaid, in marinas and docks in over 200 countries and five oceans. On the homepage, it shows how many crew and boats have signed in during the last 24 hours, which on average are a few hundred boats and double the amount of crew.

HOW DOES IT WORK?

Without registration, you can see snapshots of the sailing opportunities. You create a profile to be able to search for boats, express interest to boats, and receive interest from boats. Both aspiring crew and boats can create extensive profiles with information on lifestyle, experience, plans, and expectations. You can indicate where you are, where you wish to board a boat, and where you are looking to go. Under 'boat wanted' you can specify that you're looking for an Atlantic passage or position in a **rally,** like the **ARC.**

You can search with dozens of filters allowing for efficient and targeted boat seeking. With *QuickFind* you can automatically see the most relevant profiles matching your profile and preferences. You can save your favourite finds. You can receive an email notification when you have a new message.

Find a Crew offers two membership options: free and premium. If you're on a free plan, you can only send and receive *waves* to captains. If you both *wave* at each other, expressing mutual interest, you can start the conversation but *only* if one is a premium member. Premium allows to you send a personal message to matching members and exchange contact details.

WHAT ARE THE BENEFITS FOR YOU AS CREW?

- The platform offers a wide selection of crew opportunities all around the world.

- Users can make extensive profiles so you can learn a lot about your captain, his/her boat, and plans beforehand.
- With detailed setup and search filters the system efficiently finds the best matches for you.
- Only members logged in the last 45 days show up in search results making the boat opportunities up to date.
- See who viewed your profile the last 45 days, how many new boats registered and how many boats have updated their profile since the last time you signed in.
- Since messages can only be exchanged if one side of the party being premium, only serious requests are typically exchanged.

SAFETY AND SECURITY MEASURES OF THE WEBSITE:
- Members can go through identity verification by uploading their ID (stored on a separate secure server).
- Find a Crew has a full-time support team, providing service, and monitoring any dodgy activity. All profiles and profile updates are manually approved.
- The initial barrier for connecting between two members is an insurance safety measure for both crew and captains. This could serve as valid proof that FindAcrew.net was the first place of contact.
- You can manage your privacy settings and determine who you share your personal details with.
- The platform has a reference system.

THIS WEBSITE WON'T WORK FOR YOU IF:
- You don't want to invest time in creating an extensive profile and learning about the website features.
- You are not super internet savvy. The website needs some exploration to understand the full potential.

THE INVESTMENT
You need to invest some time to complete your profile and understand all the functionalities of the extensive system. Once done, you're not required to sign in every day. Keep your profile up to date and try to sign in at least once a fortnight when seriously looking for a crew or a position. Prices are in euro currency.

OPTIONAL: Personal Identity Verification (PIV—€13).

PREMIUM: A premium membership can be obtained any time for a period for 30, 60, 90 or 365 days. 30-day premium membership costs €49 / month. 365 premium costs €277/year.

Crewbay

Crewbay.com

ABOUT

Crewbay is an online crewing platform designed to connect newbie, amateur, and professional yacht crew with captains and boat owners from all over the world, and vice versa. The format is simple and free. On average, Crewbay has +150 boats registering each month and a typical of 150 boat log-ins every 24 hours. New design plans are in place and I, therefore, won't describe site features that are likely to change.

HOW DOES IT WORK?

Without registration, you can see snapshots of the sailing opportunities. To access profile information and contact captains, you must be a member. It's free to register.

You can use search filters and keyword search (e.g. Atlantic) to find relevant opportunities or browse the latest updated boat profiles.

Contact details are free to be shared, and you can communicate either via the platform's message system or by other contact information that has been shared. You can receive an email notification when you have a new message. You would need to login to see the message.

WHAT ARE THE BENEFITS FOR YOU AS CREW?

- The platform offers a wide selection of crew opportunities all around the world.
- It's free to register and use the functionalities for both crew and captains.
- You can choose to include any information in your profile and make it visible to any visitor.
- You can upload you CV to your profile and share it with one-click when reaching out to a captain.
- You can see when a member has logged in for the last time.

- You can create a list of 'favourites' making it easy to retrace opportunities.

SAFETY AND SECURITY MEASURES OF THE WEBSITE:
- Crewbay management checks out every registration and all photos are reviewed.
- The platform has a flagging system for spammers
- Crewbay has a reference system where members can offer feedback on boats and crew they've been connected with.

THIS WEBSITE WON'T WORK FOR YOU IF:
- You don't want to invest time in creating a crew profile.
- You don't want to receive messages by just any boat member interested in your profile.

THE INVESTMENT
Crewbay is free of charge and promises to always stay free. You would need to invest time to create a profile and browse through crew opportunities. As of 2017, they introduce a paid subscription membership that allows more access to those who are more serious about finding boats/crew.

OceanCrewlink
OceanCrewlink.com

ABOUT
Ocean Crew Link has been around since 2015 with the initial aim of connecting aspiring crew with captains for World Cruising Club's rallies, especially the **ARC.** Now Ocean Crew Link works as an introduction service to potential crew and boats looking to do any offshore passage: a boat sailing between two places at a particular time. On average, 10 to 15 new ocean sailing opportunities are posted to the site each week. Around 100+ active sailing opportunities are up at one time, and almost 10,000 users receive the weekly mailing with new opportunities.

HOW DOES IT WORK?
You can browse sailing opportunities without registration, but you must register to view details of sailing opportunities. You must subscribe, which includes a fee, to contact skippers. As a user, both for crew and

skippers, you complete a sailing profile that includes expressing your competencies on board and coastal and offshore distances sailed. The profile serves as a standard reference so that users can judge each other's abilities and skills.

You can browse passage opportunities under 'find boats' and make contact with captains that are looking for crew. You can filter a search by date, region, **rally,** experience, or financial arrangements that meet your preferences. As a subscriber, you can view the boats' profile and captains' profile.

Show interest with one click on 'Contact Captain.' The captain will automatically be notified with details on your profile. When both parties confirm interest, each party receives an email with each other's contact details, and you can exchange more information via email.

WHAT ARE THE BENEFITS FOR YOU AS CREW?

- The site focuses on ocean sailing for cruising boats.
- The site includes most **ARC** opportunities if that's what you're after.
- Both crew and captains must tick boxes in a list of boat skills (e.g. watch keeping or **'reefing'** with experienced, competent, basic or none). It's easier for both parties to figure out the capabilities of the other party. No need to find out what skills a local sailing license actually certifies.
- All opportunities contain dates, enabling older opportunities to be auto archived, keeping the site clear and focused on new opportunities.
- A weekly mailing sends out the most recent list of sailing opportunities to the entire network, not only subscribers. You could still watch attractive crew opportunities if you're not registered.

SAFETY AND SECURITY MEASURES OF THE WEBSITE:

- Captains and crew need to confirm interest before each person can see private details.
- Ocean Crew Link is set up by the World Cruising Club, a sailing **rally** organisation that has been around since 1986. With their strong network and track record, the website is possibly a less appealing place for scams.

THIS WEBSITE WON'T WORK FOR YOU IF:
- You're looking for day sails and coastal sailing opportunities.
- You don't want your personal contact details exchanged when both you and captain express mutual interest.

THE INVESTMENT

Registration is easy. You need to add some basic data to your profile before you can use the site. A complete profile needs more time investment and allows for more relevant connection. The subscription fee is US$10 for three months.

Yotspot

Yotspot.com

ABOUT

Yotspot started in 2010 with the mission to make it easier to find crew positions and contact captains directly. Overtime, this has evolved into a large yachting hub where people can find hundreds of crew jobs. The website focuses on paid sailing opportunities. Captains, as well as Crew agencies, are allowed to post to the website. The website moreover serves as an information portal on training and certifications in sailing. Their maritime training database lists over 6,000 courses. As of 2017, the website receives an average 30.000 unique visitors per month of which 50% of the traffic comes from France, UK, Spain, and Italy.

HOW DOES IT WORK?

You can view all crew and course opportunities without registration. A completed profile allows you to contact opportunities and to be contacted by captains. As crew, you can register for free. In *search,* you can select 'ocean sailing' to specifically look for ocean passage opportunities. Search broader on *sailing and/or temporary position* to see more potential options. You can opt to receive an email notification every time a new opportunity has been posted with your requirements.

WHAT ARE THE BENEFITS FOR YOU AS CREW?
- Find relevant information if you're looking to go professional in sailing.
- You can choose to make your profile private if you're worried about scrutiny from a current employer for example.

- In *my career* section of the website, you can see which certifications are next for you to obtain, including requirements, to climb on the professional sailing ladder. This is not only helpful if you're looking to (eventually) work on a boat, but helps to keep yourself informed on the existing sailing qualifications and learn what a captain is certified for.
- Due to the aggradation of crew opportunities the website serves as a one-stop shop where you can reach out to captains and crew agencies.
- You can share your profile link with anyone outside the website. It's an easy way to share your sailing resume.

SAFETY AND SECURITY MEASURES OF THE WEBSITE:
- As crew, you can only be contacted by paid members.
- All crew positions are verified by website management before placing.
- The website prevents any number, email, or website from being added to crew positions to protect you from scams, making sure you only contact each other through the website.

THIS WEBSITE WON'T WORK FOR YOU IF:
- You're looking for a leisure only ride. YotSpot focuses on jobs.
- You don't want to invest time in creating an extensive profile.
- You don't want any personal details shared with paid members.

THE INVESTMENT
As crew, you can create a free account and contact opportunities of interest. It is quite a time investment to create a completed profile.

SailOpo
Sailopo.com

ABOUT
Sail OPO (Sail Offshore Passage Opportunities) is a crew network that seeks, gathers, and creates quality offshore passage opportunities for its members. The network is predominantly USA based. The idea of OPO started in 1992 when the founder of the website was crossing the Atlantic, and many dock walkers came by and asked for a ride across the ocean. The passage allowed for some deep blue thinking and the crew network has been around for more than 20 years now. OPO also occasionally organises rallies, for example from USA mainland to Bermuda.

HOW DOES IT WORK?

Joining is free. You can preview sailing opportunities once registered. OPO allows you to create an extensive profile so captains can learn if you're a possible match. To obtain contact information and to view the profiles of captain OPO members, you must become a paid member.

Crew and captains can't post to the website. Details of passage opportunities will be e-mailed to potential crew candidates as they come up, and are approved by OPO staff. When interested in a crew opportunity you can reply with a 'cut and paste' profile to express interest and inform the captain of your competencies. On the website itself, you can check out past crew postings (without contact info) to get an idea what opportunities can be found via OPO.

WHAT ARE THE BENEFITS FOR YOU AS CREW?

- You will not miss anything if you forget to go to the website. Opportunities are only sent via email.
- OPO doesn't only mediate offshore crew opportunities, they also create them by organizing rallies.

SAFETY AND SECURITY MEASURES OF THE WEBSITE:

- All opportunities are pre-qualified through OPO admin.
- Since the network has been around for 20 years, many captains are known by the network and therefore are more trustworthy and a safety measure for crew. OPO indicates when a captain is new to the network and encourages you to ask more questions as crew.
- You can specify if you want your information to be shared with other members.

THIS WEBSITE WON'T WORK FOR YOU IF:

- You're on a tight budget.
- Not looking for positions leaving or going to the USA.

THE INVESTMENT

US$199 for an initial yearly membership. Membership renewal comes at a discounted rate of US$135.

Crewseekers
www.crewseekers.net

ABOUT
Crewseekers is a UK based family run business that launched in 1990. They are a global introductory service bringing captains and crews together. Both amateur and professional sailing opportunities from all around the world are available on the platform. This includes crew positions with private boats, **delivery** companies, sail training organisations, **charter** companies, sailing charities, and races.

HOW DOES IT WORK?
As crew, it's free to view the sailing opportunities. You can search on Ocean Voyages where you can see an overview of all ocean crew ads posted, including Atlantic crossings. You can see the date the advertisement has been placed and the date of expiry.

To gain full unlimited access to sailing opportunities you need to purchase a membership. Membership gives you access to captains' personal contact info. You can create your own personal sailing profile and share this with yacht owners when you reach out to them to join as crew.

It's free for captains to register and post their sailing opportunities.

WHAT ARE THE BENEFITS FOR YOU AS CREW?
- You can receive contact details of captains and contact them directl.
- Since it's free for captains to post a sailing opportunity but as crew you need to pay, an application via Crewseekers shows captains you're serious about the opportunity and not just browsing.
- As a member, you also receive discounts on training, clothing, and charters.

SAFETY AND SECURITY MEASURES OF THE WEBSITE:
- All sailing opportunities are checked by the website management.
- As crew, you decide who to reach out to and whom to share your contact details with.
- Amateur sailing opportunities are only listed when crew contributions (if any) are a reasonable share of daily expenses *only.*

THIS WEBSITE WON'T WORK FOR YOU IF:
- You are exploring the possibilities and not seriously looking to crew (yet). As crew, you must become a paid member to use the functionalities of the website.

THE INVESTMENT

Prices are in British Pound currency. You can choose to become a member for six months (£75), 12 months (£99), or 18 months (£135).

7Knots

www.7knots.com

ABOUT

This website may have been around the longest of all. It was set up in 2000 by a cruiser. The website is basic. One to ten sailing opportunities are posted every month, and there is an average of ten Atlantic sailing opportunities each year.

HOW DOES IT WORK?

You can see opportunities without registration. Once registered you can access contact details. There is a 'crewlist' and 'crew wanted' section where you can read advertisements and reach out. You can do a search on 'Atlantic' and see all ads posted that included the Atlantic.

WHAT ARE THE BENEFITS FOR YOU AS CREW?
- Simple, free, and to the point.
- It's fairly old school and known amongst the sailors that have been around for a while.
- You can create and publish an advertisement yourself.

SAFETY AND SECURITY MEASURES OF THE WEBSITE:

You can indicate that only registered users can see your email address.

THIS WEBSITE WON'T WORK FOR YOU IF:
- You get frustrated with basic web design.
- You don't want to share your email address. Anyone that registers can see your email address.

THE INVESTMENT

It takes a minute to register. Once done, you can freely contact captains.

OVERVIEW OF CREW WEBSITE FEATURES

Functionality	FindA-crew	Crewbay	Ocean-Crewlink	SailO-PO	YotSpot	Crew-Seekers	7Knots
Area	Global	Global	Ocean	Ocean	Global	Global	Global
Shows listings without registration	Yes, with limited information	Yes, with limited information	Yes, with limited information	No	Yes	Yes	Yes
Free membership	Yes, limited use	Yes	Yes, limited use	Yes, limited use	Yes	No	Yes
Paid Membership	€49/month or €277/ year	-	US$10 for three months	US$199	-	£75 (6 months) £99 (12 months) £135 (18 months)	-
Ease of use	★★★	★★★★	★★★★	★★★★	★★★	★★★★	★★★★
Identity verification	Yes, not mandatory	No	No	Yes	No	No	No
Shares contact details	Yes, option-ally & only with mutual interest of which one is premium	Yes, option-ally	Yes	Yes, only when member	Yes, only with paid members	Yes, only when member	Yes, only when regis-tered
Amateur	Yes	Yes	Yes	Yes	No	Yes	Yes
Professional	Yes	Yes	Yes	Yes	Yes	Yes	No
Charter	Yes	No	Yes	No	No	Yes	No
Safe & Secure	★★★★★	★★★	★★★	★★★★★	★★★★	★★★★	★★
Can you place an ad?	No	Yes, on the forum	No	No	No	Yes	Yes
Email alerts	Yes, with few details	Yes, with no details	Yes, with few details	Yes, when member	Yes	No	No
Payment methods	CreditCard	-	CreditC, Paypal	CreditC, Paypal	-	CC, DC, Paypal, Bank transfer	-

Ratings from 1 to 5 stars: 1* = Bad; 2* = Room for improvement; 3* = OK; 4* = Impressive;
    5* = Very Impressive.
Amateur: Shared or daily contributions
Professional: Paid job
Charter: You will pay for the journey)

Crew websites in other languages

- Netherlands: *omtezeilen.nl*
- Germany: *handgegenkoje.de*
- France: *bourseauxequipiers.fr* and *vogavecmoi.com*
- Spain: *genteparanavegar.com*

Forums

It's also worth checking out discussion forums that often have threads on crew finding.

Sailor forums

Popular English-speaking sailing forums:

- *Cruisersforum.com*
- *Cruiserlog.com*
- *SailingAnarchy.com*
- *Sailnet.com*

Traveller forum

Couchsurfing.org is a travel community platform focused on hosting and staying at a place for free (or just sign up to find locals and like-minded travellers and go for a hike or coffee). The website can be helpful before and after being on a boat.

Couchsurfing also has discussion groups on destinations and travel styles, including sailing and crewing. These groups are worth checking out:

- Boat Hitch-hiking group
- Vagabond Sailing
- Sailing Travellers
- Couchsailing International

It's also worth checking out sailing forums in your language.

Facebook

Search on Facebook for crew related sailing groups. Dozens of them exist, and new ones keep popping up.

Atlantic Ocean Crew

I set up the Facebook group 'Atlantic Ocean Crew' aiming to help with the Atlantic crew/boat matchmaking.

Other internet boat-find hacks

For the real inspector gadgets, here are some online boat-find hacks that are worth a try:

- Check **AIS** platforms, like *marinetraffic.com,* to see which sailing boats are in the region. Boats arriving in the Canary Islands, Cape Verde, Bermuda, or the Azores are probable to be on the Atlantic Ocean journey. Google the boat names you see on the AIS. Perhaps they have a weblog or Facebook page. Find out if they plan to cross the Atlantic. If it seems like a possible option, introduce yourself.
- Follow boats that keep a website, YouTube channel, Instagram feed, or Facebook page. These boats are followed by many other like-minded sailors. Read the comments, leave a message yourself, and interact. You may come across one that will set sail for the Atlantic soon.
- Search on social media. In particular, on Twitter and Instagram, you can do a targeted search with keywords like 'Atlantic passage,' 'Atlantic crossing,' 'Atlantic Ocean,' 'Atlantic sailing.' Or do a location-based search for different harbours, including those that might be visited prior to the Atlantic crossing, like, for example, Madeira, Gibraltar Lanzarote, Antigua, BVI. You could search on Instagram, for location 'Madeira marina', and see what content has been posted on this area. On social media, it is easy to reach out via a comment or direct message.
- Throw out lines on location-based apps like Tinder or Happn to see if there may be a boat in the region. Warning: be sure about intentions!

Navigational Hazard! Each captain has a different favourite crew platform. To increase chances of success as a boat seeker, you can choose to become a member of different platforms. This does mean extra efforts in engagement and profile updating from your side.

DO: Research credibility and trustworthiness of 'crew wanted' advertisements to make sure you're not dealing with scams. Read more on safety in Chapter 5!

DON'T: Buy a plane ticket after one or two message exchanges on the internet. Find out to the best you can if the boat you found is a good match.

Many more boat search platforms exist, and new ones keep popping up. Relevant platforms I'll add to the resources on *Oceannomad.co/ resources.*

Harbours

> *"He who is outside his door already has the hardest part of his journey behind him.*
>
> **– DUTCH PROVERB**

You can meet captains and find boats by going **dock walking**. If the season has already started, or you are simply curious, go to a harbour. While you may have less potential boats around as opposed to the internet, walking the dock is a quicker way to analyse if there are suitable possibilities. Strolling around the harbours to find a crew spot, is definitely part of the fun.

Back in the days, before the internet, **dock walking** was basically the only way how boats found crew. Still, captains may look for crew at the last moment because previous arrangements did not work out. Or they realise after the passage to for example the Canary Islands that an extra crew member may be handy. Many captains are also aware that they can pick up crew on the dock.

Make friends and success will follow. When you see a boat with solar panels, a wind generator, jerry cans, and/or two **forestays,** it's likely they are preparing for an ocean crossing. Unless you write it on your forehead, sailors won't know that you might be looking for a boat to cross the Atlantic. You need to be noticed, so you have to get out there and meet people (more about the tactics later in this section). Of course, not everyone you meet will cross the Atlantic—but they might just have that friend who will.

If you do find your boat beforehand, it is good to go to the harbour anyway to enjoy the fun, connect with fellow Atlantic-crossers and get the preparations started. Here you'll meet like-minded water-lusted people with a shared love for the ocean, with the same dreams, mindset and nomadic lifestyles.

Which harbour to go to?

You can either go to the most popular places from which boats leave for the Atlantic passage (like Las Palmas or Antigua), or choose to go to a harbour or bay where boats do initial preparations or pass 'en route' towards their last port of call before sailing out for the Atlantic. The smaller harbours and bays in Europe, the Canary and Caribbean Islands are worth checking out. The bigger marinas can be expensive and busy. Some boats prefer to prepare elsewhere 'off the beaten path.' There will be fewer boats but also fewer people looking for a boat.

Isla Graciosa, an off the beaten path island on route to Las Palmas

Here's a list of harbours and marina's where you can try your luck.

Harbours from east to west

MAINLAND EUROPE
- United Kingdom: Falmouth, Plymouth, Gibraltar.
- Portugal: Porto, Figuera da Voz, Peniche, Lisbon, Portimão, Lagos, Albufeira, Oeiras.
- Spain: Baiona, La Coruña, Valencia, La Linea Alcaidesa, Cadiz, Huelva.
- France: Brest, Antibes, Fréjus, Saint Tropez.
- Italy: Genoa, Varraze.

ISLANDS IN EUROPE

- Portugal: Madeira and Horta (Azores).
- Spain: Palma (Mallorca) and Canary Islands.
  - Lanzarote (Arrecife, Puerto Calero, Rubicon, and Isla Graciosa)
  - Tenerife (Santa Cruz, San Miguel, Los Gigantes, Marina del Sur, Radazul, Garachico.
  - Gran Canaria (Las Palmas, Pasito Blanco, Puerto de Mogán, Puerto Rico).
  - Fuerteventura (Gran Tarajal, El Castillo, Corralejo).
  - La Gomera (San Sebastián de La Gomera).
  - La Palma (Santa Cruz, Puerto de Tazacorte).

WEST AFRICA

- Morocco: Tanger, Agadir, Casablanca, Essaouira.
- Cape Verde: Mindelo (São Vicente), Palmeira (Sal), Praia (Santiago).
- Senegal: Dakar.
- Gambia: Banjul.

Harbours from west to east

CARIBBEAN

- St. Lucia: Rodney Bay.
- Antigua: Falmouth, English and Jolly Harbour.
- St. Maarten: IGY Simpson Bay, Lagoonies Marina, Palapa Marina, IGY Isle de Sol, and St. Maarten Yacht Clu.
- British Virgin Islands: Tortola.
- US Virgin Islands: Charlotte Amalie.
- Puerto Rico: Salinas.
- Dominican Republic: Luperón.
- Bermuda: St. George's Harbour.

NORTH AMERICA

- USA: New York, Newport, Norfolk, Annapolis, Hampton, Portsmouth, and Fort Lauderdale.
- Canada: St. John and Halifax.

Dozens more marinas, bays and harbour towns exist, especially in Europe and the USA, that are worth a visit for a possible ride. Find the marinas and bays well visited by sailors by on *noonsite.com,* a global database for up to date sailing information in every country.

> Hitch-sailor: *"I wish I had known that it's very hard to find a boat in the Canaries, but quite easy in Cape Verde."*

> Hitch-sailor: *"Be patient, be polite, go out there and hang around with the sailors. It doesn't have to be Las Palmas where you search; in smaller marinas, there is traffic as well, also outside the crossing season."*

> Hitch-sailor: *"I'd wish I had gone sooner to Antigua. All the boats were taken."*

> Hitch-sailor: *"I would not search on the French south coast anymore."*

> Hitch-sailor: *"I wouldn't go to the Canaries and would surely stay in South Portugal where I would be the only one searching."*

Where can you connect with the sailors?

IN THE BAR
Sailors like the bar. It's often the first thing they look for when they've touched shore. Marinas, or any harbour town, usually have one or more bars where sailors go to. It's usually the closest bar or the bar which has WiFi. Have a chat. Make friends! Sailors love to meet new people. You may not want to get too attached to other hitch-sailors, especially in the popular places like Las Palmas. It makes you less approachable. If you are not confident walking up to someone, or you feel like you would bother them, you can also just sit down in the bar and put a sign in front of you: 'Crew Available.' It makes you approachable for a chat.

STAND OUT TIP: Make a cap or t-shirt which says *Crew Available.* Or do actually write it on your forehead.

At the harbour/customs/marina/immigration offices

Captains have to go through bureaucratic procedures when arriving in a new place. Each island usually has a few 'points of entry and departure,' which make these places a good place to meet captains. Custom and marina offices can be a good spot to hang around, especially in the hour before the office opens. Those who sailed in the evening before or in the night are often waiting for the office to open. It's the right timing for a chat with a captain.

At the dock

Be curious and brave and wander around the dock to see what's happening. Start a chat, make a friend and offer your help. The sailing lifestyle can be a lonely one, and most sailors are eager to have a chat and meet a new face. Perhaps you'll get lucky and will be invited for a coffee or a **pontoon** party. You never know who you might meet there. A few thoughtful take-aways:

- Always ask for permission to come on board.
- Don't approach every single person you meet on the dock. Particularly in busy places like Las Palmas, captains and crew become annoyed by people asking all the time.
- Time it right and don't disturb captains and crew when they're working.
- Make yourself known as a cool/fun person, not as that annoying person asking everyone desperately for a ride.
- The fuel dock is a strategic point to find your boat. Boats often fuel up first before berthing in the harbour or going on anchor in the bay around the corner. Welcome the ship with a smile (and poster/CV!). A warm welcome is always appreciated when sailing in somewhere.
- Stand out tip: Rent a stand-up paddle board or borrow a **dinghy** and paddle around the harbour or bay to talk to sailors!

Cats walk the dock too

Attend an event

Hang around the harbour when there is a sailing regatta, **rally** or festivity. Sneak into the party. It's a great network opportunity to find a ride. Weekly events happening in town can be a great opportunity to meet sailors while they are in socialising mode. In Las Palmas, you have 'Ruta del Pinchos' on Thursdays, and live music in Las Canteras on Fridays. In Cape Verde, there's live music on the street on Saturday. In Antigua, you have a rum punch steel drum party every Sunday. Every destination has one of these weekly local events that are a 'must-do'. Here captains and crew will have more time to talk to you since they are not working on their zillion 'things to do' list. This is great fun!

Do a work exchange

Try to find a boat that can accommodate you in exchange for helping out (or sharing harbour fees). It will put you in the centre of all the action and brings more opportunity to meet potential Atlantic crossers. You will learn about boats, get a sense of the scene, and you will be noticed.

> *Hitch-sailor:"Search for personal contact and talk with boat owners, not only asking "Do you need crew?", but trying to make a conversation and then get to know if he needs someone or not."*

> *Hitch-sailor:"Go out and socialise. And always be clean and presentable—you never know when you will meet your next lift."*

Hitch-sailor: "Be social and don't be shy. Ask politely, and you will find somebody who will help you."

Make a poster

Get noticed and put a colourful poster of yourself on the bulletin boards: in the bar, at the laundry facilities, at the harbour office, at the bakery, in the chandlery, on the **pontoon** gate, shower door, and any other strategic place where cruisers pass. This is targeted last-minute publicity. Place your advertisement during happy-hour in the bar. It makes people curious, and they'll have a face with the ad right away. Include a photo, phone number, email address, and the date of placement. Update the date to keep your advertisement valid. Don't forget to remove them when you leave! It keeps the system working.

The advertisement I put up in Las Palmas harbour

Crew ads in Las Palmas

Team up with other hitch-sailors

In Las Palmas, someone took the initiative to list all boat seekers and spread the list around the harbour. The printed sheet included crew details like nationality, experience, skills, plans and contact details. Every few days the list was updated and spread around again by an aspring crew volunteer. This made it easy for boats to find the right crew candidate. Put yourself on that list! Or make a list yourself if the initiative has not been taken yet.

Radio networks

Use the **VHF** radio. Many harbours have their own radio channel, often called 'the net', where things like the local weather, tonight's' event, items for sale, and crew /boat wanted too are communicated amongst the cruisers! Become a radio man or women and give it a try. Prepare your pitch! Keep it short and sweet. Say who you are, where you're from, what you are looking for, and what skills and experience you can contribute, and *over*. If someone is interested, switch to a different channel to talk privately. Don't give up after the first try. Boats sail in all the time. Try it several days, if not weeks.

Hitch-sail hack: cross in 2 legs

Southern route: Canary Islands → Cape Verde → Caribbean/South America

Where in Las Palmas aspiring crew is standing in line, in Mindelo, on São Vicente island, there's hardly anyone looking for boats. Mindelo is the sailor's hub in Cape Verde where yachts often make a stop before heading into the Atlantic. Some boats only decide here, after having been at sea a few days, that they would like extra crew for the crossing. Or that they want to get rid of crew. As a crew member, this is also an opportunity to leave if the 'test' ride from the Canary Islands didn't work out as expected. You may be worried and think "what if I can't find a boat, I'm stuck there." Even if you can't find a boat, it's a lovely place to get stuck! In the worst-case scenario, you can stick around for Carnival (in either February or March) and then take a flight. At the time of writing, flight connections from Cape Verde exist to the Canary Islands, Brazil (from Santiago), and mainland Africa. May you find a ride to Cape Verde 'only,' and you feel good about it, consider taking it, and then continue the search in Cape Verde.

When I was on *Sea Ya*, we tried to find a last-minute crew member in Cape Verde (January) since one crew member left us. We couldn't find anyone! And we were not the only boat looking for crew.

Northern route: Caribbean → Azores → Europe

When you're heading from west-to-east, you can focus on finding a boat going to Bermuda or the Azores. Bermuda is a popular stop on the route. Once in the Azores, you can take a break and explore this green, natural and stunning island archipelago. I only spent one week there and cannot wait to go back and explore more. The sailing season, between May and July, is a breathtaking time to be in the Azores. As the Azores is a popular stop on the Northern route, it would be fairly easy to find a boat (or cheap flight) to take you onwards to Europe.

How did I find my boats?
I found the boats I crossed the Atlantic with in three different ways: on the internet, locally in the harbour, and through personal connections. Here's how it went.

BOAT 1: *THE BOUNTY*
(found online, in August 2014)
I started digging into this adventure in July. I signed up for a few different crew websites I found on Google, just to learn what it's all about and try it out. I encountered a few crew possibilities that seemed interesting, and feasible for an inexperienced newbie like me. I received a message from someone saying he liked my travel blog and could use a reporter for

their big Atlantic sailing adventure. I checked out his profile and website. The website (now deleted) had some nice pictures on it of young people, watersports, and a cool navigation plan that was more than 'just' the Atlantic Ocean. What most appealed to me was his drive to make this trip as green as possible. It all sounded right up my street! Somewhere around mid-August, I had a video Skype chat with the captain. Though he didn't look like the young man on the website, it all sounded perfect. He told me about the people that will be on board: six different nationalities, all young people, and one girl, who was even a sailing instructor. The plan was to spend some time island-hopping in the Canary Islands and Cape Verde before setting sail for the Caribbean. We would then continue the island-hopping in the tropics, in search for the best kitesurf and diving spots, making conscious efforts to minimise our impact on the environment. Last but not least, I could come on board for free in exchange for capturing the fun with photos and videos. He even wanted to put my blog logo on the **bow** of the boat. The plan was to set sail for the Atlantic in mid-November. That seemed perfect to me. It meant we would spend Christmas and New Year in the Caribbean.

It sounds great, doesn't it? Maybe too good to be true? Well, it was! I should have done better research. I joined this boat and left this boat. Despite the setback, I was not ready to give up and was determined to find another boat.

BOAT 2: *SEA YA*
(found at the harbour, in December 2014)
The friendly sailing community in Las Palmas offered a place to stay on board until I would find another boat. I moved on board with Captain Rudy, who happened to be from my home town. We also discovered that we had actually been in contact before via a crew website, about a passage from mainland Spain to the Canary Islands. The timing for that trip hadn't worked out in the end, but the connection proved that the sailing world is a small world (keep this in mind!).

By staying in the harbour, I was at the place to be to find a boat. Captain Rudy was also preparing to cross the Atlantic but not until mid-January. Someone who was going to crew on his boat cancelled, and he offered me a place for the Atlantic crossing. He asked for €10/day + shared food/fuel contribution, which I thought was a fair price. It took me a while to decide if I should do it or not. I was cautious after my previous experience with *The Bounty*. And would I want to spend another month in Las Palmas? There were still a few other boats looking for last minute crew: a beautiful 55ft yacht with a Russian captain who hardly spoke English, a 32ft boat with a young captain who spoke so negatively about other people. Both

Santa Claus was coming to Muelle Deportivo de Las Palmas

options didn't seem right. I realised that Christmas and New Year's Eve were looming, and not many boats would leave before then. So, I cut the knot (Dutch expression), and the decision was made. I'll sail across with the experienced and relaxed pirate: Captain Rudy. I wasn't going to rush onto just any boat because I wanted to spend more time in the Caribbean. This trip was about the journey, not the destination. Rudy had been preparing his boat for years. His boat was maintained very well. And he thought of every possible spare part that may come out helpful at some point. Two more girls were going to join the trip which I hadn't met yet, but Rudy had.

Mid-January we set sail. The six-week wait wasn't so bad in the end. I met incredible people, explored Gran Canaria inside out, and I found a super flight deal and surprised my parents for Christmas by putting myself underneath the Christmas tree! And Las Palmas has become one of my favourite cities.

BOAT 3: *CYCLOS II*
(found through personal connections, in April 2015)
I wasn't actually planning to make a crossing back to Europe. But I had to go back at some point to be maid of honour at my best friend's wedding. That's an honour to adjust the sails for. I was curious to experience what the west to east route, known as the more adventurous route, would be like. While in the Caribbean, I threw out some lines to find opportunities for sailing back to Europe. I updated my profiles on some crew websites. Also, I sent some emails to boats I had been in contact with before for the east-to-west crossing, to see if someone is planning to sail back to Europe.

I received a reply from Captain Zac. Zac and I met via a crew website when I was looking for a ride from Europe to the Caribbean. At that time, I'd already committed to *The Bounty*, so I did not follow up for the first crossing. Zac's email said that they might go back to Europe and that he would keep me in the loop. A few days later he sent me a message asking if we can have a call, and we arranged a time to talk about the trip. Based on the lessons I had learned at this point, I asked dozens of questions The *Cyclos II* is a 90ft sailing yacht that needed to be sailed to Europe as a **delivery** per the owner's request. She has four permanent crew, and two extra professional crew were brought on board for the crossing. And then there was me, the 'freeloader.' I was invited to join to balance the sexes (there was only one other girl), and with no autopilot, six **watch keepers** were needed to steer the boat. Since the chef didn't take part in standing watch and more professional crew is expensive, I could come and join as the sixth watch keeper. My experience with my previous crossing helped to gain the captain's trust and proved my 'can do it' personality.

I had a great feeling about the trip, and it matched perfectly with my plans. They were planning to leave soon though. We met in Antigua just three days later! After seeing the boat and meeting the crew, I was even more excited. I had never been on a boat that big. It happened to be the Antigua Classics, which is one of the most impressive gatherings of soulful classic sailing boats in the world. For a few days we prepared, went out, and got to know each other. It all felt very professional, safe, and right. *Sea Ya* was around too and trusted the full situation. Two days later we threw off the **bowlines** and set sail for Europe.

How did the hitch-sailors find their boat?

A few take-aways from fellow hitch-sailors on searching a ride:

> *"I recommend to network with other sailors and be wary of captains who take on crew only to get money. Paying for expenses is normal. However, the game some captains play is that you stand on the shore watching them sail off with your money in their pocket."*

> *"Never give up! It's possible, even for people who never stepped on a boat before! Be patient, brave, open and always smile and share positive energy!"*

> *"Do your research! Spend the time making sure the boat you're on is safe and everyone on there is compatible."*

HOW DID THE HITCH-SAILORS FIND THEIR RIDE?

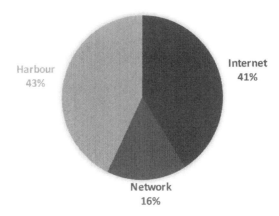

"*I wish I had known about the spectacular group feeling and support within the community of Atlantic crossers. They were much more professional and helpful than I had thought. If I had known this, I would have been less anxious about getting in contact with people beforehand.*"

"*Take your time, be flexible about destinations, do not set a fixed destination. Do have alternative ideas in case you get stuck somewhere. Enjoy the search as part of the adventure.*"

How did the surveyed captains find their crew?

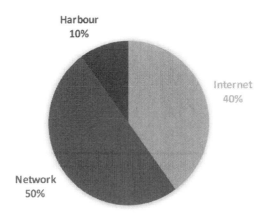

3.2 WHEN TO START SEARCHING?

Some boats start searching for crew as early as one year beforehand. Some boats decide a few days before departure that it might be handy to get extra hands on board. Sometimes crew leaves vessels and replacements need to be found. Opportunities arise anytime. You can start searching, or decide to do this, anytime. Just check whether you need to apply for a visa since this differs per nationality. You may need to apply in advance. Make sure you checked out chapter two for details on the best time to catch a ride. To increase the chances for a successful match, it helps if you:

Start the investigations and communications early.
For the east-to-west crossing, most listings on crew websites show up between June and November before to the start of the season. ARC boats often search for crew earlier. From September, there is much more demand for crewing, and more crew is looking into it. It becomes more competitive. If your profile pops up beforehand, you are more likely to be noticed. For the west-to-east crossing boats start looking for crew from January/February.

Let people know as soon as you decide to sail across the Atlantic.
Let friends, family, and colleagues know that you are looking for a boat to cross the Atlantic. They will keep this in the back of their minds and will think of you if they hear of a sailing opportunity. Who knows who your friend may know! Also by letting others know, you stay more determined to make your Atlantic crossing happen!

Meet up!
If you think you find a good match online, try to meet before the trip. Spend some time together to figure out if this could work. If it doesn't work out, you can continue your search without declining other opportunities because you have already committed to a boat.

Time your chatting

When hunting in the harbour, speak to a captain or crew member when they are not in the middle of something. Say 'hi' when they are having coffee, lunch, beer, or are waiting for the toilet, cashier or their turn at the marina office. Boat works are never ending, and captains are busy. Especially in Las Palmas, they tend to duck away if they see you coming since you won't be the first.

I've seen people find a boat within a day; I've also met people who gave up after two months. Whatever happens, don't forget to enjoy the journey, explore the islands and make the most of the experience! It's all part of the fun.

No matter what, if you stay determined you will find your boat.

3.3   CAPTAIN'S CHOICE

I surveyed 32 captains who crossed the Atlantic and took extra crew on board. What did they say?

What are captains looking for?

"The more experience, the better, but this is not necessary. I've had very good crew with hardly any experience."

"Watch-keepers must be keen and willing to learn. Most of all, I look for laid back personalities who will get on well and help out everywhere when needed."

"Clean, non-smoking, and willing to share expenses as fewer boats now crew with all the electronics."

"It depends on the position. A watch leader must be a confident sailor and be able to carry out duties on deck without much explanation— plus be trusted with the boat while the captain sleeps!"

"Coordination and skillfulness are more important than actual skills because if one is skillful, they are likely to pick up any skills.

"Good social skills, good manners, a common language, experience in sailing, knowing how to cook, people who have sailed before and know what it means to be on a boat."

Many captains don't place too much emphasis on finding experienced crew, but rather seek out the right personality and mindset.

"Honest, friendly and happy people with a great attitude, who don't want to change the world for the better, but change themselves for the better.

"Making sure they have the right skills and will fit in with the permanent crew."

"I look for someone who is keen and has the same views as me about the industry. A passion for sailing and working on yachts. Someone who is willing to put in the extra work and show initiative. Someone you don't have to be nagging all the time."

"The ability to understand that you are crossing the Atlantic in a small boat. You must have a good sense of humour and be able to deal with people in confined spaces. You have to be able to help turn your hand to whatever is required, and be able to laugh at it if it doesn't work out."

"Help sail the boat safely, asking questions and demonstrating an ability to piece together the knowledge I am willing to share."

"They should not bring hard case bags and preferably less than 15kg luggage per person. Not that the weight matters, but usually crew who travel with more bring a lot of useless things such as hair dryers, excessive technology equipment, etc. If you set a limit, it makes people think and set priorities. But I prefer if they only bring what they could carry for one km without having to stop, rest or change how they carry it. This usually works out the best, not because they bring less but they can actually think of what is essential and important. Those are the people I don't mind sharing a life raft with if worse comes to worst.

"Some experience, but most important for me is a willingness to learn, strength and fitness, and someone who is not prone to seasickness.

What captains find most challenging to find

"Someone who is passionate about sailing. It is tough these days because most crew just want the free ride and the party. They don't understand the work that has to go into the delivery of a vessel. So, they do not put in the effort.

"Someone who we could rely on during night watches."

"The right personality."

"A likeable person who is like-minded and has experience in sailing."

"Crew willing to sail off the beaten path. Crew with at least some experience, crew ready to share the cost of food (no other expenses shared). Crew with a meaningful profile."

Top tips from the captains

"Listen, listen, and listen! Don't say you have experience if you don't have any, and especially not that you are a quick learner. I'm only interested in what they can do even if it's milking a cow because that is a skill that requires coordination, a little courage, and is not learned just by watching, like most tasks on a yacht.

"Get some experience and dress tidily. You are asking for a job or being let into someone's home. If your grandparents wouldn't let a stranger through the door wearing odd clothes, why should a stranger or a captain?"

"Offer to do the horrible jobs. For example, grab your snorkel, dive in and clean the bottom of the boat. That will impress every boat owner/captain."

"Make sure the boat you're on is sound and make sure the people you're sailing with aren't idiots. . . ."

"Get a good idea of what the condition of the boat and other crew is. Check what the safety and first aid equipment are on board. If the captain will explain this all to you in detail, then he is a responsible captain."

"Be honest and open about your level of experience."

"Buy a boat."

"Try to make contact as soon as possible, if possible months ahead. Be prepared time and moneywise to meet the prospective captain before the crossing. Go to the hot spots like Las Palmas and allow a lot of time to walk the dock and meet people. Socialise with them over some weeks. The best way is to be recommended by someone. Do not approach skippers with the idea to sail with them but with the intention to make a friend. If you have become a friend, you can ask to sail with him. But to make a friend takes time, so bring the time and have money to live in a room for e.g. 4–8 weeks."

"Prospective hosts are unlikely to be interested in the fact that you have just ridden a mono-cycle across the Sahara. Nor do they care whether you plan to wander when you reach the far side of the pond. I recommend that you restrain yourself from advertising your skill at juggling, tai chi, or sculpting statues from metal or marble." (2)

"Make it clear that you realise that you are asking for a favour. Make it clear that you know that a yacht is a very private home. It is not a ferry, a hotel, or a youth hostel. Recognise the fact that you will be getting under the fellow's feet, and let him know that you aim to minimise your impact in his life. Forget all about being a laid-back dude. Instead, show respect for this person whose help you are seeking, and be the very model of Perfect Behaviour." (2)

3.4 YOUR CREW PROFILE

You might be a newbie in the sailing world with little or no sailing experience. I was. What can you put in your online profile or harbour poster to make yourself stand out?

Show *who* you are in your profile. What makes you unique? What value can you bring? What you can include.

A close-up photo (An action shot is even better)

- Hobbies and interests
- Skills and strength.
- Sailing experience
- Your reasons for crossing
- Your dreams
- Your passions
- Your mission
- References to confirm your experience or personality
- A link to your website, About.me page, Facebook profile or Instagram account, where prospective captains can learn more about you.

No sailing experience? No worries!

Don't worry if you don't have sailing experience. An extra pair of hands and skills is often welcome when making an ocean passage, but so is someone fun to chat with. Sailing experience is desirable, but for an ocean passage a positive attitude, a strong sense of responsibility, balanced personality, proactive attitude (to a certain extent!), and kindness go a long way. An ocean crossing is more about **seamanship** than sailing. Seamanship is about fixing things, solving problems, and being inventive, handy and a great team member. Highlight your enthusiasm, your story and any other skills and beneficial characteristics you have. This can be much more valuable and interesting than an experienced sailor who is negative, smoking, and dirty. Of the 58 crew that filled out the survey, 29 had none or little sailing experience. 27 of those found a boat and crossed the Atlantic. It can be done!

> Hitch-sailor: *"Be friendly, useful and problem-free. You don't have to be experienced—there's not much 'sailing' while you get into the trade winds—all you need is resilience, a strong will, friendliness and mental toughness."*

You surely have some knowledge or skill to bring to the table! What skills or knowledge can you contribute? Here are a few skills that can catch a captain's eye if he or she is looking for crew:

Languages, babysitting, cooking, local knowledge, fitness, strength, sports instructors ((free)diving, kitesurfing, yoga, Pilates), mechanic, computer, electrical engineer, diesel engineer, fixing engines, radio, fishing, medical, writing, photography, video, babysitting, musician, cleaning, sewing, painting, mast-climbing, fridge Tetris, teaching languages, comedian, massage, carpentry, master fisherman, dietitian, meteorology, storytelling, joking, marketing, website builder, social media nerd, destination knowledge, (marine) biologist, fixing things, making knots, sprouting, baking, plumbing, fixing ropes, trip research, resistance to seasickness, offshore sailing comfort, CPR, first aid, soldering, communication equipment, IT, website, dinghy, fundraising. . . .

TOP-TIP: Make an 'about you' page on the internet where boats/captains can read about you, your skills, dreams, and reference statements. About. me is free and easy to set up.

Licenses
If you do have the money and want to increase your chances of success, expand your skills. If you want to find a real job on a boat at some point, these certificates can be helpful:
- STCW10 (Standards of Training, Certification and Watch keeping for Seafarers). This is a basic safety certificate where you learn about personal safety and survival, firefighting, first aid/CPR, and personal safety and social responsibility.
- ENG1 Medical Certificate. This is a basic medical check confirming that you are fit.

A few more takeaways
- Always profile yourself online as you are in real life, and vice versa.
- Never lie about a skill or experience. Be honest.
- Look presentable.
- Obtain references that confirm your skills and/or personality.
- Smile! In real and on the phone. This is fun! A genuine smile will open many doors of opportunity.

Hitch-sailor: "Don't lose hope. I had to send more than 1,000 applications before I found a possibility. The worst problems happen because of human mistakes. It's important to scan the rest of the crew, the captain, the boat and yourself. Use your common sense before making any decision."

Hitch-sailor: "Don't be a 'hippy' trying to cross like you're hitch-hiking. Clean up, look sharp, and speak languages. Be professional while you march around the docks and sailor bars."

3.5   YOUR SEARCH CRITERIA

What should *you* look for? These are the points I suggest to initially bear in mind:

A minimum of 3 crew

- I wouldn't recommend joining a boat with a captain only and definitely not as a girl (with a male captain)—unless you really know the person and know how to handle the boat perfectly.
- Someone always needs to be on watch. If you're only two, it will make the trip much more tiring.
- The more people, the more fun. To a certain extent.

Characteristics of captain and crew.

- You can be on the most advanced yacht in the world, but if the people you cross with are not the right match, it's going to be a long ride!
- Can you speak the same language?
- Do you share some common interests?
- Age. Of course, age is just a number, and no one should be judged by that, but that said, as a 20-year-old you might not want to be on a boat with just +70-year-olds.
- Are you OK with smoking on board, each other's eating habits, other habits.
- More on figuring out if it's a good match in Chapter 5.

A boat of minimum 36ft.

The smaller the boat, the rockier the ride and the slower it goes. Small sized boats can definitely be seaworthy. For the sake of comfort, I would put the minimum at 36ft if you're going with complete strangers.

Experience on board

You want to cross the pond with a capable, experienced crew. What qualifications does the captain (and other crew) have? What kind of boats has the captain sailed before? If he is new to the game (which can still be okay), who is there on board to bring the experience to the table? More about assessing the experience in Chapter 5.

Seaworthiness

Is this boat capable, and equipped to cross an ocean? Is the boat new or recently refitted? This might sound appealing but have things been tested? I have met many boats who suffered huge delays because of new stuff that didn't work. More about this in Chapter 5. Stepping on a new or just refitted boat is almost a guarantee for a delay, or worse failure, and a complete change of plans.

Destination

Are you looking to go to a particular place? If South America is the final goal, try to find a boat that is going there. If the Mediterranean is the aim, hopping on a boat going to the UK is not ideal either. Catching rides 'on the other side' can be as complicated and time-consuming as crossing the Atlantic.

This is what I was looking for
- Boat of minimum 36ft
- Experienced captain/crew
- Technical/engineering knowledge on board
- Minimum 3 crew, preferably including at least one more girl
- Dutch, English or Spanish speaking captai.
- Destination: don't care
- Similar interest.
- Preferably non-smokin.
- To be part of some kind of adventure/conservation project

I didn't manage the last two, so I just accepted the smoking situation and created my own project that eventually turned into this book. I would use the same criteria again for my next search. Though crossing on a boat smaller than 36ft would be exciting too! Also, I am much more cautious now about the seaworthiness of the boat and the reliability of the captain.

DO: Realise that it's unlikely you will find a boat matching exactly what you are looking for.

DON'T: Cross an ocean on a boat that has made fewer than 1,000 miles after buying or a recent refit. Testing time is essential.

Important, but to a smaller extent:

The navigation plan

Does the boat leave from a destination you can practically and financially reach? And does the boat go to a destination where you can disembark and make your way to the place you want to go? If you're planning to go to Brazil and the boat is going to St. Maarten, you will have a long journey ahead in the Caribbean. It's only when the **hurricane** season approaches that most boats make their way south. Or if you are in Curacao and you find a boat in the British Virgin Islands to sail to Europe, be aware that a flight within the Caribbean may be more expensive than a flight to Europe or the USA.

Timing

When is the boat planning to leave? Does this work with your schedule? Keep some flexibility in mind with this, since boats often don't leave according to schedule.

3.6 SOLO FEMALE TRAVEL

"As a girl, it must be easier to find a ride, right?" I hear this a lot. While it may be 'easier' to find a boat you still want to feel safe, secure and comfortable. There may be more opportunities but maybe less suitable ones. The sailing world has simply more guys than girls, and more male than female captains. It is nice to have a balance of sexes on the boat, so that you may get more invitations as a girl, but not all with the same intentions!

As a woman, I recommend to the following:
- Narrow down your search criteria to a boat with a minimum of three, or preferably four people.

- Check online profiles carefully. On many of them, captains can indicate if they are looking for romance.
- Don't put a bikini photo as your profile picture. That's asking for a certain type of attention.
- Have a video call beforehand (easy through Skype, WhatsApp or Facebook messenger)
- Ask for a résumé and references before accepting anything.
- Avoid a boat with only men on board, unless you are 100% happy and confident about it.
- Get your own **bunk** or **berth.** If you share a cabin, share it with another woman, or at least have a separate bunk, until you know fellow crew. It's not normal to share a cabin with the opposite sex due to 'limited space.'

3.7 COUPLE TRAVEL

What if you like to crew as a couple? Is it easy to find a boat? I've seen many posters of couples that are looking for a boat together. Most of them find a boat. If your relationship is strong and you can show this, you'll increase your chances. Captains don't want to take the risk of relationship problems on board. A fighting couple can ruin the experience for the rest of the crew. This has happened more than you would think!

I do believe it's easier to find a boat by yourself. You are more approachable when you are alone. But being a couple has the advantage that you can share a cabin. This is easier than asking two strangers to share a bed, especially when they are the opposite sex. As a couple, you'll be more likely to find a boat run by another sailing couple.

When you think you found a boat, make sure to navigate to Chapter 5 to find out if it's the right boat.

4

ATLANTIC-PASSAGE HARBOURS

*"Land was created to provide a place
for boats to visit"*

—BROOKE ATKINSON
(Journalist)

THIS CHAPTER PROVIDES HARBOUR AND DESTINATION INFORMA-**TION** on the most noteworthy Atlantic sailing hubs that I all have personally explored. For an extensive list of harbours along the route, see 'Which harbour to go to' in Chapter 3.

4.1 PALMA (MALLORCA, SPAIN)

La Palma is the capital city of the island of Mallorca. It's the centre for superyachts. This is one of the biggest harbours that I've ever seen. There seem to be more boats than cars in the city. It's actually comprised of many small harbours and pontoons built next to each other, each having a different owner. If you come here in September, you might be lucky enough to join a yacht setting sail for the Caribbean soon. Many of them leave 'Palma' in October. Check out the Facebook group 'Palma Yacht Crew' for helpful info on everything sailing, event, and accommodation related in Palma and Mallorca. After arriving in May, I wanted to absorb the local vibes, and through that Facebook group, I was able to find a lovely room at a local house for €15/night.

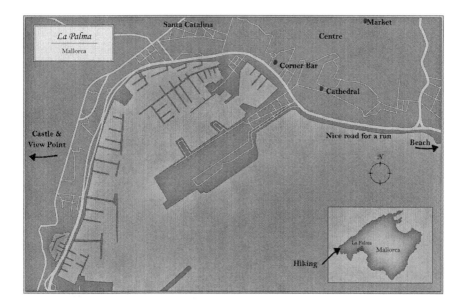

What to do.

- Must visit: The Cathedral.
- Meet the sailors in the Corner Bar.
- Explore the vibes in the characteristic Santa Catalina neighbourhood.
- Try the local delicacies at the market at 'Mercat de Santa Catalina' or 'Mercat de l'Olivar.'
- Stroll or run Avinguda de Gabriel Roca.

4.2 GIBRALTAR

Gibraltar, a British Overseas Territory, is located at the merging point of two seas, the Mediterranean and the Atlantic. This particular location made Gibraltar a strategic military point in history.

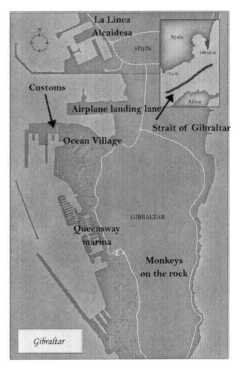

Gibraltar (often called 'Gib') is one of the best bets to find a boat in continental Europe. Many boats sailing out of the Mediterranean make a stop in Gibraltar to fuel up, shop tax-free, or wait for a good weather window to sail the Strait of Gibraltar. In Gibraltar sailing boats mostly go to Queensbay Marina and Ocean Village. Just on the other side of the border, in Spain, La Linea Alcaidesa is another marina where you may find your ride.

It's an industrial place but an interesting one to visit. The rock of Gibraltar, a spectacular landmark, is what was known by the Ancient Greeks as the northern pillar of Hercules. The southern pillar is in Morocco. Hercules set his giant feet on both continents and split them apart.

Gibraltar's rock and its surroundings are a fascinating place for wild-life watching. Its location is on the migration route for both whales and birds. Gibraltar lies next to the natural park of Los Alcornocales, one of world's largest cork tree forests. This park is a mountainbikers, hikers and climber's heaven. Access is easy but be aware when out there. Your trail may be occasionally blocked by some bulls, donkeys, cows, horses, pigs, or goats giving away a music play with their bells. Uphill exercise efforts are rewarded with magical views of the strait and Morocco. Add the fragrance of pine trees and eucalyptus, migrating birds above you, and your expedition becomes priceless!

What to do?

- Walk across the border with Spain and back
- Watch the airplanes landing right in front of you
- Say hi to the Monkeys on the rock
- Go for a hike or bike ride in the Alcornocales natural park.
- Make a day (or multi-day) weekend trip to Tarifa, the most southern point of mainland Europe and one big outdoor playground.

Practicalities

- Gibraltar is a cheap place to fly into from the UK. You can also reach Gibraltar by flying to Malaga or even Seville. Or by boat of course!
- Check if you need a visa to enter. Gibraltar is outside the **Schengen** zone.
- By being in Gibraltar you may be able to pause the visa clock if you have a **Schengen** visa (check the latest).
- Gibraltar is well connected with bus lines to Spain and a ferry to Tangier (Morocco).
- The Strait of Gibraltar has strong currents, strong winds and a lot of traffic. Do you research when sailing through.

The view of Gibraltar from the sea

4.3 LAS PALMAS (GRAN CANARIA, SPAIN)

Las Palmas, a city on the northern side of Gran Canaria, is the capital of the Canary Islands. This is where Columbus left Europe to discover what is now the Americas! 'Muelle Deportivo de Las Palmas' is the most popular harbour and a central hub to stop, shop, and prepare for sailing out to the Atlantic. In total, I spent about three months in Las Palmas. This city exceeded all my expectations. It's an ideal mix of island and natural living with all the luxuries and cultural ambience of a city.

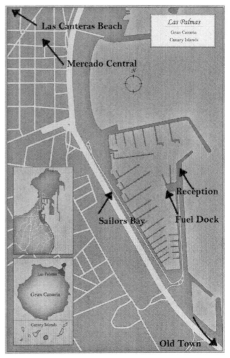

I love the Las Palmas sailing community. It's the perfect place to meet water-loving people with a shared love for the ocean, with the same dreams, mindset and nomadic lifestyle. You can meet all kinds of adventurers determined not to wait for retirement to make their sailing dreams happen. Some are sailing around the Canary Islands; some are just chilling in this harbour enjoying la vida Española or making a difference for a healthy ocean. Some are preparing for the Atlantic Ocean passage.

The ARC and ARC+ sailing rallies depart from Las Palmas in November every year. The harbour can be pretty hectic during the weeks prior to these events.

Meet sailors around the marina at the reception, the Sailors Bay bar, the laundry machine, or just walking or rowing around the harbour. You can also sign up for the 'Club.' You pay €20 for one week and are allowed to make use of the WiFi, swimming pool, gym, as well as accessing more networking opportunities to find a boat.

Muelle deportivo de Las Palmas and Las Palmas city in the background

What to do?

IN LAS PALMAS

- Head for the old town every Thursday evening for la Ruta de Pinchos. For €2 you can get a beer, a tapa and great Spanish ambience in *la calle* (the street).
- Every Friday, and sometimes on Saturday, there's live music on the streets in Las Canteras.
- Visit the church in the old town where Columbus made a prayer before he sailed out. For a small fee, you can climb the stairs to the top for a beautiful view.

ELSEWHERE ON THE ISLAND

It's fun to take the bus and explore the mountains for a day, or weekend. Gran Canaria is an island with one of the highest elevations in the world. Almost 50% of the island is a Biosphere reserve. With lots of greenery, hiking, biking and climbing trails outdoor fun is guaranteed. Put your sport shoes on and go on an adventure. This can also be an excellent crew bonding activity.

Exploring Gran Canaria

Practicalities

- Hostels in the Canary Islands go from €15/night. You can also stay with a local—Airbnb and *couchsurfing.org* are well represented throughout town. For your own convenience, don't stay too far from the harbour. For food, plan for another €10–€20/day. If you eat where the locals eat, you can have a beer or tapa for just €1.
- Las Palmas marina is a 30-minute walk from the old city centre, and a 20-minute walk from the popular boulevard, Las Canteras beach (Great surf spot too!). There's a bus stop close to the marina, or my preferred option: rent a bicycle (+/− €75 / week)!
- The central market (Mercado Central) is a great place to source your food. You can have your fruits and veggies delivered to the boat from here with reduced packaging. The places around the Mercado Central also provide budget friendly provisions. The old town has another market (Mercado Vequeta). On Sundays, there is a farmer's market at San Lorenza. The Indian Supermarket at the end of Las Canteras is a great place to find all sorts of spices, seeds, nuts, and teas at reasonable prices. Read more food provisioning tips for the crossing itself.
- The Pharmacia on Plaza Santa Catalina in Las Palmas gives over-the-counter antibiotics to ships.

4.4 MINDELO (SÃO VICENTE, CAPE VERDE)

Cape Verde (Cabo Verde in the local language) is an island archipelago in Africa, lying west of the Western Sahara. The island group is located 850 nautical miles southwards from the Canary Islands. Cape Verde became independent from Portugal in 1975, so they speak Portuguese and use the escudo currency (100 escudos = around €1). Cape Verde consists of 10 larger islands and five smaller ones, scattered across a relatively large region. Every island is unique, and also quite a distance from any other (average 100 miles between islands). Cape Verde is a blend of Europe and Africa and used to be the centre of the slave trade.

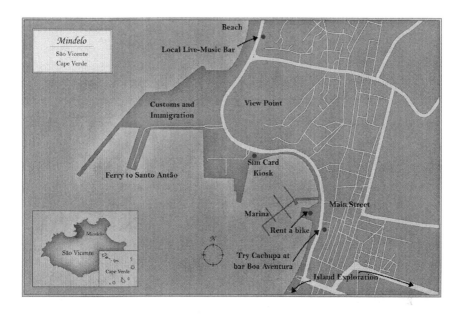

São Vicente has a happy relaxed island vibe: music in the street, people chilling, strolling, and smiling. Many boats make a stop here to re-stock, fix things, de-board crew off the boat, or simply get a taste of the country. São Vicente is the island with the most (though still quite restricted) yacht facilities in Cape Verde. It is less touristy than other Cape Verde islands like Sal and Boa Vista. A visit to São Vicente allows you to absorb the real Cape Verde. The climate is mild and dry during the sailing season. Around 80,000 islanders live on this island, mostly in Mindelo.

Mindelo

Mindelo is the cultural capital of Cape Verde. It's the biggest town on the island of São Vicente. It is a vibrant town and a great base for island exploration. There is beautiful Cape Verdean live music all around, good food, and a relaxed island atmosphere. Friendly locals, adventure seekers, stranded sailors and off-the-beaten-path travellers are all on island time here. Fiesta, celebration and dancing in the street are part of the daily routine.

The harbour is called Porto Grande. It used to be the most important harbour in the Atlantic. There is a little marina where boats can dock, although many boats choose to anchor in the free (but windy) bay. They all come in their dinghies to the same spot: the floating bar. This is where you will meet sailors if you're looking for a boat. This bar has 'yachtie' prices. If you walk into town, you'll find numerous cafés and bars with local and cheap coffee, WiFi or food.

If your boat search in Las Palmas isn't working out, consider going to Cape Verde. When I was there the first time, there were plenty of boats looking for crew, including our boat, and not many hitch-sailors around. Also, when I was there the second time with the ARC+, numerous crew members left boats, and some boats were looking to replace them.

Practicalities

- WiFi is available all over the island. For the fastest connection, you can buy a local SIM card—for €5 you get around 2GB of data.
- Food & restaurants—Mindelo has an abundance of restaurants in all sorts of price ranges. The 'local' bars and cafes are cheap and well worth a try. For a quick and healthy local style meal turn right out of the marina and hop into 'Boa Aventura', 100 metres further on the left side of the street.
- A local Cachupa (the national dish) is around 200 Escudos (€2), beer is 120 escudos (€1.20), and the local **Grog** (rum) is 100 escudos (€1). You'll need a little patience to get your food.
- Transport—São Vicente has an international airport with direct flights from numerous European destinations.
- Get around—To explore the island, you can rent a bicycle, hike, take a haiku (bus), aluguer (shared truck ride), or taxi.
- Thoughtful takeaways—Don't give money to beggars, especially the children. You might think that you're helping, but this just motivates them to stay out of school.
- Distances between the Cape Verdean Islands are large (100–150 NM)
- May you get stuck in Cape Verde and really want to go to Brazil, two flight connections exist (with TACV to Recife and Fortaleza) from the island of Santiago in Cape Verde.
- The islands in Cape Verde are connected with flights and a few ferries.

Sailing practicalities

- Clearing customs and immigration goes on **island time** so bring your patience. You have to visit two different offices, about a ten-min-ute walk from the marina.
- At the time of writing you are not required to buy a visa when you sail into Cape Verde (as opposed to when flying in).
- There is a fuel and water dock. Especially here water is a precious resource so don't just rinse down the deck.
- For a small fee, you can tie your dinghy to the floating bar. It's the safest option.

What to do?

- **EVENTS** Besides the daily happenings on the streets, the big parties are Carnival in February and the Baía da Gatas Music Festival in August. It could be cool to time your visit with one of these events! Every Saturday a stage is set up in the main street and local musicians come out to play. The famous Cesaria Evora was from Mindelo and used to perform here before she passed away.
- **KITESURFING** Salamansa is about a 15-minute ride from Mindelo and is awesome for wind or kite surfing. A ride with the local *aluguer* costs about 100 escudos (+/−€1), while a taxi will charge about 900 escudos (€9). Hitchhiking and taking the bus are also options.
- **WINDSURFING** São Pedro next to the airport is ideal for windsurfing with windsurf gear available for rent. Kitesurfing is prohibited here.
- **HIKING**
  - For a short hike and great view, it's nice to walk up the hill on the northern side of the harbour. From here you can see the whole crater Mindelo lies in.
  - For a bit more adventure, hike up to Monte Verde to see a stunning sunset over the island. It's about a 12km hike from Mindelo town—a great workout before sitting on your ass on a boat for two to three weeks!
- **MOUNTAIN BIKING** Just outside the marina to the right you can rent mountain bikes from the little tourism office.
- **ISLAND HOPPING** The island next to São Vicente, Santo Antão, is a short ferry ride away, and is a stunning island with mountain backdrops and lots of greenery. It's a natural paradise for hiking, biking, and canyoning. You can rent bicycles in Mindelo and take them on the ferry.

4.5 RODNEY BAY (SAINT LUCIA)

Saint Lucia is one of the busier islands in the **Windward Island** chain. It's the island where both the **ARC** and **ARC+** make landfall. Rodney Bay St. Lucia is the most advanced place when it comes to recycling facilities and waste disposal. Therefore, it's a good place to arrive after making the Atlantic passage. It's not a departure place for an Atlantic crossing.

Boats generally leave more up north in the island chain.

The Street Party every Friday night in Gros Islet is a cool local event happening close to the marina to get into the Caribbean vibes. The vibe is a lot busier and more commercial in the north, while the south has endless natural gems like waterfalls, hot springs, hikes, flora and fauna waiting for you to be explored.

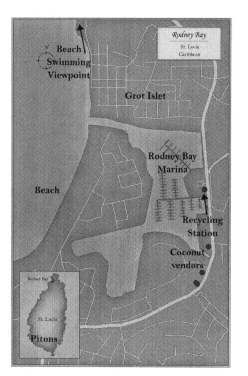

What to do?

- Zip a coconut
- Mingle with the locals at Gros Islet
- Anchor, dive, hike, and have a chillax session at the hot springs around the Pitons.

Practicalities

- Currency: EC (Eastern Caribbean Dollar) and US dollar.
- Coconut Index: EC$2 Turn right outside of the Rodney Bay IGY marina, walk a few hundred metres until you find trucks with coconuts.
- Cool town: Soufriere. A charming local town in the midst of all the adventure potential. There's a local vegan food-van making delicious plant-based burgers.
- Get around: With the local bus, you can easily go around the island. Bus stops exist in the street.
- Good to know: A taxi ride from Rodney Bay to the Hewanorra international airport can be as much as US$80. The bus is a way cheaper alternative for which you need to calculate a bit more time. You'd have to change buses in Vieux Fort or walk the last few kilometres.

Moored between the pitons

4.6 ANTIGUA

Antigua & Barbuda are a twin island nation where you can explore a new beach to explore every day of the year. Antigua is a big sailing hub in the Caribbean. It's a popular place for superyachts, as well as other boats sailing up and down the **Windward Island** chain in the Caribbean.

Each year in mid-April, the south coast of Antigua has the most beautiful scenes of boats racing against each other. It's the most impressive gathering of sailing yachts I have ever seen. The Antigua sailing event spans two weeks. The first week is for traditional wooden sailing yachts, while the modern yachts start to race during the second week. This event attracts many other boats to Antigua, so plenty of potential crew opportunities, and 'yachtie' parties! It's the time that boats start crossing back to Europe and the best place to be in the Caribbean at this time and the best place to find a ride. 'Antigua Yacht Crew' Facebook group is an online "Crew Helping Crew" discussion group on Antigua.

Antigua has two main ports of entry which are English Harbour and Jolly Harbour.

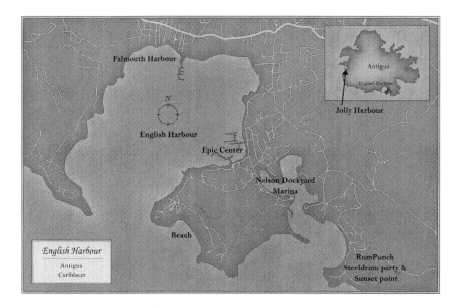

The bay of English Harbour

English Harbour and Falmouth harbour are part of the Antigua's National Park. Falmouth harbour is the superyacht harbour. There is a big notice board here where you can post your crew advertisement. Many smaller yachts are anchored in the bay. Jolly Harbour is another port of entry and exit, located on the west side of Antigua.

What to do?

- Check out Nelson Dockyard Marina (English Harbour). Once the base of the British Admiral Horatio Nelson's fleet in the 18th century. Now a World Heritage scene.
- Hang around during the Classics and the Sailing Week. Mingle. Perhaps you can join a race as crew. Crew drop outs and heavy weather make boats want more crew. 'Rail meat' (body weight ballast) is always desired to balance the boat.
- Go to the sunset rum punch steel drum party on Thursday or Sunday at 'Shirley Heights' on the top of the hill. From here you have a spectacular view over English Harbour. If you're lucky, you may see the green flash at sunset. Be careful with the rum punch!

Practicalities

- Currency: EC (Eastern Caribbean Dollar.
- There is no scheduled bus system on Antigua. You can identify buses by their license plate. You can flag a bus down anywhere.
- The Antigua sailing scene is not cheap. Many people hanging out here earn high yachting wages. If you're on a budget it can be hard to tag along. Be prepared.
- Have a proof of exit or captain letter when entering the country.

4.7 ST. MAARTEN

St. Maarten is divided between two nations: The Netherlands and France. English is widely spoken on the Island. Although French is the main language on the French side. St. Maarten is not secret on the tourist map. Jumbo jets fly in and there is no shortage of resorts, shops, casinos, and clubs. This island is well connected with flights from the USA and Europe, and tax-free. The French side is greener than the Dutch side. The airport runway lies next to a popular beach. You can almost touch the planes when they are landing.

St. Maarten is a popular sailing hub. Arguably the busiest in the Caribbean. Hundreds, if not thousands of boats are scattered across the bays and marinas. The Simpson Bay lagoon is one of the largest lagoons in the Caribbean. The border between the French and Dutch side goes right through the middle. Every first Monday of the month there is a sailors' flea market, where second-hand gear is sold. It could be a good place to find a good jacket for the West to East crossing. Or you can sell your gear if you don't need it anymore. Shops on the French side

are generally cheaper than the Dutch side. If there's anything special you need; this is probably the best spot to find it in the **windward** and **Leeward** Caribbean Island chain. Second hand, or new. St. Maarten is a duty-free island. There are marinas in both territories. The Dutch side is the busier and the chances of finding a boat are higher. If you're French, you'll surely have an advantage on the French side. St. Maarten has a radio net every morning where cruising related topics are discussed. 'St Maarten Yacht Crew' Facebook group is an online "Crew Helping Crew" discussion group on St. Maarten.

What to do?

- A few times per season there are laser regattas at the Yacht club. You can rent a laser and become a temporary member (+/– US$65 per race day). You can also rent a laser at Kim Sha beach (US$10 see).
- Go hiking. Cool trails in the mountains are awaiting you!
- Check out the jumbo jets flying over at Maho beach (don't cling to the runway fence, people have died from jet blasts doing that!)

- Take a bus to Mullet beach. Nice vibe here and sometimes good surf.
- St. Maarten is famous for the Heineken Regatta, held in March.
- Join the *NaturefoundationSXM.org* for a beach clean-up.

Captain and crew meeting places

MARINA'S WITH HIGH BOAT-FINDING POTENTIAL
- IGY Simpson Bay
- Lagoonies marina. Popular cruisers hang-out with an effective and well-visited marine bulletin board to place your 'Crew Available advertisement.
- The bigger boats are in IGY Isle de Sol (on Snoopy Island—with crew barbeque on Fridays), Palapa Marina and Port de Plaisance.

POPULAR BARS WITH THE SAILORS
- Lagoonies.
- The 'Dutch Yacht Club' sailor's bar next to the bridge. Especially Friday afternoons are busy. There's also a bulletin board.
- Soggy Dollars (with Salsa class on Tuesday 8 pm and a salsa band afterwards).
- Fat Turtle (on Snoopy Island).
- Clubs: Pink Iguana (Live-music), Dirty Sanchez, and Tantra.

Practicalities

- The currency of Dutch St. Maarten is the Netherlands Antilles Guilder, while the official currency of the French side is the euro. In both sides, the US dollar is widely accepted.
- Budget food-tip: Falafel at Little Jerusalem opposite Soggy Dollars.
- Getting around: Bus US$1.5.
- Coconuts: It's hard (but possible) to find a coconut for sale. You can better just work on your climbing skills. The palm trees are there.

4.8 VIRGIN ISLANDS

The Virgin Islands are made up of the British Virgin Islands (BVI), the United States Virgin Islands (USVI), and the Spanish Virgin Islands (which are part of Puerto Rico and also the United States, Spanish

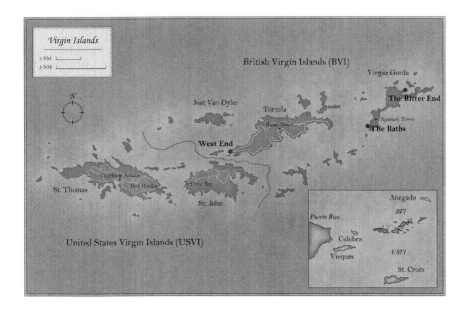

speaking). Many boats end their Caribbean season in this Island Archipelago. It makes a good departure point for the Atlantic Crossing and a potential place to find a ride.

BVI

Road Town (Tortola) is the commercial centre of the BVI. This is where many boats provision and clear in. West End (Tortola) is another sail boat hub, with a customs office, where you have a chance to find a boat. The Bitter End is an ideal chill zone in the North Sound of Virgin Gorda. It's relatively affordable and a good place to hang out while searching for a boat. Willy T's on Norman Island is a popular stop for yachties and party animals. The Baths are a spectacular natural rock formation on the island of Virgin Gorda. I could spend weeks exploring this gem.

USVI & Puerto Rico

Red Hook and Charlotte Amalie in St. Thomas are popular cruising stops and your best bet to find a ride. St. John is almost entirely a protected nature park with loads of hiking and diving potential. If you have the chance to sail via the Spanish Virgin Islands (Culebra and Vieques), do it! Salinas in the south of Puerto Rico is a popular place amongst sailors with a potential to find a ride. For the islands in USA territory (USVI and

Puerto Rico) you'll need a valid ESTA stamp in your passport, which you need to apply for online a few days before entering the country. You can only receive the ESTA stamp when entering USA territory via scheduled transport (flight or ferry), not under sail. Check the latest visa situation when planning to go there.

4.9   HORTA (FAIAL, THE AZORES)

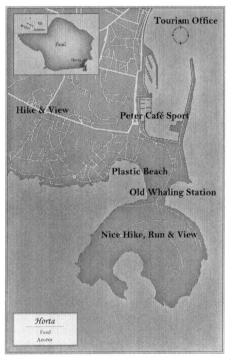

The Azores are a green and flourishing island archipelago in the middle of the North Atlantic. The island group is an autonomous region of Portugal. It consists of 10 islands, with each island having a unique identity of its own. Their volcanic origin has given the islands impressive natural scenery with cones and domes, caldeiras (craters) and caldeira lakes, caverns, caves and thermal springs. The waters around the Azores are rich in marine life and are especially famous for bigger creatures such as dolphins, sperm and great whales, and marine turtles. It is likely that you will spot them here when arriving or leaving the island.

The northern route season overlaps with springtime. From the hot and tropical Caribbean, you'll arrive in a green flourishing dream land. If you have spent some time in the relatively expensive Caribbean, it is a pleasure to sit down on a terrace and have a coffee, tea, beer or wine for just €1. Definitely try one of the locally produced teas or wines.

Faial Island is the most important port of call for the international yachties. For centuries, the Horta marina on Faial Island has been a strategic place in the trading world. Today, more than one thousand yachts make a stop at Horta when crossing the North Atlantic from the Americas to

Horta, Faial

Europe. In this marina, you'll find thousands of paintings from all the different yachts that have passed this port, making it the most colourful marina in the world. So, if you're on a boat, don't forget to leave your painting!

What to do?

IN FAIAL
Within walking distance from the Horta Marina:
- Hike the different hills walking distance from the harbour in Horta. The views are just spectacular!
- Visit the old whaling station, a five-minute walk from the harbour. While you're there, check out the microplastics on the beach. You'll be amazed about the amount of manmade materials that washes ashore here.
- Peter Café Sport is the place to be. Every sailor making landfall in Horta goes to this bar. The atmosphere is fantastic. It's filled with sailors waiting for spare parts and weather windows. The bar is famous for its cheap gin-tonic. When I was there it cost €2.80 for a G&T. In 2018, they have their 50th anniversary!
- Make a painting of your boat in the marina.

ELSEWHERE ON THE ISLAND
- Visit the fascinating Geopark museum and lighthouse, located between and underneath the ashes of a recent volcanic eruption in 1957.

5

SAFETY & HAPPINESS CHECK

"Keep trying. Stay humble, Trust your instincts.
Most importantly, act. When you come to
a fork in the road, take it."

— YOGI BERRA
(Sportsman)

YOU'VE FOUND A BOAT. Congratulations! You must be thrilled and excited. You are one step closer to making the sailing dream a reality. Or to finding yourself in a living hell.. You're going to be 'stuck' with the boat and crew for a few weeks, 24/7, so it has to be safe, fun, and the arrangements need to be clearly spelled out. You must figure out if it is the *right* boat for you. But how do you know if it's the right boat, if you have never experienced sailing life before? What is normal and what is not? What can you expect from this ocean adventure? What is expected from you? What agreements should you make?

Don't let your eagerness to make the trip override your investigative spirit, instinct and judgement! Go through the safety and happiness checklist in this chapter to find out if the boat is a good match. Discover the strengths, weaknesses and interests of the captain, crew and boat. Put your critical hat on and do your homework. It's not 'just' a ride.

5.1   WHAT COULD BE WRONG?

What dodgy things happen?

- Scams. Classically, the matter is about a 'too good to be true' crew position where money is asked in advance. And the position is indeed too good to be true!
- Unsafe behaviour because of alcohol, drugs, and unstable personalities.
- Sexual intentions.
- The boat is planning to traffic illegal goods, like drugs, or people!

You could be ripped off, sued, or sink. It happens! Don't be too naïve to think it won't happen to you. Seamen are a special 'breed.' Mostly in good ways, but not always. In Chapter 7 you can find more suggestions on how to minimise risk as a crew member. The best action you can take to minimise risk is to hop on the right boat. Investigate!

5.2 HOW NOT TO CATCH A RIDE

Before I give suggestions on how to assess the happiness and safety situation, I will tell you my story about my first attempt that failed. I will also tell you about the moments where I should have trusted my instincts more. Other hitch-sailors with similar experiences are quoted too. It is not my intention to put you off in any way, on the contrary! With this I simply want to sharpen your antennas so that you board the right boat with the right captain and crew for your adventure.

I've been slow travelling around the globe for ten years now. Mostly alone. I've travelled to all sorts of 'off the beaten path' regions and countries, travelled together with many 'strangers,' and found myself in dozens of challenging situations. I have never felt anxious about a situation except for one time: the first time I was going to cross the Atlantic.

SV *The Bounty*
(December 7, 2014: Gran Tarajal—Lanzarote)

My last Facebook update to friends and family
"A broken water pump, bad weather, leaking hatches, last-minute crew changes, delivery issues, solar panel installations, Spanish mentality, lice . . . The Atlantic Ocean crossing boat had some delays. TODAY is the day we set sail, safe and sound, into the pond! After a quick stop

for fuel and buying charts we will take off for the Atlantic. Xmas at sea, New Year's in the Caribbean! I'm super excited! We're 8 people on a 44ft boat! A super interesting crew group. A big psychical and mental challenge! The stories from the ocean will follow . . . I have the cameras ready! I wish everyone a great great great Xmas! Xxx Suzanne PS. The map tracking on my website will stop working after 50 miles, so no need to call the emergency services if you don't see the boat moving."

Wow. To say that "luckily" that didn't happen is an understatement! Thank you, **Neptune** for stirring up the seas that night and making us go into Las Palmas marina, as opposed to just fueling up! Let me take you through the process that led to leaving this boat.

What happened?

So, I found this boat. I boarded the boat. Then I left the boat, just before taking off for the Atlantic crossing. We had built an amazing crew team within a few weeks. Six nationalities, all with big dreams and beautiful life stories. We worked hard to make the boat ready. It had been an incredibly intense and fun time. We were supposed to be on the ocean already. We had some delays due to a leaking water tank, a broken water pump, bad weather, leaking hatches, a **winch** that had to be installed, last-minute crew changes, delivery issues, solar panel installations, Spanish mentality, and lice. No problemo! The most important thing is that the boat and crew were ready to make the crossing. Afterall, it's not just a ride. We fixed it as a team. We had our 'last beer' in Bar Brazil Gran Tarajal (Fuerteventura) . . . seven times! Seven times the last dinner; seven times the last run on land because we were going to leave 'mañana'. We already provisioned one week ago for the crossing since we were under the impression we were going to leave! Still, nothing major, we were able to laugh about it. But the thought niggled; do *all* these things really still have to be solved when you're about to set sail across an ocean? There didn't seem to be much time for testing. And why wasn't any of this communicated before? The plan was to leave two weeks ago. No way that was even possible.

The plan was to just stop for fuel and a chart in Las Palmas and leave for the Atlantic. It had been a rough sail from Fuerteventura to Las Palmas. Five of us got seasick. We were literally throwing up over each other. Eventually we went into the marina, where it appeared we were still not ready. The water tank was still leaking, there were bugs in the food, there appeared to be more things to be fixed and to be arranged that we didn't know about. Which is okay—although I'd like to, I don't *need* to know everything. But every day there was something 'new' that hadn't been mentioned before. Departure was not going to happen at least for another few days. I was starting to lose trust in the situation.

An increasingly uneasy feeling told me that this was not the right boat and captain to make the crossing with. Too many weird things were in the air, and it was taking all my energy. The crew team gave me energy. We were a really great and fun group. This kept me on board. Also, I had made a commitment, so I wanted to stick to it. Last but not least, this was my dream! But what if the situation turned out differently than expected and communicated beforehand? I had doubts.

What exactly was it about *The Bounty* that made me feel unsafe?

- At the first meeting with the captain he talked in a negative way about the rest of the crew. I had not met the crew yet.
- The captain easily changed crew in a way that was very unpleasant. Ultimately seven were kicked off the boat. The rest left voluntary. Most had paid serious money in advance and didn't get their money back.
- I had my doubts about the number of people we were going to cross with: eight on a 44ft boat. That's a lot of people on a small boat! When emailing and skyping with the captain, we were going to cross with five people. That's what I signed up for. Once I was on board, the plan changed to six, then seven, then eight! There were eight proper **bunks** but not enough storage for food and spares. I also questioned whether we were carrying sufficient water (suggested calculations in Chapter 7).
- The captain just seemed too keen on the money (each crew member paid €35/day! On top of sharing food/fuel/marina fees).
- I had my doubts about the captain's judgements. You must respect the captain's decisions, but setting sail 'for fun' when there's a storm announced on the radio? That's asking for trouble. Because (I assumed because he said so) he knew the area and local weather patterns, we placed our trust in him and sailed out. We ended up losing the oars and fuel tank from the dinghy. We had to go on **deck** to get the sails down, holding on to the mast for our lives. Half of the crew threw up. There was even a **Mayday** on the radio! It was an unnecessary risk we took.
- The boat was purchased just a few months before the Atlantic crossing and was still being refitted while I was talking to the captain about the crossing. I hardly even knew what that meant. I thought, 'an upgrade,' great! But, it turned out it means a lot of trouble. Things had not been tested and no time had been planned for testing. Endless fixes needed to be done to make the boat ocean worthy. Too many situations came up and made me question if this was normal.

- The plan was to go via Cape Verde. It would be a great test! Suddenly the plan changed to the Atlantic without any particular reason. There would be really no way back. This made me nervous.
- I had my doubts about the captain's stimulants. A lot of Cokes and Red Bull were being consumed each day. Everyone can, of course, decide what he or she throws in their body, but these drinks contain stimulants and affect the mental state of mind.
- I was supposed to share the cabin with the captain as well as do the watch keeping shifts with him. This would not give me *any* private space or talking time with other crew. I'm sure there were no sexual intentions. But it was uncomfortable for sure! My advice: always distrust a captain that wants to share the cabin with a crew member.
- I realised that maybe some manipulative techniques were being used to keep me on board. For example, putting my logo on the boat, an offer to earn €5/day per crew member by helping to find them and making sure they paid, keeping me away from the other crew by inviting me for dinner.

The combination of all of the above was just too much weirdness! I went for a walk, to put the adventure in perspective. Having my logo on the boat was cool. With all the fixes that had to be done, I had no idea if the boat really was safe. On the internet, the boat project was all about adventure sports, nature and sustainable living. In reality, it wasn't about that. The non-profit concept appeared to be a bit too much about money and not about sustainability at all. This was still okay. I could make my personal twist to that. But the anxious feeling in my head, and not feeling 100% comfortable about the captain wasn't worth it. I lost trust in the situation. A 44ft boat is too small for disagreements. Imagine if things go tense, in the middle of the ocean where there is no escape? Peace of mind and freedom is worth so much more.

I packed my bag and left with two other crew that got kicked off the boat the same day, I rented an Airbnb. I felt such an intense feeling of freedom when I woke up on land the next morning.

Two days later the whole crew left the boat: the old and the new replacement crew. I wasn't alone in thinking that the situation was not as it supposed to be. Everything escalated after I left. The police and court got involved. For everyone else leaving was more difficult because they had paid for months of cruising in advance. Since there was not enough proof to make a valid case, several of the youngsters lost thousands of euros. The money had already been spent. But even money means nothing compared to your life and peace of mind.

The Bounty eventually sailed across two months later. I'm not sure how and with who. Now, the boat has a new owner. I came across *The Bounty* in Dominica, with my logo still partly on the *bow* of the boat. The sailing world is a small world!

It was a good learning experience, that's for sure, and I have no regrets. I am happy to share my lessons learned, to help you have a smooth ride. Looking back, I should have left that boat so much earlier! I should have researched better and not even have hopped on in the first place. The fantastic sailing community in Las Palmas offered their help and kept encouraging to realise the dream. Relieved and enjoying the Spanish sunshine, I just continued with my mission to find the right boat with a happy bond between crew and captain, which eventually led me to *Sea Ya*, and a successful crossing.

~~~~~~

If I could give you only one piece of advice, it's to always listen to your instinct. When in doubt, don't do it. When you go for an ocean crossing, there is no turning back.

I am not the only one with a story like this. I asked the hitch-sailors for lessons learned. What would they do differently if they could start again? Here's their take.

Lessons learned from the hitch-sailors

"Searching for a "good" captain . . . because he was so awful!"

"Take more time to cross with nice people."

"Believe more in what I feel when I meet the captain for the first time."

"I would like to get to know not only the captain but also the crew before we do the crossing."

"Be more confident that everything will be ok."

"I would only do financial dealings with the captain, i.e. not get involved in complex financial dealings with the crew or any third party."

"I would be very careful about picking an experienced and skilled captain."

"You can find rides for €10/day. It doesn't have to be €25/day. Don't jump at the first opportunity to ride—it's your life—check the boat and the experience and credibility of the captain and Hitch-sailor."

"I would take it easier, not rush my choices as I did, because the right captain would have come, I'm sure of it."

"I wish I knew more about the experience and qualifications of the captain. He was very stressed and that was affecting the whole crew. He was pushing the boat too much, going faster than it should have gone. That was stressful and tiring."

"I wish I had known that many of the captains participating in this phenomenon aren't honest or mentally stable. That's not to say there aren't many "good captains" too. However, many try to cheat innocent people out of their money."

*"I arrived at Cape Verde but that is where I got off. Prior to my arrival at Las Palmas, the **winch** on the **port side** had rotted out underneath and had to be re-fiberglassed, which was done there. Also, the AIS could only receive and the radar didn't work. The centreboard became stuck in down position on the leg from Las Palmas to Mindelo. When we arrived in Mindelo we were seemingly good to go for St. Lucia until another crew member decided not to go. That put the entire crew with the captain down from four to three. The captain confronted me with an ultimatum on my decision to continue or not and would not answer any questions until I gave an answer. I decided it was best to get off and return home rather than travel on a boat with continuing issues."*

Don't let these stories make you too nervous about finding a boat. Just don't accept an offer too quickly out of desperation or desire. It's not worth it. Do your research to avoid putting yourself in an unhappy and unsafe situation. So here we go!

5.3 THREE-STEP BOAT & CAPTAIN ASSESSMENT

You have found a boat to cross the Atlantic. It's now time to put on your investigative hat, research, and assess the situation. Is the boat and captain you have found the right one for you? Learn as much as you can about the captain, crew and boat before you commit to spending weeks together at sea.

If you found a boat online, exchange loads of messages, ask questions, and talk to each other on the phone, preferably with video. Don't just commit via email. Try to figure out as much as you can before you book tickets. It can all sound amazing on the internet and turn out to be a disaster in the real world. Be prepared to walk away if the situation is not as claimed.

Hitch-sailor: "The first feeling you have when you meet the crew is the most important. Follow it."

Hitch-sailor: "Be sure to make a test trip for one or two weeks closer to land before doing the Atlantic or any other ocean. There is no stopping and getting off in between! And stand by your rights and thoughts—if the captain/crew does pick on you, get off the boat."

Hitch-sailor: "Sailing most of the time is the easy part, the hardest is the cooperation between the crew and the captain."

Go through these three steps that help assess if it's a good captain, crew and boat-match for you to cross the ocean:
A. Background check
B. First call or conversation
C. The Full Situation Assessment
   1. Happiness
   2. Safety

A. Background check
Do your research on the background of the boat, captain, crew, and plan.

- Search details and photos on the boat, the name of the captain, and names of the crew.
  - Do a Google Search

- Has there been any media exposure (crimes, disasters, judgement failures)?
- Possibly the captain or crew have a website or blog. Check it out!
- Search on social media (Check Facebook, Instagram, Twitter, LinkedIn.)
- Become Facebook friends. A timeline can say a lot about someone's personality, values, and beliefs.
- Search the sailing forums
- Once in the marina, ask around about the boat's and captains reputation.
- Check the route the boat is planning to make.
  - Can you match the boat plan with your plans.
  - Could you arrive and depart from the place where the boat is and will go to?
  - Do you need a visa for this route?

Still happy? Continue the conversation and investigation!

B. First call or conversation

What to ask when having the first conversation about the trip.

If you connected online, have a phone call to get to know each other. The main purpose of the call is to get a feel for the boat and the captain. Don't make it an interrogation; facts and details can also be asked via email. I strongly recommend to make it a video call so you can really connect with each other.

If you met in the harbour, after general chatting, this is what you can ask to figure out if it could be a safe and happy match.

Be sure you talk to the captain. It could also be the owner that is looking for crew, who is sometimes not the captain of the boat. If that's the case, talk to the captain as well. Also talk to fellow crew members before confirming your place on a boat.

QUESTIONS YOU COULD ASK

Small talk (phone)
- Where are you now?
- How has the sailing been?
- How is the weather?

Captain & Crew
- How long have you been sailing?
- Who else will be on board?
  - How many crew?
  - Characteristics (age, nationality, background, interests).
  - What experience, skills and licenses are represented on board?
- What do you expect from me as being crew? During preparation, during and after the trip? Read more on mutual expectations.
- Will there be smoking on board? If so, to what extent?
- Will it be a **wet boat** (alcohol allowed) or **dry boat** (no alcohol)? If wet, to what extent? The answer will tell you something about the attitudes of the captain toward safety and boat management.
- I'm vegetarian/vegan/gluten intolerant. Are you cool with that?
- I have medical condition X. Are you cool with that?

The plan
- Figure out intentions. Why do you want to make this trip?
- The passage plan
  - What will be the port of departure?
  - What is the planned date of departure?
  - Will we be sailing and stopping anywhere else before or after the ocean crossing?
  - What is the passage plan?
- Will it be possible to meet up beforehand?

Financial agreements
  - Which costs are we sharing? (food/fuel/harbour-mooring/custom and immigration fees)?
  - Do you ask for a daily contribution.
  - Who pays for transport to and from the boat?
  - Any other costs I should bear in mind?

The boat
- Tell me about the boat! What is the boat like?
- Under which flag is the boat registered?
- How old is the boat? Has it gone through any refits?
- How many miles have you sailed on this boat?
- Equipment

- Is there an **EPIRB?** Life raft? **Satellite phone?**
- Is there **foul weather gear** on board?
- What engine does it have?
- How do you generate electricity?

Boat preparations
- What fixes have to be done beforehand?
- What is the provisioning plan?

You don't need to ask all these things on the phone or dock. Anticipate depending on how the call or meeting goes. If you make any agreements on the phone, re-confirm any spoken agreements by email. And then go for the full situation assessment!

C. Full situation assessment

Before you set sail, you must get to know each other and the boat. Don't just fly in and set sail the next day for the ocean. I strongly suggest spending at least three days together to be able to figure out if it's a good match. Meet up beforehand, fix things together and go for a sail. This will give you an insight into the captain's personality, values, competencies and problem-solving skills. And it works vice versa of course. Preferably go for a multi-day test sail. It is also a good idea to go out together for a crew-captain drink or dinner. You can get to know people on a different level. You need to have a good feeling about being in a tiny space together. They say that boats get a foot shorter every day. So put on that investigative antenna!

> Hitch-sailor: *"When meeting the crew, take a week or so to get to know them better, and only do the trip with them if your gut feeling is right."*

> Captain: *"The weakest link is the human being."*

I have divided the full situation assessment into two parts: happiness and safety. You don't need to find answers to all of these questions. Try to figure out as many as you can, so you can make an informed decision whether this boat is the right fit for you, and you are the right fit for the boat, or not. Don't be afraid to ask questions. It shows that you are curious, serious and trustworthy. Many questions don't have right or wrong answers. Answers help to inform, prepare, and clarify expectations. Make your judgement.

HAPPINESS CHECKLIST
This happiness checklist will help you to figure out if it's the right boat, captain, and crew—*personality-wise.*

Feeling

- Do you like the captain? It's a simple question to ask yourself, but an important one! Does he treat not only you, but also other people with courtesy and respect.
- Do the captain and fellow crew have a positive attitude?
- Do you feel comfortable around him/her/them?
- Is there like-minded crew on board? Do you get along with the personalities on board? Do they have good energy? No signs of depression or mental instability? Take the time to figure it out! Don't only talk about sailing things. Do you share interests beyond the sailing life?
- No-goes to discuss on a boat: religion and politics. You can touch the waters on shore and accept each other's beliefs, but then leave it. You don't want any conflict or arguments at sea. On the other hand, if you sense racism, sexism or very different political opinions, you might want to jump ship before you sail out.
- Living standards. You will enter someone's home so you have to adapt. To what extent can you do that? Can and do you want to deal with a smoking or drinking (avoid excessive!) captain? What is the captain's attitude towards the use of alcohol during sailing and the ocean passage? Will there be drinking during the passage? A cheers to **Neptune** before take-off or at the half-way point is okay. But beers or Gin & Tonic every day during an ocean crossing? This can be risky and you might want to avoid that. Alcohol dulls the senses. In dire situations, when *everybody* needs to be at their best, alcohol is a dangerous companion.
- What about drugs? Don't make it the first thing you ask, but *do* ask if drugs are or have been used, and to what extent. It says something about someone's personality and responsibility.

Intentions

- Why does the captain or crew want to do this trip? Is it a dream coming true or is it to escape and go to the other side as quickly and cheaply as possible? If it's the latter, investigate why!
- Are you happy with the planned destination of the boat? Depending on the time of the year, going from a random Caribbean Island to South America might be as complex and expensive as going from Europe to the other side of the Atlantic. The same counts for Europe. Is the boat going to northern Europe, for example the UK, or heading for the Mediterranean? This will be a different route once leaving the Azores. Sailing from the UK to the Mediterranean is a two-week trip, and most likely longer since the Bay of Biscay doesn't always have a good weather window.
- Is the captain predominantly after your money.
- Is the captain looking for a relationship or sex (girls, watch out for this!)?
- Are you sure the captain is not involved in any illegal business like trafficking or smuggling (I've actually met a captain with this intention!—this happens!)?
- Will you be in the marina or on anchor? Would it be easy for you to go to shore?
- Will you go sailing around the islands before sailing out for the Atlantic.
- If island hopping, before and/or after the ocean passage, do your interests align? Some only want to sail, some rather just drop anchor in the next bay and don't go ashore, some prefer to explore islands inside out, others prefer to just tick the 'been there, done that' box.
- Can you prepare and provision the boat together? Discuss the menu and provisioning. Food is such an important part of your happiness on the trip. You need to have this well sorted so that every crew member is happy. More on food happiness and provisioning in Chapter 8.
- What will the watch-schedule be?

Hitch-sailor: "Although a sailing boat can bring you to remote places and gives freedom in a certain way, it also limits your freedom. You cannot always go ashore when you feel like. Even if *you are willing to swim ashore, some anchorages are not suitable to do so because of the distance or boat traffic. You will have to wait until everyone is in the **dinghy** and you have to be back at a certain time. Also other people on board might not have the same interest in exploring the island, maybe they just want to have a cocktail in a bar and use the internet."*

Boat

- Does the boat have a comfortable watch-keeping place? You will be on watch for dozens of hours. Is there a **bimini** providing shelter from sun and rain?
- Are you happy with the cabin and **heads** situation? On some boats you have your own cabin, on most boats you share a cabin, and on some boats you sleep on the sofa in the saloon, or maybe just the cockpit. Is this okay for you? Who are you sharing the cabin or bed with?
- Are you happy with the power generation situation on board? Perhaps you can charge your laptop, maybe you can't. Perhaps you have medicines that must be kept in the refrigerator at all times. Does the boat have the resources for this? A boat generating power through solar and wind rather than burning fuel, would make the ride much purer, and friendlier to the environment, without noise, smells, and fuel burning generators. What has your preference?
- Are you happy with the engine? Are you satisfied with the carrying capacity of diesel? And water?
- Does the boat have a working autopilot? If not, are you happy steering with x crew on board?
- Is the boat clean?

~~~~~~

I was once invited for a coffee on a boat that was planning to set sail across the Atlantic soon. He was still looking for a crew member. I'm always curious to the boat interiors and see how the real seaman have made their boat their home. While sipping the coffee and looking around to observe the museum of this boat, I saw a little cockroach scuttling around in the corner. And then I saw another one and another one. Suddenly I saw them everywhere! It makes me even itchy writing this. Once there's a cockroach on a boat they're difficult to remove. They lay eggs and will multiply. You don't want to cross the Atlantic in a cockroach zoo! I can only imagine what a nightmare that could be. I left after coffee and double checked my clothes to make sure not to bring the insects onto another boat.

SAFETY CHECKLIST

This safety checklist will help you to figure out the capability of the captain, crew and boat in terms of *safety and responsibility*.

Navigational Hazard! Some of the wording about sailing and boat parts in the checklist can be an obstacle. They've been marked bold. Navigate via the Glossary waypoint to check the meaning.

Captain

- What experience does the captain have? Ask for a résumé of sailing experience, including qualifications, coastal and offshore sailing experience, and miles covered. Learn what the qualification certifies.
- Ask for references!
- Ask questions to try to assess experience and competency. Try to assess **seamanship** skills, including weather, emergency, navigation, and technical aspects. Dare to ask and don't assume every answer is the right thing to do. Example questions (Be careful with making it an interrogation—just to give you some ideas):
  - Where have you been sailing in the world?
  - What's the longest passage you have made?
  - Have you experienced a storm, a fire, or a **man overboard** situation? If so, what happened and how was the situation solved?
  - What do we do when there's a man overboard?
  - What do we do when there's a fire?
  - Have you been in a storm before? Whether it's a yes or no, what do we do when there's a storm or heavy weather?

- How will we navigate when the electrical toys die? Have you navigated with a **sextant** before?
- Can you show me how to tie a bowline?
- When do you decide to go motor-sailing?
- Ask questions about the boat to learn about how prepared he/she is:
  - When was the life raft serviced? Can I see a blueprint of the boat? Do you have a map of all the **seacocks?**
  - Which spare parts do we have on board? Have you ever replaced the fuel filters and **bilge** pump yourself (testing his/her ability to fix items by using the spares)? Any captain should have basic electrical system knowledge and fixing ability.
  - How much fuel does the boat carry? How are we going to use it?
  - How much water does the boat carry? How much do we expect to use each day?
  - How old are the rigging, sails, engine, batteries? When have they been last serviced?
- If the captain is not so experienced, is there other competent and experienced crew on board?
  - Is there technical knowledge on board? If not, is the captain or crew a problem solver? Handbooks and manuals could perfectly lead to solutions. Check if those resources are on board.
  - What other skills are there on board?
  - What is considered and implemented for crew safety?
  - When on board:
    - Are you shown around the boat to learn where all the safety equipment is?
    - Are man overboard and fire procedures being talked through and practised?
    - Ask if you can have a look through the **logbook**. This can give you some insight into the boat's past as well as in the captains' responsibility.

Even when you feel happy and safe with the captain and crew, what about the boat.

Seaworthiness and the state of the boat

Your life depends on the condition of the boat. To a large extent, the state of the boat is also a reflection of the captain's personality and capabilities. The best boats can be very messy. Look through the mess; there might be loads of preparations going on. If you don't know about certain aspects, ask other captains and crew for their opinion. Find answers to the following safety aspects:

- If you're not there locally (yet), ask for recent photos of the boat.
- Is the boat newly bought? If so, how many miles have been made? Have things been tested?
- Has it just been refitted? If so, how many miles have been made? Have things been tested.
- Is it well maintained? Old boats can be the most robust out there. Don't let the age of the boat put you off.
- What's the repair and maintenance history?
- Is the boat in the same state as claimed? Or do you foresee yourself readying the boat for another month or two? This is okay if you are okay with it (you can learn a lot!), but be aware you might be 'used' as a free boat worker.
- Check (or have someone to check) the engine (room), electrical wiring, hull, rig, and sails. This is super important!
- Request a copy of the most recent boat survey. A captain should provide you with one. If he or she gets resistant about providing it, ask and wonder why.
- Is it clean? Look at the galley, fridge and **navigation desk.** Look carefully for insects. You want to avoid that at all costs. Bugs in pasta and rice are actually not uncommon, and some sailors go ahead and eat it.
- How much fuel and water can be carried?
- Equipment
  - Is there an offshore life raft with enough passenger capacity and with a valid inspection check? This is a must.
  - Is there an **EPIRB?** This is a must.
  - Does the boat have an **AIS** receiver?
  - Are there life jackets & safety harnesses for all crew?

- Man overboard equipment (a lifebuoy or ring and a MOB pole (also called **DanBuoy**))?
- Sufficient amount of (valid) flares (red parachute, red handheld and smokers) on board (not just those in the life raft)?
- Is there a back-up steering device (like an emergency tiller)?
- Are the **jackstays** well-placed?
- Are there sufficient fire extinguishers on board?
- Are there paper nautical charts on board of the departure and arrival destination, as well as of the Atlantic Ocean?
- Is there a well-equipped **grab bag** (with communication tools, sun/wind protection, food, water and medical supplies), placed in a location where you can quickly grab it?
- Is there a well-equipped first aid kit, including prescription drugs and pain relief?
- Is the boat well-equipped with spare parts? Think about the engine parts, filters, electronics (GPS, compass, **VHF** Antenna), sail repair stuff, lines, sails, pumps.
- Is there a working radar? If the boat is fibreglass, is there a good radar reflector? You could also check the "radar signature" by asking another yacht how the boat looks on their radar from a distance.
- Does the boat have autopilot? And/ or sufficient capable crew?
• How much time will be taken to prepare the boat before setting out for the Atlantic?
• Have new installations been tested?

Communication equipment

• Is there a **satellite phone** on board? Or another device to send/receive data at sea for weather info and/or emergencies?

Other aspects to check

• Is the boat insured? Does the insurance allow the number of people on board? Make sure you cannot be held liable for any major damage.
• Is there **foul weather gear** and a **life jacket** for you on board? This can save you loads of money.

- Do you know each other's capabilities as crew? If not, is there the opportunity to get to know each other on this level before sailing out?

GOOD TO KNOW: All you *really* need is water, food, and a (paper) chart of the Atlantic. The rest is a bonus, safety measure, or an extra headache! Equipment can make the ride more comfortable and safe but also more complicated. Every addition costs maintenance and money. Every boat has its problems. Boat works are ongoing. Stuff breaks and has to be repaired all the time, so don't freak out. This is perfectly normal. And you actually learn most on boats where things break. It just makes it extra important to figure out if the captain is well prepared.

It is vital that you get along with the people on board, trust in the captain's abilities, and feel safe. What does your instinct say? If you can't come to a well-informed decision, or if something is nagging inside of you, don't do it. Opportunities come along all the time.

Again, and I cannot stress this enough: follow your feeling. If you are not sure, do not do it! No matter how desperate you are to cross the Atlantic, how much you might be paid, or how cool the boat is, nothing is worth more than peace of mind and your life. It should be fun, not a nightmare.

You will always have to adjust in some way. Therefore, be clear on each other's limits and expectations, and make agreements accordingly.

These checklists are not exclusive and only created to help you identify safety and happiness to a certain extent. It will never be perfect and there will always be a risk. But what's life without it?

> *"Never was anything great achieved without danger."*
>
> **– NICCOLÒ MACHIAVELLI**

5.4 EXPECTATIONS AND AGREEMENTS

For both crew and captain, it should be clear what the agreements are. Know what the captain is expecting from you. What are you expecting from the captain and the trip? It makes it easier for you to prepare, anticipate, and do what you are expected to do. What expectations should be communicated? What should you agree upon?

Captain: "Their expectations of a free ride, thinking they will save on airfare. Also, their expectation to be taught to sail for free. When I am off watch, that is my free time or rest time, not sailing school time."

Financial agreements

Be clear about the financial arrangements for the passage. Consider:

- How much will you pay (or when lucky, even earn)? Not just the amount itself, but also know *what* the amount covers: daily contribution, fuel, harbour fees, food, and/or customs (total customs amount (boat + crew) or the crew fee only)? Many captains communicate a daily contribution, e.g. €10/day, but quite often this does <u>not</u> include food, fuel and harbour fees, which you would then need to calculate on top of that. Depending on the number and budget of the crew you should figure an extra €5–10/day for food, fuel and harbour fees (x30 days, which is a reference point for the time on the ocean, plus a few days for departure and arrival). Read more on the cost situation.
- Does the daily contribution start as soon as you are on board (including harbour time), or only at sea?
- When will you pay (or get paid)? I suggest you pay <u>no more than </u>50% beforehand (after meeting the captain in real life!). If you are getting paid, it's normal to get paid afterwards.
- Who will pay for the transport to and from the boat? What does this entail? Only flights? Or also the bus, trains and taxis that you may need? If flights are covered, have the captain book them. My flights were covered a few times, but I had to do a lot of chasing for weeks after arrival to receive the money. Do realise that covering flights is not common for newbies.
- What happens if you end up sailing to a different destination than agreed, or you get stuck in, for example, the Azores or Cape Verde, because of breakage? Do you have to pay for those days? Or if the trip can't be continued, will the captain contribute to your flights out of there (which can be costly!).

- What happens when something breaks on the boat? What happens if you break something on the boat? What happens if the boat damages to another boat? Is there insurance.
- When worse comes to worse, what happens when the boat sinks? When will search and rescue services be mobilised? Does the boat and/or you have insurance for this.
- Does the boat insurance cover the amount of crew on board?

Don't make assumptions. Ever.

My assumptions cost me a few hundred euros. I arrived at the Canary Islands assuming that the boat was ready and we were going to sail out five days later. Three weeks later we were still fixing things. This type of situation can be okay, and you can learn a lot, but it's disappointing if you were told otherwise before you hop on, especially if you are paying.

I was going to meet The Bounty in Tenerife. So I booked a flight to Tenerife. Later, I was told it's better that I come to La Gomera, another island in the Canary Islands. No problem, that's just a ferry ride away. It also took a few more days before the boat reached the harbour in La Gomera. Again, no problem, I was happy to explore Tenerife some more. With sailing in general, it's hard to guarantee to be at a certain place at a certain time. After all, we are dependent on the weather. I understood. Weather can cause delays; technical stuff can cause delays. Plans can change. But change upon change is not standard and a bad sign. It was high season in Tenerife and ferries and accommodation were not cheap. The extra spending for accommodation and a ferry ride added around €100 more to the costs of the trip. I was under the impression that I could crew on the boat 'in exchange for' taking photos and writing stories. Upon arrival, it appeared that I was also expected to share costs for food, harbour and fuel. Again, no problem. I figured it was fair. But this had not been communicated to me beforehand, and turned out to be another few hundred euros extra. Apart from the unexpected costs, there was also the passage itself that I assumed to go different. While we were supposed to sail out a maximum of five days after I arrived, we ended up sailing the Canary Islands for weeks, fixing things, waiting for spare parts and looking for more crew. Again, no problem, I was happy to see some of the Canary Islands, and the most important thing was to make sure that the boat is ready for the crossing. But, this also added another batch of euros to the personal costs. Eventually, after three weeks sailing around the Canary Islands, it became clear to me that the whole situation was different from what had been agreed and expected. Not to mention that new 'situations' were cropping up every day. So I left—which cost me even more as I had to find accommodation. I lost a few hundred euros by leaving The Bounty (for provisioning costs, harbour share and by incurring extra costs on land after leaving).

Do: Have your expectations clear, be sure you're on the same page, and clearly document any agreements made on how much will be paid, and when.

Don't: make assumptions. Ever. Everyone perceives things differently. What may be obvious and logical for a captain may not be obvious to you, and vice versa.

SCHEDULE & ITINERARY

- How certain is it that the boat can be at a certain place a certain time? If not certain, which is very likely in sailing, don't book your ticket too far in advance. This pressures captains.
- Are you living on a schedule while the skipper has none? If so, find a way that works for both.
- When and where do you expect to arrive after the passage? How likely are changes?
- Can you stay on the boat after arrival? I suggest not committing to any sailing after the crossing since you may change your mind after an intense time at sea. Do find out if it's even possible to stay on the boat. If you are sure that you will *not* stay on board after arrival, also make this clear. The captain can plan ahead for another crew member that he or she may need.

After arrival in Tobago on *Sea Ya*, I could stay on board for as long as I wanted. *Sea Ya* was planning to sail the **Windward Islands** of the Caribbean, and I was welcome to join them. It was a tempting option, but I decided to leave the boat in Tobago. I simply fell in love with the island and wanted to feel and explore the essence of it. My time together with the *Sea Ya* crew had been wonderful, but I was excited to adventure on my own terms again. Life on someone else's boat requires a lot of adaptation. As I had not committed to any sailing after the ocean passage, and captain Rudy and crew Noor are just awesome, it was no problem at all to leave the boat.

After arrival in Palma de Mallorca on *Cyclos II,* I had to leave the boat the following day, as it needed to be prepared for the owner. This was known to me up front, so I looked for a place soon after we arrived.

~~~~~~

PREPARATION & PROVISIONING

- How far in advance will you join to help prepare the boat? One of the best ways to get to know a captain and fellow crew is to spend time together fixing things. It's also an excellent introduction to the boat and you can learn a lot. Going on board well in advance of the big trip can be a good way to ensure if it's the right match. Be aware you could get involved with *a lot* of boat works, also if you're a paying crew member. On The Bounty, the crew were actually paying (35 euro + shared costs) to work on the boat. This might be reasonable for a few days, but once it stretches into a few weeks, including fixing non-essentials, the captain is taking advantage.

- To what degree has the provisioning been planned? Do you have a say in this?

- If you share the costs for food, be clear about each other's budget, food habits, and time on board. Make agreements accordingly.

- Provisioning is a joint effort and it's all about give and take. Everyone should be happy. If budgets vary, you can agree on getting all the basic foods together and put the luxury foods on your own account.

- If you are a vegetarian or vegan joining an omnivore boat, you should talk about it with the captain and crew beforehand, for two reasons:
  - Emphasise (if you agree) that you don't have any problem with other people's diet, or with cooking food you don't eat yourself, and that you do not expect others to cook extra or different for you. Emphasise you'll make sure you'll get your nutrition to stay fit. It should not be so much of an obstacle for crew, but beneficial (Especially financially)!
  - You should be clear up front if you prefer not to chip in for the costs of products you don't eat. The bill might turn out reasonable but it can really add up. You are not just buying for one dinner; you're stocking up a month of food. Meat, fish, cheese, and sometimes alcohol (if it's not a '**dry boat**'), make up the biggest part of the bill.

O n *The Bounty* it cost €600 to provision for eight people. We were all on a backpacker budget and were happy with basic food. Not too much luxury.

On *Sea Ya,* we also provisioned for €600, but for four people. We did not set a budget beforehand—we just loaded up with what we thought we needed and (I) had a heart-attack at the cashier. On top of this €600 we still had to hit the market for fresh produce.

DUTIES

What are you supposed to do as a crew member? Make sure to have this clear. Generally, the captain expects you to be part of the crew and share all duties like helping with provisioning, cleaning the boat, cooking, watch-keeping, fixing things along the way, and contributing to clean the boat on the other side. If you are joining mainly as a cook, engineer, photographer, or babysitter, then clarify with the captain whether he or she expects you to be part of the watch-keeping, sail changes, and cooking duties or not.

PUT AGREEMENTS INTO WRITING

All the above can often (but not always) be negotiated. Some boats let you sign a ships' agreement, that every crew member has to sign beforehand. If this is not the case, be proactive and create an agreement yourself. It may not seem necessary during happy bonding times, but at a later stage it may come in handy. Put agreements in writing, so you can refer back to it easily if you have forgotten the details, or when disagreement arises.

Suggested details to include:

- Full names and contact details of both parties.
- Where you've met.
- Money agreements (be specific with which costs will be shared (food, fuel, harbour fees, customs & immigration, maintenance), and who pays for transport (flights, buses, taxis).
- Agreed time frame and destination(s).
- Duties.
- Trial period / Change of plans. (What if it goes differently than planned or someone is not happy?)

- Liability & Insurance information.
- Medical information.
- Repatriation.
- Contact details of a friend or relative.

Once you commit, commit (unless a situation is not as claimed!). Not everything can be ideal. Captains also put big efforts into finding the right crew member. It's not cool to break the deal and make him or her do a search all over again.

> Hitch-sailor: *"Things escalated on the boat I was supposed to sail the Atlantic with. It got so bad, we had to go to court. No one was charged because of lack of evidence. I wish I had more proof."*

WHAT ELSE CAN YOU EXPECT?

Many things may seem obvious for the captain or an established sailor, but not so obvious to you. What else can you expect? What is expected from you?

- Expect to adapt. Remember that you are entering someone else's home and living space.
- When out sailing or doing boat works, "the captain's will is law." You have to respect a captain's decision whether you agree with it or not. Suggestions are welcomed but arguing is not appreciated. Therefore, it's extra important before embarking that you feel safe and comfortable on that boat with that captain. Be clear on what the boat rules are and the captains' way of working is. Every boat is different and every captain is different. Pro activity is often welcomed but don't act if you're not 100% sure what you're doing or 100% know the boat. A simple push on a button can break a mast!
- Captains are legally responsible for the boat and crew's safety. In pressure situations some of them can shout. Don't take this personally. But this should only be temporary, not constant.
- Expect to work hard. Have a positive and open attitude, be loyal and take part in all tasks on board. Whether you are paying or getting paid, there are duties to be done on board. The list is never ending.
- Expect to have a small space to store your stuff. So don't bring a lot and definitely not a big (and hard) suitcase.

- Expect to share a cabin, maybe even a bed (but not with the opposite sex unless you're a couple).
- Expect not to shower often. Every drop of water is sacred.
- Expect things (sails, systems, pumps, tech) to break. But try to not break anything!
- Expect to get seasick (this isn't the end of the world. I get seasick and still take any opportunity to sail. It's worth it! More about this in Chapter 7).
- Expect it to be a rocky and humid ride. Not all days but many days, in both ways. I thought I could actually write a book on an ocean crossing, but it was far too rocky, and humid, as well as difficult to keep the laptop charged up.
- Expect at least a month at sea, so don't make any other obligations during that period.
- Expect that others, including the captain, may be as excited as you are. Many of them are doing this for the first time and are working and planning towards an ocean crossing for years.

Expected the unexpected with an open mindset and just let the adventure happen!

6

TAKE-AWAYS FOR THE CAPTAIN

*"Accept the challenges so that you can feel the
exhilaration of victory"*

– GEORGE S. PATTON JR.
(Senior Officer US Military)

FOR A SAFE AND HAPPY PASSAGE, the collaboration between the captain and crew is essential. Extra crew for an ocean passage can give a captain more sleep, reduce costs, increase safety, and add more knowledge and fun to the journey. Well informed and prepared crew can make the trip more pleasant and safe for you as a captain. Though the focus of the book is on crew, this chapter presents a few take-aways that can help you as a captain when welcoming crew on board. It also good for crew members to read to get an idea what a captain is getting him or herself into by taking *you* on board.

6.1 BEFORE YOU TAKE ON CREW

Do you really want crew? If so, what kind of crew? Ask yourself:

- Are you comfortable having strangers in your personal space and giving them responsibility over your boat?
- Do you need experienced sailing crew or rather fun people on board with maybe less experience but other qualities?

- Does your insurance cover extra crew? Is crew paying? Does your insurance allow that? If someone gets hurt, the captain is responsible.
- Are you comfortable taking responsibility for the safety of someone you hardly know.

You open your home and let strangers on board. You want to know if it's the *right* stranger. As a captain looking for crew, you can ask:

- Résumés and references.
- What have you done on boats before? Ask beyond the answer of 'watch-keeping' and 'trimming sails' to be sure they know what they're talking about. Many only know sailing via books or a day sail. This can be okay, but if you're looking for experienced crew, you want to be sure the crew member is competent. You could ask crew with 'experience' for the procedure to put in a **reef** on the **mainsail**—this will show you if they have real experience or not.
- Have a video call, meet up beforehand, and take the crew out sailing, preferably on a multiday trip. That's when you get to know people and their value. Spend at least three days with the crew before setting sail for the ocean.
- Can the crew member you take on board as a cook, actually cook? At sea?
- Is crew eager to learn and ready to work? Have they experienced living with limited power and water?
- What was their worst experience with an owner or captain?
- Can crew commit to at least a month?

6.2 CREW MANAGEMENT—ON SHORE

What to think of on shore?

- Be clear on what you prefer and expect. Inform crew about any other preferences, rules, ways of working on your boat. Rules and habits are different on every boat. Crew comes with diverse backgrounds and experience. For some crew, it's common sense not to open the **hatch** above the electronics. For some, it's not. What responsibilities does the crew have? What do you want them to do and what not? Will all duties (provisioning, cooking, watch keeping, cleaning) be shared? It could be nice to write this out on paper, so you don't forget to mention anything, and crew can repeatedly read this.

- Make your expectations clear to the crew. Communicate! Perception = reality. How you perceive the world is not how others perceive it. Everyone has their own reality. Your crew stays motivated if there is clear communication on what's happening, what will be happening, and when time allows, even better if you can explain why. With understanding the why comes responsible action.

- Which costs are you sharing? What is included? If you want to share costs, let the crew know upfront what this includes: food, fuel, booze, harbour/**mooring** fees, marine park fees, custom and immigration fees (boat fees + crew fees?)? Perhaps you're hoping to share boat check-ups, maintenance costs, and marina fees. Be transparent about this to your team. Paying crew may see themselves more as a passive passenger. It can also have insurance and legal implications if the shit hits the fan. If you want them to be a full working crew member, be clear about this.

- On land, the crew usually wants to do all sort of different things. It can help to schedule and structure work days. Set hours whether it's a full day or half day. It is nice to know as crew that you start at 8.00 am, have lunch at 12.30 pm, and you'll have some free time after 4.00 pm. It's not fun and motivating to just hang around the boat waiting for something to happening.

- Make crew in charge of a particular area. Have someone in charge of the expenses, someone in charge of the provisioning, someone in charge of the weather. This has appeared to work well on boats and keeps crew motivated and engaged.

- Be sure all crew has valid passports and complies with visa requirements in the next port of call.

- Be aware of medical conditions of crew and drugs prescribed.

- If crew flies in, provide them with a captain letter (download a template on *Oceannomad.co/resources*). They may need to show this at the airline/immigration.

- Often crew leaving need to have proof of onward travel to be able to be signed off the crew list. Make sure they have this before you go to customs, so you won't be delayed or charged!
- Make crew familiar with all equipment on board. Especially the safety equipment.
- Go through the terminology on board, especially essential if your crew has different nationalities.

On *Eau Too* our captain created a fun game. He listed about 40 "boat parts." As crew, we had to figure out where it all was on the boat. A great and fun way to learn about what is where on the boat and agree on terminology. Also, we had a little **knot** class to learn what were the preferred knots on board, for what and when to use them. Simple, engaging, and fun.

6.3 CREW MANAGEMENT—ON THE OCEAN

What to consider on the ocean?

- Communicate! When time allows, communicate what's happening.
- What do you want to be woken up for? To what extent can crew make decisions when on watch? Are you happy with crew changing or trimming sails, put in **reefs**? Or do you want to be woken up?
- Also during the crossing, have someone in charge of the weather forecast, rigging checking, **bilge** check, **guardrails** and whatever else needs to be monitored. The crew will get a sense of ownership, and the boat will stay ahead of breaking things.
- Have a daily meeting, for example during dinner when often everyone is awake, talk about what's happening with the weather, boat, food and fun things. It's an opportunity for everyone to have a say and it may prevent tension from building up.
- Talk in miles, and not in time. You never know what will happen.

Communication is essential!

6.4 MAKE A DIFFERENCE FOR A HEALTHY OCEAN—AS CAPTAIN

What can you do as a captain to minimise your footprint and contribute to positive change for the ocean? Along the journey, I've learned and picked up some ideas. On top of the crew suggestions, what can a captain do? Here are a few ideas to minimise environmental impact as a boat captain or team.

- Plan your first or second destination after the crossing to be a place where you can dispose of your waste properly. Do boat works, which often involve a lot of waste material (like oil, bits and pieces of sowing, paint) in places where facilities exist to dispose this harmful waste.
- Decrease your boat's carbon footprint.
  - Source your power from nature. Solar panels, wind generators and hybrid generators can supply you with enough power. It's a one-time investment and set-up, but will then save you and the environment lots of fuel.
  - Buy parts second-hand.
- Do your research on low-impact anti-fouling (bottom paint).
- Make an effort to provision consciously.
- Take a **mooring** buoy if available. Always anchor in sand or mud. Never anchor in a seaweed or coral bed, to prevent important habitats from getting damaged. If it's hard to tell, have someone jump overboard to check out the situation.
- No one wants to swim in their own or other people's poo! Empty your black tank at least 12 miles from the coast!
- Learn more about why the ocean is so important, what's going on with the ocean and how you can individually make a difference.

Find links to tips and resources on how to green your boat on *Oceannomad.co/resources.*

7

PREPARATION: ON LAND

*"The adrenaline and stress of an adventure are
better than a thousand peaceful days.*

- PAULO COELHO

HOW TO PREPARE AS A CREW MEMBER? What should you pack?
What skills can you work on prior to the trip? What to bring and
download for on board entertainment? How to prepare to stay fit
and healthy? How to prepare for research and science projects? How can
friends and family follow you? What is seasickness and how can you prepare for that? What to prepare when arriving by boat in a new country?
This chapter makes sure you are ready!

7.1 THE PACKING LIST

Less is more; less is more; less is more! But packing for months at sea,
with no idea what the weather might do, what a regular day will look like,
which shores will be visited, and what the next adventure will be? What
To Bring?!

A few days before take-off, I definitely mastered the art of chaos. I
packed at my parents' place where I have a cupboard with some
clothes, books, and adventure gear. Every year when I make a visit, I stock
up with vitamin M and D (Mum & Dad), reorganise and get ready for the

next adventure. But, besides the art of chaos, I also master the art of packing for multi-adventure trips.

~~~~~~

I have made an extensive list of the most important things to consider to bring as a crew member, for a pleasant, safe and happy ride. I didn't have all these things, and you'll be fine if you don't have all. You don't need much at sea. As a general rule, if you can live without it, leave it at home. Storage space is worth gold on board. You won't have much. If you have already committed to a boat (and are sure about it!) before leaving your home base, ask what's already on board, so you don't have to bring it. What boats usually (but not always) have for you: towels, bed linen and a **life jacket**. What boats sometimes have for you: **foul weather gear** and a head torch. First, I will present the list for easy reference. After the list, I provide some commentary on different items to help you figure out whether they may be necessary for you or not.

The List

LUGGAGE
Duffel bag
Waterproof day backpack
Different coloured bags for storage
Waterproof bag/box

SAFETY
Life jacket
Personal **AIS** or **GPS**

SAILING GEAR
Gloves
A pocket knife

CLOTHES
1 waterproof jacket and pants
1 sweater
2 tee shirts
1 long-sleeved shir
2 tank top
2 fast drying shorts/board short

7 underwear
1 long breathing/quick drying pants
Thermal underwear or leggings
2 pairs of warm sock
Warm hat /beanie
Clothes to sleep in
1 set of decent clothes for on shore
Swimwear
For girls: 2 sports bra/top

SHOES
1 pair of flip flops/sandals
1 pair of **deck** shoes or neoprene socks
1 pair of hiking/running shoes

SUN PROTECTION
Sunscreen
Lip balm
Sunglasses (polarised)
Sunglasses neck cord
1 bandana
1 cap
1 cap leash
1 big hat

GIRL STUFF
Hair ties and clips
Menstruation cup/pads/tampons

TECH GEAR
A SIM-unlocked phone & charger
Laptop/tablet & charger
E-book reader
12V USB charger unit
Music machine & earphones
Camera
Head torch
Universal adapter
A clock/watch

TOILETRIES AND SLEEPING
Towels & bed linen

Earplugs
Sleeping mask
A sleeping bag
Multifunctional all in 1 soap/shampoo
Tooth brush, powder/paste, and toothpicks
A scrub/washing glove/sponge

HEALTH KIT

Seasickness pills/wristband
Supplements
Mineral/electrolyte hydration solution
Food/snacks that you like
Personal medicine/glasses/contact lenses

TOYS & ENTERTAINMENT

Mask, snorkel & fins
Games for on board
Books
Movies
Music

PAPERWORK & MONEY

Valid Passport (and visa if necessary)
Cash
Debit card
Credit card
Proof of vaccinations
Proof of onward travel

OTHER USEFUL ITEMS

Refillable water bottle/bidon
Filter water bottle
A notebook and pen
A sewing kit

ALSO COOL

Your country flag
Picture of family and/or friends
Hammock for on the boat and lime time
A USB solar charger
GPS device

Notes on the packing list

LUGGAGE

- **DUFFEL BAG** Unless it's a huge catamaran, a boat does not have storage room for a hard suitcase. A waterproof duffel bag is ideal; you can fold it into a small size. A 50- to 70-liter duffel bag is a good size. The smaller, the smarter you will pack.
- **DAY PACK** A 20- to 25-liter waterproof day backpack is nice for day hikes and shopping. It's also helpful in **dinghy** rides from the boat to shore to keep things, like a laptop or camera, dry.
- **STORAGE BAGS** Chances are you will only have one small cupboard or drawer to store your stuff. It's helpful to have different coloured (non-crispy/noisy) bags to be able to easily find what you need on a boat that never stops rocking, and where usually someone is sleeping. A few years ago my mum made me a few cotton storage bags which I still use as travel organisers (one bag for the shirts, one for the shorts, one for the electronics, one for the bikini's, and one for the underwear) (Thanks, Mum!). There are also easy to make from an old t-shirt.
- **WATERPROOF BAG/BOX** Electronics are not made for life on the sea. You only need one wave and hatch not properly closed to have your phone, laptop or hard drive ruined. Also, on the boat it just easily becomes humid and salty, so you better protect it. A waterproof bag is well worth the investment. With rice and cloth, you can make moist absorption sachets you can put near the gear to soak up humidity.

SAFETY

- **LIFE JACKET** An ocean- worthy life jacket is different from the one they have for you on the ferry or below your airplane seat. Those used on sailboats are advanced and expensive. Usually, two or three life jackets are on board. For extra crew, extra jackets need to be purchased. Captains often provide these but certainly not always. Be sure there is one for you on board. The most comfortable one will be one that is your own. Consider investing in one yourself. You will wear it for dozens of hours during the ocean crossing (during night watches and when doing fore**deck** work). In Europe and the USA, life jackets are reasonably priced (€100–200). In the Caribbean gear prices are sky high. They come in all sorts and sizes. Life jackets are graded by flotation capacity. A 150N (N stands for Newton and refers to how buoyant they are) jacket is the minimum standard for offshore sailing. Life jackets should at least have a light, reflector and spray hood. Also, harnesses should be on board, so you will able to clip yourself. Life jackets carry gas cylinders to inflate them. If you are planning to fly with a life jacket, contact the airline in advance to receive approval to carry one.

- **PERSONAL GPS** A personal tracking device is a cost effective possibility that allows text communication, location tracking, and emergency alerts in the unlikely event that you get lost at sea, or anywhere. This may be welcome to have if you're doing solo watches or plan to explore foreign lands on your own after the sailing adventure. Note that some boats have '**Personal Locator Beacons (PLB)**' which are 'emergency only' devices you can carry in your pocket. Like the **EPIRB**, PLBs are registered to the boat. Very few boats provide these. It's a requirement in the ARC. These devices are expensive though—I personally don't have one. Just don't fall over board. Ever. If you choose to bring a personal GPS, check registration procedures. What you want to avoid at all costs is, that in the unlikely event, search and rescue services are needed, several centres get activated due to signals from different devices, that may not be registered to the boat. This could be costly!

SAILING GEAR

- **GLOVES** I never had gloves, and I never thought I needed them unless I was a pro. Then I caught my finger in the **winch** and realised it would be good to have some sailing gloves!
- **POCKET KNIFE** A pocket knife/ yacht knife can be useful for fixing, cutting, measuring, chopping, and opening the beer when you arrive. Boats have tools too; it's not a must. But who knows, it may save your life in an emergency! If you pack a knife, pack one with a blade that is at least partly serrated (this allows for much better rope/line cutting). The knife should be able to cut through +1 centimetre of synthetic line.

If you're racing, which only a few ocean crossers do, you may want more advanced sailing gear for the ocean crossing.

CLOTHES

You can have all sorts of weather: from freezing cold and wet to tropical heat. Most likely there will be chilly days and squalls! The northern route requires more warm clothes than the southern route, and wet weather gear is a must. The answer: bring layers! You'll need enough to stay warm and dry, without having to backpack around the Caribbean or Europe carrying heavy sweaters and advanced jackets. On all three trips I needed long pants and a jacket about half of the time. On all three trips I also got soaking wet numerous times. You'll thank yourself for having a good waterproof jacket and for having a dry set of clothes. It would be more comfortable to have **foul weather** sailors' jacket and pants, but you don't need advanced sailing gear just for the crossing. Unless you're going on a racing boat or a different route than the common Atlantic routes, a rain jacket and rain pants and warm clothers can be sufficient.

No one cares what you look like at sea. Opt for comfortable stretchy, fast drying and breathable fabrics to be comfortable. Cotton clothes can get humid and heavy. We can look like hippies on board but bring something presentable to wear for on shore. A long sleeve shirt is nice as protection from the sun (opt for white, breezy, and with a hoody even greater to protect from the sun in your neck). Fast drying shorts are better, as opposed to cotton or jeans shorts. Running shorts with an inside legging or pants can be great too! The fellow crew won't have to gasp at your pants when you are climbing up the mast or **winching.** Usually, it's hot in the sleeping cabins. Bring boxer shorts and a shirt or top for sleeping. Don't forget a beanie (for warmth at night) and a cap (to protect your face from the sun).

WHAT'S REALLY ESSENTIAL AT SEA?

- A wind/waterproof jacket.
- Wind/waterproof pants and/or a good pair of fast-drying pant.
- Thermal underwear or leggings to wear underneath waterproof pants, for warmth (*if* you don't have proper **foul weather gear**).

SHOES

Shoes don't have to be sailing-specific shoes. I used my multi-purpose trail running shoes for sailing, walking, running, dancing, and everything. They did the job just fine. Just keep in mind that your shoes might not survive wet and salty conditions. So consider bringing two pairs. Also, not all captains allow you to wear the same shoes on land as on **deck**. On every island you touch shore, you will find places to explore and hills to climb where the roads are usually not that great. Good multi-purpose trail/running shoes allow for island exploration. Take those with good ankle support. Not once, but twice after leaving the boat and hitting the land, I sprained my ankle.

On **deck,** you have to be careful with black soles. They can leave marks on the **deck.** As an alternative to shoes you can also bring neoprene socks to keep feet warm. On my first Atlantic adventure I did not have good shoes, but I did have my freedive gear which included a pair of anti-slip neoprene socks. These turned out to be perfect for keeping my feet warm during night watches. The anti-slip sole also helped me work on **deck** without sliding! You can find these socks at most dive shops.

SUN PROTECTION

- **CAP** A cap is a must. A hat leash is Neptune's greatest invention. This is a clipper between your cap and t-shirt, which, in my case, prevented my cap from going into the ocean about 283 times.
- **SUNGLASSES** Polarised sunglasses are favourable at sea to view deeper, sharper and clearer. You can better see the dolphins swimming underwater at the bow. A neck cord prevents your sunglasses from going overboard.
- **LIP BALM** I thought lip balm was nonsense up to the point I actually got blisters on my lip.
- **BANDANA** A bandana was another life saver. I had a multi-purpose headband/scarf/bandana thingy to protect my head from the sun, to stay warm at night, and to keep the hair out of my face in the wind. It made sure I at least have a few unbroken hairs left over after a sailing trip. It's also great to put around your neck when it's cold.
- **PERSONAL BIMINI** A big hat is an excellent protection against the sun. I didn't have one, but I wish I did, especially on boats with no

bimini, this saves you from turning into a lobster.

- **SUNSCREEN** Bring a good ocean friendly sunscreen.

GIRL STUFF

- **HAIR TIES AND CLIPS** Bring something to fix your hair. Otherwise, your hair will be all over the place. All. The. Time. And gone after the crossing. The wind and salty air will destroy your hair. Tie up your hair for safety. Try to protect your hair where you can if you want to have something left on the other side. Anyway, breaking a few hairs is a worthwhile small price to pay for this adventure! I've also seen crew members shaving it all before the crossing. It must be very liberating! This saves lots of hairs sneaking into all the little corners on board. If you dare, have a so-called crew cut.

As for healthy hair. . . . The hairdresser laughed at me when I finally paid a visit on shore. *"When was the last time you've been? Last year Christmas?" "No, it was only two months ago. . . ."*

- **MENSTRUATION** Can you just throw tampons over board? No, you can't! Be prepared for the monthly menstruation madness. Find suggestions on how to tackle this at 'ocean friendly bottom units'.

TECH GEAR

- **A SIM-UNLOCKED PHONE & CHARGER** A sim unlocked phone is handy, so that you can use local SIM cards. This can save you an enormous amount of roaming fees and anti-social time in the WiFi bar. Protect it well with a waterproof cover. Bring a charger from which you can disconnect the cable from the plug, so you can use 12Volt power outlets.

- **FILM & PHOTOGRAPHY** On all boats I crossed with, I was the only paparazzi on board. Memories are certainly best captured with your mind, in the moment—but capturing the adventure with a camera can also create nice memories to look back on later. Smartphones do the job these days. Protect the gear well.

- **LAPTOP** You might want to bring your laptop. Take some precautions and don't expect to be able to charge it on board. On some boats you can, on some you can't. Power is a limited resource. It's more important, that navigation equipment and radar can run. Protect your laptop well from moist with a waterproof bag.

- **MUSIC MACHINE & EARPHONES** Music, podcasts and listening books make the journey very pleasant! Possibly you can just listen to music on your phone, or get a mp3 player or iPod. More music suggestions below. Bring earphones or headphones, so you don't disturb other crew.

- **E-BOOK READER** An e-book reader can be handy since you can have a whole library on there and the battery life lasts for weeks. It's also possible to read your e-books on your phone. Though nothing beats a real book.

- **CHARGING** A little portable solar panel charger could be helpful. Though usually charging phones and tablets is not a problem. You need a 12V USB charger for that. These are popular on board so it can be helpful to bring your own.

- **HEAD TORCH** Often head torches are on board, but it's still handy to have your own for reading, getting up in the night without waking anyone up, and for when you arrive on the other side. It's great to have a head torch with a red 'night watch' option—bright white lights affect your sleep rhythm, and blinds you and fellow crew.

- **UNIVERSAL ADAPTER** Europe, the Caribbean and the Americas have different power outlets. Bring a universal adapter so you can plug in everywhere. Especially in the Caribbean, it's not easy to find one.

- **A WATCH OR CLOCK** Even though you will completely lose track of the dates and time of the 'real' world, your routine on board is determined by the clock. "What time is it?" is a question asked before, and on every watch shift. A watch is also handy to put an alarm every 10–15 minutes to be sure you don't forget to scan the horizon.

TOILETRIES & SLEEPING

- **TOWELS AND BED LINEN** are usually present. Not always, so I recommend bringing at least one towel and pillow cover/sheet and/or sleeping bag.

- **EARPLUGS** Good earplugs (perhaps invest in custom made earplugs) can help to dampen the noises on the boat. Be sure to only wear them when appropriate.
- **SLEEPING MASK** that covers your eyes can help you get a good rest; you won't be woken up by daylight, or fellow crew turning on the light (or just grab a shirt to cover your eyes).
- **SOAP AND SHAMPOO** Whatever shampoo, soap or shampoo product you bring on board, remember that it all drains straight out to the sea. Choose biodegradable! A simple soap/shampoo bar or multifunctional soap is a responsible solution. You can also wash your clothes with that.
- **WASHING UNIT** A sponge or washing glove is handy to give yourself a quick wash. Baby wipes can also be useful, although most options are very bad for the environment, and your own health due to the chemicals they've put in. Opt for biodegradable ones.
- **TOOTH CARE** Bring a good toothbrush, paste or powder, and toothpicks. You don't want any tooth problems on board, and you don't want to bother fellow crew with your bad breath. Opt for untreated wooden tooth sticks so you can throw them over board. It can get stinky if toothpicks perforate the bin bag. Rinsing with sea water is a really good mouthwash (tip from my dentist!). I rinse with sea water every day now.

HEALTH KIT

- **SEASICKNESS** Bring something for seasickness. Seasickness remedies are available in pill, plaster, and wristband form. Scopolamine is the ingredient that many find to work best, but comes with some side effects so be aware of the dosage. Also, an antihistamine ingredient is believed to be helpful. They can help make the first day or two of your trip much more pleasant. If you're really afraid of getting seasick (which you shouldn't, it's not so bad), get the plasters. They are powerful and work for a few days. I know many sailors that prefer them. I personally don't. I prefer seasickness over the side effects (dry mouth, drowsiness, anxiety, feeling tired and down). I also know now that I can be a competent crew member, even when seasick. You have to find out what works best for you and the boat. Test your seasickness medicine before you go on board to see if you're okay with any side effects that you experience. Some people don't experience any side effects. Read and learn more on preparing and dealing with seasickness.

- **SKIN BRUSH** If one thing is good for our health, it's circulation. And since it's a lot of sitting on your ass at sea you might want to brush it up a little. A dry skin brush is superbueno for circulation of the lymphatic system. It's like a carry-on wellness centre.

- **FOOD & SUPPLEMENTS**
  - A happy crew is a well-fed crew. Being 'well fed' means something different for everyone. Food on board is all shared, and you should have a say in what's being provisioned. You should also try not to be too complicated for your fellow crew, so if you have particular tastes, bring some goods of your own to keep yourself satisfied. I can be obsessive with tea, so I was sure to bring some tea excitement for myself. Also, I prefer not to compromise my vegan values, unless there really is no other option. Preparation makes the difference.
  - Diet—If you are gluten intolerant, vegetarian or vegan, it's smart to prepare a bit more in the food department. More on food in the provisioning chapter.
  - Supplements
    ○ Bring a good natural multivitamin supplement. The food situation on board might not be as healthy as you're used to. Especially in week three, when the freshness is gone, you'll receive fewer vitamins and nutrients from food. You'll surely survive, but to stay super powered supplement when necessary.
    ○ Bring some probiotics to keep your digestion process healthy. With a lot of sitting and little fibre and movement, it's easy to get constipated.
  - Coconut oil is incredibly versatile - it can be used as a mouthwash, hair mask, infection fighter, basically everything! Choose for cold pressed, and an organic certified brand. Some non-certified brands are manufactured with coconuts that are picked by enslaved and abused monkeys. Shop consciously.
  - Have a few sachets of vitamin C/electrolytes for when you feel dehydrated or seasick. Dehydration happens very easily at sea.

- **MEDICINE/GLASSES/CONTACT LENSES** Bring enough supplies of whatever medicine you take. You might not be able to find it on the other side. Have a spare set of glasses or contact lenses.

Sailing Vegan

It's not easy to be vegetarian or vegan on board if no one else is, but definitely doable! As a sailing vegan, you need to be extra prepared to make sure you get the nutrition you need. Surely you will survive, but you probably don't want to turn to all the crappy processed food either and bring your health down. What to bring to stay healthy? I only eat plant-based food and this is what keeps me super-powered:

- I travel with a mix of seeds and dried powdered greens (wheat, barley or whatever I've been able to find), and add this to my water or breakfast. We thrive on green vegetables, and you won't get many fresh greens at sea. Proper dried foods still contain most nutrition benefits.
- A natural multivitamin and B12 supplement.
- A bag of nuts (peanuts, almonds, brazil nuts).

Still, you will have to adapt a lot. It's a nice physical and mental challenge. Don't worry; you'll survive. It will make you treat every leaf of lettuce as gold for the rest of your life.

TOYS & ENTERTAINMENT

On two of the three crossings, I brought my kitesurf and freediving gear. You need to ask the captain in advance if there is space for gear like that! There wasn't really space on *The Bounty*, but I was happy to sleep with my kite. Surely there will be space for a snorkel set. The underwater world in the Caribbean is truly spectacular. You won't regret it. Find more suggestions on the personal on board entertainment set in 7.5.

PAPERWORK & MONEY

- **PASSPORT** A passport is the one and only thing you *really* need to enter a new country. Check if your passport is still valid long enough after arrival. Some countries require 90 to 180 days' validity on arrival. A passport cover could be a good idea too. I think if my passport gets wet one more time, they don't let me enter new territories anymore. Protect this official document.

- **MONEY** An Atlantic crossing will be a rare period in life where you don't spend any money for three whole weeks (though before and after the crossing it can get excessive if you're not careful). Bring plenty of cash and an extra credit card. In the Caribbean, ATMs often don't work, are empty, or swallow your card. Or all of your cards, like I experienced in Tobago. It's good to have a back-up. Cash cards are becoming more available and less risky than credit/debit cards. Euros are also accepted in Cape Verde (and in the French Caribbean). US dollars are widely accepted in the Caribbean. Europe mostly has the Euro.
- **PROOF OF VACCINATIONS** Check if you need vaccination evidence for the destination you might visit. For example, if you're planning to go to Central or South America you need proof of yellow fever vaccine.
- **PROOF OF ONWARD TRAVEL** You may need to show a proof of onward travel when disembarking. More on that in the Landing and Leaving chapter.
- **VISA** Check if you need to apply for a visa in advance.

OTHER USEFUL ITEMS

- **FILTER BOTTLE** On one boat we had more beer than water on board—no joke! The captain heard that beer was expensive in the Caribbean (after investigation: not cheap, not expensive. Average beer costs €2). Our tank water was okay to boil for tea and coffee, but not for drinking. On another boat we had a proper drinking water filter and a **water maker**—but this is luxury and not the norm. If your boat does not have a water filter on the tap to make it drinkable, get yourself a filter water bottle (also encourage the captain to install a water filter). A personal filter bottle is useful on a boat, but also when travelling in regions where tap water is not drinkable or loaded with chloride. When travelling with a filter bottle, you can prevent hundreds of disposable plastic bottles from ending up in the trash pile, in just one month.
- **REUSABLE BOTTLE** A reusable bottle/'bidon'—is also handy to have on board and on shore.
- **NOTEBOOK & PEN** You will have a lot of time to think, and the salty air will keep fresh ideas coming, so bring a notebook! Your mind will expand with all the deep blue thinking you will do. It's nice to keep a diary and write down what you see, feel, hear, taste, think and do. It's

easy to forget about this after the adventure. Write down the new insights and experience! Just don't forget to do something with it once you're on the other side. A pen is useful too. Some captains don't want their pen leaving the **navigation desk.**

- **REUSABLE BAG** To be able to make a positive difference while shopping.

ALSO COOL

- Your country flag (small–max 30cm x 20cm). You have to be careful with official flag regulations.
- Picture of your family/friends.
- Hammock for on the boat and **lime** *time.*
- Rum for Neptune!

WHAT NOT TO BRING

- Too much!
- A hard suitcase. There is no storage space for that.
- Too many (winter) clothes. You'll end up wearing the same things anyway. No winter clothes needed in the Caribbean.
- Too many shoes. You'll be mostly barefoot on the boat (some captains demand wearing shoes).
- Too many creams and oily cosmetic products.
- Hairdryers and electric razors.
- Your surfboard, mountain bike and sea scooter (without asking captain in advance).
- Unfinished work or school projects that can't wait a month.
- A return ticket ;-)

Budget & ocean friendly packing

We have become accustomed to obtaining the easiest and cheapest thing available without really questioning or investigating the route this 'thing' has taken to get to us. Or the route it takes when it's not 'ours' anymore. We all have the right intentions, but in our busy lives convenience is the prevailing priority and norm.

A big part of your contribution (or destruction!) to a healthy ocean starts with the packing preparation. Being well-equipped and prepared allows you to create positive change in many ways. We can do more than simply packing light, compactly and purposefully for our own sake. Our greatest and most exciting individual power: the power of choice! To a large degree, we can choose what to eat, drink, wear, believe, say, do, create, and buy. Each choice comes with its consequences, good or bad. Do your best to make whatever choice you make a good one for you and the ocean! Not sure what the best choice is? Ask questions, research, explore, and find out! How can you pack smart, on a budget while minimising your carbon footprint, your trash trail, and the number of chemicals polluting the environment and your body? What can you choose to be best for your health, your wallet, and for the world that you call your playground?

Here is some food for thought on actions you can take to make the packing challenge more affordable *and* better for the environment:

- Be creative and inventive. See what you can reuse, borrow, swap, buy second-hand or make yourself. Don't buy new if you don't have to. Ask you surrounding. Check the local newspaper, Facebook groups, sailing stores, and the internet for second-hand marketplaces.
- Pack light. It saves the boat, fellow crew members, and yourself loads of energy (and money). Pack with purpose for the trip and destination. What do you really need? By packing layers, you only need one jacket, one sweater and a few shirts. If you end up packing heavy, and realise further on that this is not convenient, like most girls do (I'm still guilty!), give your clothes away. There are people who can use them.
- Arrive prepared or source sailing gear locally. Las Palmas is a good place to find any necessary sailing gear. Explore shops beyond the marina for affordable gear as well as any boat bits and pieces. Sailing gear in the Caribbean is extremely expensive. Prices can be double or triple compared to Europe or the USA. If you do need to source in the Caribbean, St. Maarten and Trinidad are your best bets. The busier harbours, like Las Palmas and St. Maarten, also occasionally organise sailing flea markets.
- Buy from local providers to shorten the supply chain, which decreases transportation energy cost, use of packaging, and increases benefits for those down at the bottom.

- If you buy online, buy from a warehouse near you to avoid a package going from plane, to ship, to ferry, to truck, around the world. If you order online from the islands, it takes time (up to a month!). Having packages delivered to the islands (including the Canary Islands) has many variables and risky logistical factors because of customs procedures. Delays and lost items are not uncommon. You will have to pay import tax, and your package comes with more plastic and emissions.
- Support the small entrepreneurs and creatives and go against mass consumerism. We live in a demand driven society. Where there is demand there is supply, so by supporting the change-maker businesses, instead of the lobbying profit-making guys conveniently presented to you on page one in Google or at eye level on the shelves, we can make a huge difference. Help the good brands, those without lobbying power and big advertising budgets, to hit the mainstream with the power of your dollar.
- Don't just buy something because a company says it's 'eco', 'sustainable', 'organic' or 'green'. These have become fashion words. Certifications are a step in the right direction but don't just take that for granted either. When a brand is a certified B-Corporation, it's using business as a force for social, environmental, and economic good. So that's a good step. Read labels, read stories, and ask questions.
- Reduce and eliminate your plastic trail. Society has made it hard for us to avoid plastic. Plastic convenience has become the norm. We don't even know anymore what is made of plastic these days. Massive amounts of crude oil and chemicals are used to produce polyester, nylon, and other synthetic stuff (all plastic) for your backpack, clothes and technical gadgets. That shampoo bottle I used ten years ago, is still out there, somewhere. Yours, and those of seven billion other people, too. We're still producing more plastic every day, and the biggest problem with plastic is that it never ever disappears. Learn more about the plastic challenge and solutions. Help to turn the tide by choosing alternatives:
  - Choose gear made from natural fibres and material. Choose sustainably sourced cotton, wood, bamboo, coconut fibre, and even seaweed as an alternative to plastic.

- Try to restrict whatever you use, eat, store or pack as close to nature as possible. Think, what would grandma do?
- Stuff made from recycled materials is better than new. It helps to create awareness. *But,* recycling is not the solution! Recycling costs a lot of energy and eventually it still adds to the trash pile. Rethink—refuse—reuse—reduce—recycle—and if no other option . . . waste.
- Reduce packaging waste—Especially in the cosmetics department we can reduce a lot on plastic waste. Almost all toiletries come in plastic packaging and are thrown 'away' once finished. Choose a hairbrush, hair ties, toothbrush and razor made from other materials than plastic.
- If you order online, kindly request to use little packaging and without plastic tape. Demand minimal or better NO packaging in general wherever you go.
- What to pack things in? It all revolves around plastic these days, and it's not really practical to travel around with a dozen glass jars, is it? Look at what you already have on hand for packing. Packing cubes and travel organisers are handy, but most of them are made of plastic. Any bag does the job just as well so just see what you already have lying around. For shampoo, you can reuse empty pill bottles, or whatever boxes or packaging you can find. Ask friends and family for this as well. It gives you more options and helps to increase awareness. You can even sew an old T-shirt into a bag, so you don't have to buy any fabric. If you don't have the time or possibility to make something yourself, get a few (organic!) cotton bags you can use to organise your packing. Also, keep a spare for when going shopping! Stainless steel food containers are useful to store food items. Find alternatives. There are plenty of creatives and entrepreneurs out there developing biodegradable, plastic-free wrappers, bags, boxes, and bags.
- Reduce the chemicals. Cleaning products, cosmetic products and plastic products are often loaded with harmful toxins that drain straight into the sea (or your body). Read more in the Ocean Love & Conservation section on ocean-friendly sunscreen, shampoo and soaps, cleaning products, and outdoor gear.

- As budget travellers, as you and I may be, cheaper is not always better. Go for the durable and degradable option. In the long run it will be cheaper and healthier for you and/or the ocean because you don't need to buy a replacement or fix it, whether it's your travel bag or your body!
- Still got paper or plastic packaging? Have it all removed before hopping on a boat.

Let the dollar be your voice and a reflection of your values and your love for the planet! With conscious packing, we can create a ripple effect. We can have a positive influence on fellow sailors and locals to contribute to creating awareness of solutions out there to make this world a better place. To learn more about what's actually happening and how you can make a difference, navigate to the Ocean Love & Conservation section in this book

Download the packing list and find recommendations on what I use and why on *Oceannomad.co/resources.*

7.2 SKILLS TO WORK ON

What can you do, physically and mentally, to prepare? Whether or not you have already found a boat, it's good to be ready for 'all hands on **deck.**'

Sailing basics and terminology

Learn about the basics of sailing. Read a book, watch YouTube videos, or if your budget and time allows, complete a crew competency course. Learn about basic marine navigation, weather reading, **deck** procedures and safety, sail set-ups, **seamanship,** maintenance, **points of sail,** using **VHF** radio, and tying knots. Educate yourself about the basics of the boat. The different bits, parts, sails, actions, ropes and life on a boat is pretty much a different language. It helps to know what the captain or fellow crew member is actually talking about, especially in urgent situations! Pull 'that thingy' or steering the wrong way when the captain says 'head up,' isn't helpful, and can be dangerous. Learn the ropes!

On an east-to-west crossing, many boats sail **'goosewings'** or **'wing-on-wing,'** meaning two headsails, one on each side, often **poled** out.

Or instead of sailing straight **downwind,** they make angles and **jibe.** Or perhaps your boat has a **cruising chute** or **spinnaker.** Dig into the sailing slang and figure out what it all this means!

Sailing Wing on Wing

It's a journey, and you will also learn as you go. That's how I have learned so far and am still learning something new about sailing every day. Even the most experienced sailors never stop learning.

Go nuts with knots

Sailors talk a lot about 'knots.' We have two types of knots: *knots speed and tying knots.* I explain both.

Speed in knots

At sea, different measurements are used than on land. The wind, as well as the boat speed, are indicated with 'knots.' Why knots? Back in the days when there was no **GPS,** the sailors let out a rope with knots tied at regular intervals, overboard. As the ship moved forward, the number of knots that had gone over the ship's **stern** was the boat speed. This method was called 'the Dutchman's log'! **1 knot = 1 NM** (Nautical Mile) per hour. A knot measures speed and a nautical mile measures distance. Nautical miles are used for navigation. A nautical mile is equal to one **minute** of **latitude** or **longitude.**

So if you go six knots **SOG** (Speed Over Ground) for one hour, you have sailed six nautical miles (NM). 6NM is a pretty good speed to average. If you average six knots from Gran Canaria to St. Lucia (2,700 miles), it will take you (2,700/6) 450 hours, 18–19 days. That's if you go in a straight line, which of course you won't. Logically, wind speed is higher than boat speed, unless you're surfing a wave.

15 knots of wind is a comfortable wind speed where the boat will be pushed forward at a decent pace, and the waves are not too high to throw you around. At sea, you will soon become familiar with this terminology. Perhaps you're more acquainted with the **Beaufort** scale (see table below), which is often used to express wind speed in weather forecasting.

BEAUFORT WIND SCALE

Force	Wind (Knots)	Description	On the Water
0	Less than 1	Calm	Sea surface smooth and mirror-like
1	1–3	Light Air	Scaly ripples, no foam crests
2	4–6	Light Breeze	Small wavelets, crests glassy, no breaking
3	7–10	Gentle Breeze	Large wavelets, crests begin to break, scattered whitecaps
4	11–16	Moderate Breeze	Small waves 1–4 ft. becoming longer, numerous whitecaps
5	17–21	Fresh Breeze	Moderate waves 4–8 ft. taking longer form, many whitecaps, some spray
6	22–27	Strong Breeze	Larger waves 8–13 ft., whitecaps common, more spray
7	28–33	Near Gale	Sea heaps up, waves 13–19 ft., white foam streaks off breakers
8	34–40	Gale	Moderately high (18–25 ft.) waves of greater length, edges of crests begin to break into spindrift, foam blown in streaks
9	41–47	Strong Gale	High waves (23–32 ft.), sea begins to roll, dense streaks of foam, spray may reduce visibility
10	48–55	Storm	Very high waves (29–41 ft.) with overhanging crests, sea white with densely blown foam, heavy rolling, lowered visibility
11	56–63	Violent Storm	Exceptionally high (37–52 ft.) waves, foam patches cover sea, visibility more reduced
12	64+	Hurricane	Air filled with foam, waves over 45 ft., sea completely white with driving spray, visibility greatly reduced

(5)

Tying knots

Another kind of 'knot' is the physical one. Lines are to be tied, and things are to be fixed. The solution is often a *knot*. Tying knots and knowing when to use which knot is one of the most useful skills on a boat. With many different types of boating knots, it can be overwhelming for a newbie. Why do you need knots on a boat? To join two ropes together, to make a loop at the end or in the middle of a rope, to attach a **mooring** line to the dock, to attach the fenders to the **guardrail,** and for many more situations.

Most useful knots on a sailboat

BOWLINE *The* most useful knot on a boat. This knot won't go untied if there's no pull.

CLEAT HITCH / OXO To tie a line to a **cleat.**

CLOVE HITCH This is a handy knot because it can be tied quickly and adjusted easily. It is used for securing **fenders.**

FIGURE-EIGHT KNOT Mostly used to make a stopper at the end of the line, preventing it from going out of a **block.**

Once you think you know how to make a knot, practise it ten times, every day, with your eyes closed, behind your back, on one foot. Practice makes perfect.

If you only learn one knot, make it a **bowline**. A bowline can be used as a safe option in many situations. Two bowlines can also be used to attach two lines together. Visualise it by keeping the famous rabbit story in mind: The rabbit comes out of his hole, goes around the back of the tree, and then goes back into his hole.

You can ask a sailor to teach you the basics, or ask the internet. You can find many animations and videos online showing you, step by step, how to make a certain knot. Keep in mind that sailors have different methods and preferences to tie certain knots. As long as it holds, any method is fine.

Find links to videos and animations to learn about knots (if you don't have anyone to show you) on *Oceannomad.co/resources.*

Weather reading

Learn how to read the weather, on charts as well as from changing weather patterns when looking around. This can literally be a lifesaver! I'm surprised how many captains don't check the weather forecast before sailing out. Being up-to-date on the weather is the most sensible pre-vention measure you can take to reduce risk. Study the weather patterns on your planned route, and learn how to read **grib files,** simplified weather data charts. Grib files are low data files and are therefore easily downloadable at sea with a satellite connection. PredictWind is a useful website and app for accurate weather forecasting and downloading Grib weather files. *NOAA.gov, Passageweather.com, Windguru.com, Windy. com,* and *earth.nullschool.net,* are other sources for weather checking. The last two provide a visual view of the wind and currents. Check those out now and then, to visually learn about the wind and **current** systems.

Fishing & preparing flying fish

If you're planning to catch fish on your trip, learn how (& how not) to fish in advance, and prepare accordingly with the right gear. I've seen too many fishing lines end up in the sea because of bad preparation or the wrong gear. Flying fish can sometimes make for an effortless and free dinner—we had plenty! Attracted by light, they 'fly' on board and then die. So, you might as well eat them! Look up in advance how to prepare and eat flying fish.

Safety

Learn about sea survival, maintenance of safety gear, life rafts, storm sailing, firefighting, search and rescue procedures, seasickness, and com-munication at sea. If you have the budget for a course, consider obtaining the **STCW10** certificate. This is a basic safety certificate where you learn about personal safety and survival, firefighting, first aid/CPR, and per-sonal safety and social responsibility.

If there's one thing you learn about radio, learn how and when to do a **Mayday** call. A Mayday is a distress call in situations when there is an immediate danger of loss of life or the vessel. For example, when the boat is sinking, there's a fire not under control, or someone on board is seriously injured. Familiarise yourself with the radio on board. Learn how to turn it on. Know where the distress button is and how to use it. All crew members should know how to use it in the event of an emergency. What to say when you need to call for a **Mayday:**

MAYDAY, MAYDAY, MAYDAY
This is [VESSEL NAME] (say it three times)
Call Sign
MMSI
MAYDAY
Call Sign
MMSI
My position is [**latitude** + **longitude**]
Nature of distress is (Sinking, fire, etc.)
I require immediate assistance
We have # persons on board
Any other information that can help (vessel type, colour, life raft on board?)
Over

Learn more on Safety & Risk management and what you can do to minimise your risk and consequences as a crew member, in the next chapter.

First Aid and/or CPR

First aid and **CPR** are good skills to have in any situation, but especially on board where the nearest doctor can be weeks away. Check with your nearest Red Cross for a first aid course in your neighbourhood. *SimpleCPR.com* is an online training resource for first aid and CPR. 'First Aid, CPR, and AED Essentials' is a good book on the topic.

7.3   PREPARE FOR SEASICKNESS

Seasickness: a phenomenon that keeps many people land bound. What is seasickness? What actually happens when you're seasick? Most people, including captains and professional crew, get seasick, some more severely than others. It's quite normal, especially during the first few days of an ocean passage. Seasickness is caused by a conflict between what you see and what you feel—the body is moving, but with no fixed reference point on the ocean, the eyes don't register the movement. It is kind of like having a short circuit in the brain. According to the most common theory, the brain, unable to resolve the conflicting messages, concludes that you are hallucinating. It thinks you have ingested poison. The vomiting response is part of the body's defense mechanism to expel the toxins. Prepare for seasickness so you can hopefully avoid it. But even if it does hit, don't worry. In almost all cases, it can be treated, and it *will* pass. I have only heard once about a person who couldn't get over seasickness. He decided to step off board in Cape Verde and not cross the Atlantic.

Captain: "I'd suggest a quick study of sea sickness, as understanding its causes can be very helpful.

I was not going to miss out on this trip because I might get seasick. Then I might as well become a couch potato. I didn't know beforehand, but it turns out I do get seasick. Every first day at sea it is the jackpot for the fish. But after day one or two, I'm 100% fine and even better than those who take seasickness medicine. I'm a better person being seasick than having the side effects of the pills, so I choose not to take them unless it gets really nasty. Seasickness pills do really work for most people. They just make you feel a bit 'meh,' sleepy, and quiet.

How to prepare for seasickness?

- Have seasickness medicine, ginger candy, biscuits and mineral electrolyte solution as part of your kit.
- The day before:
  - Eat super healthy and light.
  - Be well hydrated. Drink plenty of water. Don't drink alcohol, coffee or black tea. That dehydrates.
- A few hours before sailing out:
  - Take seasickness medication.
  - Have your clothes, head torch, sunscreen, water bottle, sickness bag, and all you need for watch and sleeping, ready to grab. You'll be okay doing watch, and you'll be fine lying on your back in bed with your eyes closed. It's just the areas between bed and **cockpit** that are the challenging zones to navigate when you're seasick.
  - Have some crackers ready to nibble on.

More on dealing with seasickness at sea in the Ocean section.

7.4 STAY HEALTHY

We can only be our best if we feel our best. As crew you are on board to help everything run smoothly, so better stay healthy on board. Besides seasickness, a few of the biggest health risks on board are sunburn, dehydration, food poisoning, insect bites, wounds, contaminated water, and just general well-being. How can you personally prepare to stay on top of your health on an ocean crossing?

- Be well rested before the crossing. Have an early night the day before sailing out—this might sound like common sense, but the parties in the harbour town are always tempting! It doesn't help to go to a rum punch party the day before setting sail, so have your 'party night' a few days earlier.
- Do you have a specific diet, allergy or medical condition? Prepare for that yourself and inform fellow crew in advance.
- Any tooth problems? Have it checked before you go! There's no dentist on the ocean.
- Do you need any vaccinations for the places you're going to visit? Check this well in advance, as some vaccination need to be shot ahead of time to be effective.
- Bring a reusable water bottle and have it with you to remind yourself to drink enough.
- Also, include a filter water bottle as part of your kit, so you have clean drinking water at all times (unless the tank gets contaminated with saltwater—highly unlikely).
- You'll be sitting on your ass a lot. Start fit and stay fit. See the health kit for more suggestions on what to bring. Also, provisioning makes a huge difference to how you will feel for the weeks at sea.
- Have a cap, sunglasses, and sunscreen, unless you want to turn out like a lobster or get sunstroke.

Hitch-sailor: "Get a lot of rest before the crossing, as you don't sleep much with the shifts. Go for a sail before the main crossing, and be part of the pre-trip duty."

Hitch-sailor: "Within three days I felt like a smashed banana!"

Find tips against feeling like a 'smashed banana' when at sea in Chapter 10.

7.5 ONBOARD ENTERTAINMENT

Your time will mostly be spent sleeping, watch-keeping, doing sailing manoeuvres, eating, and chillaxing. Here are some ideas for entertaining yourself during down time.

Reading

Bring a good book, or ten! A good read on stars, meteorology, ocean wildlife, the Caribbean or Europe will surely trigger your interest when on board. Most boats have a good collection of sailing-related books on board. Lots to learn in there. These are often expensive books that you wouldn't normally buy for yourself as a crew member, so take the opportunity to read and learn.

You can bring electronic books on your phone, tablet, or eBook reader. Download them in advance. Perhaps bring one paper copy. You can have a book swap with the library on board. Also, most marinas have book swap places. Other reading you can think of:

- Download a (free or paid) course from an online learning platform.
- Download articles you come across the weeks before and read them offline while at sea.

Games

Keep the mind sharp. Bring some games that won't blow away, such as magnetic chess, checkers, Sudoku's, or backgammon.

Apps

The phones and tablets these days are one big entertainment centre. There is usually enough battery power to charge these devices. There are many applications that can be of great fun and use this journey. Download and install apps in advance.

Podcasts

Perhaps you can't read on that rocking boat. Or you just want to have your eyes closed. Or you don't want to wake up your cabin buddies with a reading light. Or you just want to enter a conversation with someone else than the people 'you're stuck' with. Podcasts are great for learning new things, stimulating your mind, and getting new perspectives on the world. Only on land, we often don't take much time to listen to them. Podcasts exists on basically every topic you can think of.

Music

Download plenty of music. Out of seven people on *Cyclos II,* no one had really prepared for this. I think I can sing Jack Johnson songs backwards now, since it was one of the 2.5 albums we had on board. Remember you won't always have a data connection, so download your favourite tunes when you're still in a good wifi zone. If you're heading for the Caribbean, learn some reggae songs so you can join in on the local Caribbean karaoke shows. It can also be fun to bring your own instrument, but be mindful about how much everyone else will appreciate this (or not!).

> Captain: *"If someone has a guitar on his back, I turn around and pretend I'm not seeing him. I don't want that noise on board."*

Movies

Charging a laptop takes a lot of power. Some boats allow for this, some not. Movies are also suitable to watch from your phone or tablet. Find recommendations on ocean, adventure, and sailing related books, courses, apps, podcasts, music, and movies on *Oceannomad.co/resources.*

7.6 PRE-DEPARTURE RESEARCH & ARRANGEMENTS

What else to research and arrange?

- Read stories and watch videos of people who have made the crossing. The stories are fun to consume, and it gives you a good idea of what it will be like. Many of the people I surveyed kept a blog. You can find the links to their stories on *Oceannomad.co/resources.*

- Research insurance options that cover ocean sailing, and the countries you are planning to visit.
- Prepare for Citizen Science research projects. In Chapter 16, I offer some suggestions for ways you can contribute to research with sought after data you can collect during the crossing. Research and write down the protocols before you start sailing, so you know what to bring and what to do at sea.
- Research and write down basic meal ideas and recipes, especially how to bake from scratch. Most boats have ovens, so fresh bread, cookies, and cake can be a big happiness-maker on board. A few ideas in the provisioning and cooking at sea section.
- Let your bank know about the countries you'll be visiting. Withdrawing cash from Spain, then Cape Verde, then different Caribbean Islands may look odd to the bank. They can block your card. I had both my bank cards swallowed in Tobago, which was a bit of a pain, and put me on a budget **coconut** only diet for a few days.
- That said, arrange multiple bank cards and have back up cash with you. Dollars and/or euros are accepted almost everywhere around the Atlantic. Currencies can be exchanged locally.
- Check if you've paid your bills for the coming month(s).
- Scan all your documents and have a copy backed up online and on a USB stick.
- Research your onward travel for once you will leave the boat. Up next!

7.7 ONWARD TRAVEL PLANNING

"She stood in the storm, and when the wind did not blow her way, she adjusted her sails."

— ELIZABETH EDWARDS

Don't plan too far ahead because it is extremely likely that the initial plan will turn out differently. This is a rule that applies to sailing (and life) in general. Variables to consider: weather, breaking things, waiting for spare parts, fixing things, situations with the crew—the list goes on.

You never know what is going to happen, but you can be sure that some change of plan will take place. You don't want to arrive in the Caribbean and have missed your flight. You also don't want to arrive in the Caribbean and have to fly out the next day. If you really do want to book your ticket in advance, be relaxed about it and don't hassle your captain to hoist more sail or turn on the engine because the time frame is getting critical for you to catch your flight. A captain might take unnecessary risks to get you there in time. There is no point in stressing. I would also not commit to any onward travel plans with the boat for the Caribbean. You might have enough of the rest of crew after the crossing, or you fall in love with a person or island and decide to stay and explore more. Keep your plans open and stay flexible.

My 'plans' often fell apart—but a change of course can lead you to wonderful experiences:

- I was 'planning' (more hoping) to reach the Caribbean before New Year's Eve. This didn't happen so instead I just explored Gran Canaria some more, and surprised my parents for Christmas. Both priceless experiences.
- On *Sea Ya*, we 'planned' to have four crew, but one crew member ended up leaving the ship in Cape Verde. Although we were sad initially, it did give us some extra space and comfort on the boat.

- We 'planned' to go to Trinidad, but in the middle of the Atlantic, we decided to go to her tropical sister, Tobago—an island I completely fell in love with.
- On *Cyclos II*, we 'planned' to stay two days in the Azores. In the end, we needed to wait for a spare part to arrive, stayed for a full week, and allowed us to explore this natural paradise.
- As I'm writing this, I am supposed to be sailing the Mediterranean on a big sailing catamaran. However, when I arrived at the planned port of departure, it was clear that the boat wasn't even close to being ready. It's still on the dock which worked out well—Now I have the time to write this book.
- *Eau Too* was supposed to pick me up in Gibraltar. One crew member left, and all hands on **deck** were needed to sail the boat from France. So I made my way to France and hopped on to help with that.

Stay calm if things work out differently than you imagined. That said, it's good to do some research for 'the other side.' What to research in advance?

- Research the destination you're heading for. Once you are on the adventure, you'll be either getting the boat ready, sail, or socialise. There won't be much time to do the research. On most island destinations, the WiFi isn't that great either.
- If you have no idea where you'll be going, it could be good to research at least some options. You might stay on the boat, or you might not. After all my ocean crossings, I preferred to leave and move around on land. This isn't easy on a budget, especially in the Caribbean. Expenses on land can add up fast, so it's good to do some research in advance, kind of know what to expect, and possibly have some options lined up. Not only for yourself. You have the responsibility towards the captain to have your exit plan in place. Chapter 'Back on Land' will get you started.
- If you're planning to leave the boat after arrival, you may need proof of onward travel from the country of arrival. This can be tricky if you don't know yet where you will be going. This is the case in many countries so it's best if you can plan ahead for this. Learn more in 'get stamped off.

- Research visa situations, routes, and distances between destinations. Definitely part of the fun! I love looking at maps and zooming in and out of Google Earth to get an idea of what I'm getting myself into. It's part of the pre-excitement, and helps you adjust course for the adventures to come.
- Research if you need any vaccinations for the area you might be going to. Some countries, especially in South America, require proof of yellow fever vaccination.
- Research about the visa situation (up next!).
- Research if your insurance covers you in the country you are going to.

See 'On the other side' for an impression on what to expect.

> **DO:** For any and every trip, ensure you have the correct visas in place before you travel. Investigate the visa requirements for your nationality and your intended destinations on both sides of the Atlantic.
>
> **DON'T:** Buy a return ticket. It will not go as planned and you'll appreciate the coconuts, turquoise waters, weather and Caribbean lifestyle so much that you don't want to fly back right away anyway! The same applies when going from west to east. This is a more adventurous route with less predictable winds, so you can't know for sure when you will be on the other side.

7.8 VISAS

The one thing you do need to carefully plan for is the visa situation. You will be crossing borders, and you don't want to get yourself or your captain in trouble. When you join a sailboat, you will be added to a crew list. This list is submitted to port authorities by the captain. It is your responsibility towards the captain to ensure that you can legally enter that country. You may need to plan ahead a little bit. Depending on your nationality and your further travel or working plans, different visas and rules apply.

When arriving in Europe and not being a European citizen you may need to have a **Schengen visa** sorted in advance. This visa covers most European countries, and allows a maximum of 90 days stay (over a period of 180 days). 90 days should be enough time to find a boat. If you're looking to find a boat from east to west, and don't board a boat to the Caribbean before your visa expires, I would not risk overstaying. What you could do, is to go to Cape Verde instead. Many boats sail there from the Canaries, and it 'only' takes 5–7 days. It is likely that you will find a boat to go to the Caribbean/Americas in Cape Verde. In the worst-case scenario, if you don't find a boat, you can spend more time in Cape Verde. Both times I've been there, I actually didn't want to leave. At the time of writing, you don't need a visa to sail into Cape Verde with a European passport. Another option is to go to Gibraltar that is outside the **Schengen** zone. You can try you luck there.

For most of the countries in the Caribbean you don't need to apply for a visa in advance to enter as a tourist. For the United States (including the US Virgin Islands and Puerto Rico), you have to make arrangements beforehand. Also, if you are planning to work somewhere, you may have to arrange a suitable visa and/or work permit beforehand.

7.9 WHAT TO TELL MUM?

You have to make the announcement to your loved ones. If you don't come from a sailing background, sailing across the ocean might be perceived as a big risky thing to the parents/partner/kids/friends. No matter how experienced or well-travelled you are, the mums and dads want you to be safe. A smooth and informed approach helps.

How can you make your parents, friends, or loved ones feel comfortable about you taking off on this adventure?

- Give the home base contact details, such as the satellite phone number, captain's number, and details of crew members and their family. Nearly all boats making an ocean crossing will have **satellite phone** and/or SSB radio on board. Both systems can send and receive text and email when you're out of the coastal radio zone. They are expensive to use, so don't expect to be able to call home except in an emergency. Family and friends can often send messages to the phone for free though, so that's cool! My parents sometimes also called with the captains' parents. It helped them understand more about the sailing life.

Mum checking our position

- Show your family/friends how to use *marinetraffic.com*. If the boat you are on has an **AIS** transponder, you are traceable in the **VHF** radio zone. Tell them that the boat can disappear from the radar when you're out of the radio zone (+/− 50 miles from coast). You don't want them to call Search & Rescue because your boat has disappeared from the map! Mums have done this before and it can turn out to be a costly call.
- Some boat may have a tracking device that sends out a **GPS** signal every hour or so. Boats joining the ARC all carry a tracker that can be followed online.
- Let them know that boats are so well equipped these days and numerous safety measures are in place. The captain might even allow you to make a phone call with the **satellite phone** when you get halfway to assure them that you're safe and well. Texting and GPS tracking are sometimes possible as well.
- Assure them you've thought it through, can support yourself, have a plan, and a back-up plan.

7.10 CONNECTIVITY

To avoid high international roaming costs or dependency on WiFi bars, buy a local phone card (SIM). In Spain, you can get a SIM for €10 and get €10 credit with it. Orange and Vodafone work well in the Canary Islands. In Cape Verde, I paid €5 for 1GB of data, which worked faster than the WiFi in the bar. You then don't have to look for WiFi in bars and cafes, and can just focus on socialising instead! Digicel and Lime work well in the Caribbean. You can use the same card for many different islands without extra roaming costs. The local shacks sell them, and most towns have a Digicel or Lime shop. A SIM card costs EC$15 (+/− US$5) and you get EC$10 credit with it. For EC$20 you get one gigabyte of data.

With Whatsapp, Facebook Messenger and Skype, it's easy to make video calls. By having just a few dollars of Skype credit you can call any landline for a few cents only when on a 3G network.

Need to receive physical mail before or after arriving? You can share harbour addresses or have something sent to the local post office with the mention 'hold mail'. I've had stuff sent to the Canary Islands, the Azores and Grenada. If you can, avoid having something sent to the Canary Islands, as you may have to pay import tax there.

You may or may not have a transponder on board that sends a signal to the satellite to indicate your position. Check beforehand and update your mum. Some **satellite phones** allow for text messages to be automatically posted on Facebook. This is a cool feature to keep friends and fans updated about your journey. Sort this out beforehand when you're still in the WiFi zone.

I highly recommend cancelling or change the settings of your newsletter subscriptions and Facebook notifications, or you'll go crazy on the other side. You can set up an autoresponder for your email saying you'll be off the grid for a while.

8

PREPARATION: ON BOARD

"The beautiful thing about the ocean is, all there is out there is what you take with you."

- PAUL DUNN
(Sailor)

HOW TO BE READY THE DAY YOU LEAVE? How to provision? What other safety measures can you take as a crew member?

8.1 GET TO KNOW THE BOAT

- Learn where the boat parts are: lines, sails, shackles, **winches,** sail tracks and **reefs.** It's an opportunity to figure out the boat. The captain of *Eau Too* prepared a fun game. He wrote down different names for different parts of the boat. As crew members, we had to discover where it all was. I could tell you a list of boat parts here now but why not go on a little exploration yourself? It's part of the fun! The same boat parts can have many different words. Agree with your crew team which words to use.

- Learn where all the holes in the boat are!
- Check where you can hold on to yourself once the boat is moving without breaking things or yourself.
- Sharing a cabin? Discuss preferences on tidiness, storage, and privacy.

- If you can, pick a bed **stern** side or **mid-ship. Bow berths** can be very bumpy on the ocean! On the other hand, in the bow, you won't hear much engine and autopilot noise.
- Ask about the rules on board.
- If something is not right or feels wrong, discuss it with the captain so the situation can be solved.

8.2 PROVISIONING

Now the fun really starts! Provisioning is one of the most important parts of the preparation. A well-fed crew is a happy crew, so properly organise, plan and execute provisions for the boat. Your health and happiness for the next few weeks depend on it! Captains usually have their hands full preparing the boat, so it's likely that you will be part of the provisioning team. And believe me, you *want* to be part of it. I've stocked up for numerous Atlantic crossings, as well as many other multi-week boat trips so I know how much food can make or break the experience! Well-organized provisioning can save lots of time, money, and waste. Here are some key points from what I have learned.

Make a plan
Planning tips:

- Discuss dietary requirements, allergies, budget, and preferences together before you head to the shop.
- Don't be afraid to have say what foods you prefer. With a zillion different (lifestyle) diets these days, it's hard to cater to everyone's preferences. Everyone needs to adjust. But there should be happy-food for everyone, so speak up. If lots of oil, salt or sugar drives you crazy, be sure to mention that at some point. I've been with grumpy crew because the food was so oily all the time. Something easy to avoid, but if fellow crew doesn't know, then it won't be catered for, for sure. Three weeks at sea is a long time to eat food you don't like.
- Are there any allergies or other dietary restrictions on board? Be flexible and compromise on preferences for the sake of overall on board happiness, but nobody should be stuck with food that might make them ill.

- Who's paying? If you're 'going Dutch' and share expenses, which is most common, talk about what you're going to share. Are you stocking up and sharing food (and expenses) just for the crossing? Then plan and chip in for that. There should be food that everyone likes, but you shouldn't have to chip in an extra €100 because the captain wants to stock up on some rosé wine to have in the Caribbean.

- If you buy staples like rice, pasta, or couscous, etc., discuss what kind of rice to get. White rice might be cheapest, but it has been stripped of its nutrients. If everyone is okay with that, no problem. Realize that whole grain options have more nutrients, will give you more balanced energy throughout the day, and would be better for happiness and fitness on board in the long run.

The receipt. Woopsy!

- Make meal plans (e.g. seven-day menu) and calculate quantities (see suggestions on quantities below. If you just go shopping without having calculated quantities, you will end up buying far too much. I have seen people stock up more meat than they would even eat at home.

- Don't plan heavy meals for the first few days. Until everyone gets his and her sea legs on, the appetite is usually low.

- Buy basic ingredients that allow you to cook from scratch. It's healthier, fun to cook, allows for flexibility (for weather, diets, a seasick chef, etc.), and there is less packaging waste.

- Buy food that will last long. On *Sea Ya,* we had a fridge but had to turn it off to save power, so the perishable food ended up moist and spoiled quickly. We didn't have much freshness left the last week.

Be prepared for that, and stock up with enough dry fruits, nuts, and seeds. This kind of food lasts forever and is nutrient dense.

- If you can't live without marmite, chocolate, or a zillion different teas, and it doesn't fit the boat budget, just buy it yourself. You will thank yourself for that later.
- Before you head out to stock up and come back with a massive volume of edibles, create space.
- Keep it as simple as possible. Provisioning is already complicated enough.

The banana boat

Did you know that it's bad luck to bring bananas on a boat? For all sorts of reasons: Crew members can slip on the peels, bananas come with deadly spiders, fish don't bite on the day bananas are discovered, several ships carrying bananas have disappeared, and they release stinky methane when they go bad. On the boats I've been on, we've always stocked up with bananas, and we all luckily made it to the other side. What is true for sure is that bananas make the other food spoil more quickly. They are great to eat when you have sea sickness symptoms, which also usually happens in the first few days. (Most of) The bananas you find in the Canary Islands, Cape Verde, and the Caribbean are de-li-cious and nutrition rich because they are locally produced. If you bring bananas on board, store them away from the other fruits and vegetables. Buy some green bananas to maybe even have bananas in the second week of the voyage. If they all start to get black, you can make banana bread!

Minimise your provisioning footprint

It is important to be mindful about what we bring to sea and to shore at our final destination. Pollution is one of the greatest challenges our health and the health of the oceans faces today (learn more about the why in Chapter 13). The ocean is not a dumping ground, and in particular on the islands, the waste disposal facilities are limited. Landfills are small, and waste is often dumped near the road or burned. Even the waste in the landfills is often burned. How can we as sailors best tackle this issue?

It all starts with the preparation! Here are some ideas:

- Do your very best to buy products with as little packaging as possible.
- Opt to land at a destination with recycling facilities in place.
- In Spain, Cape Verde, and the Caribbean, plastic bags are still widely used, and supermarket staff will give you one by default (especially if you have your food delivered). Always bring your own shopping bags and decline the plastic.
- Choose consciously what you buy; be mindful about what you bring on board in the first place:
  - Buy in bulk to have less packaging. You can store smaller amounts in reusable containers.
  - Paper towels are favourable and frequently used on board. But in many cases a good old reusable cloth can do the job. If you do use paper towels, obtain unbleached biodegradable ones without ink (ink is a kind of plastic). White paper towels are treated with chlorine which is a dangerous toxic for your own and the ocean's health.
  - Cleaning products. Use biodegradable washing liquid for your own and the ocean's health. It all drains straight into the ocean. Alternatively, vinegar and water combine to make a great cleaning product, for the boat interior as well as your hair.
- Try to avoid buying from a supermarket, as much as possible. Supermarket products are generally wrapped in multiple layers of plastic, and at the checkout they put everything into plastic bags (especially when they deliver), even if you ask them nicely not to. Supermarket produce is often chilled and will go bad way quicker! Go to the local market instead of the supermarket for your provisioning. It is not only the cheapest option, you are supporting the local entre-preneur, and reducing plastic waste. More on this in "Hit the Market" below!
- In the Caribbean islands, Saturday is market day. While you can provision the other days of the week as well (except for Sunday), on Saturday islanders from all across the country make their way to the capital towns to sell their produce.

Avoid buying items with lots of wrappers, such as candy, biscuits and tea (in Spain and Cape Verde, many brands even wrap individual tea bags!). If you do happen to buy wrapped items, try to get rid of as much packaging as you can at your departure point, if waste disposal facilities are in place.

What happens if you go to the supermarket in Spain

- If you have foods delivered, see if the sellers can take back the plastic bags, cardboard and boxes. You shouldn't take cardboard on board anyway as they can be a source of unwanted bacteria and cockroach eggs.
- Choose products with recycled packaging or packaging that you can reuse yourself.
- Reuse items as much as you can– bags, containers, jars, boxes, etc.
- Opt for cloth napkins instead of paper.
- Opt for wooden pegs, instead of plastic ones.
- If you don't have a water filter on board and need to buy bottled water, choose the 20-liter bottles and a pump, as opposed to six-packs of 1.5-liter bottles with an extra plastic wrapper around it. Water bottles are one of the biggest ocean polluters and unwanted in the Caribbean. More on water as a limited resource.
- If you need to buy any pots, pans, or plates, go for cast iron or stainless steel. These materials are easy to clean, durable, recyclable, and less toxic compared to plastic.
- Have the right size pots/pans for the number of people on board, so you don't have to overuse water or gas.
- Opt for wooden utensils: they are durable and collect fewer bacteria than plastic.

One of the prettiest beaches in the Caribbean: Salt Whistle Bay

We live in a world where convenience and profit still dominate the scene. Think about what's more important: short-term convenience, or maintaining a healthy ocean for future generations? As individuals, we can walk an extra mile to source a better choice. Read more about how to deal with waste on the ocean in chapter 10, and on the other side in chapter 11.

Food choices, quality & quantity

FOODS THAT DO WELL ON PASSAGES
- Long-lasting fresh fruit: lemons, apples, oranges.
- Long-lasting vegetables: pumpkin, butternut squash, garlic, onions, cabbage, sweet potatoes, beetroot, carrots, cucumber, tomatoes (technically a fruit;)), olives, olives, and olives.
- Grains: Brown rice, quinoa, amaranth, millet, couscous, pasta, and flour to make bread, biscuits and cakes.
- Beans: Lentils, chickpeas, other peas, green beans, black beans, any beans.
- Canned foods: lentils, chickpeas, beans, fruits, coconut milk, corn, vegetables, capers, gherkins, sun dried tomatoes, coconut milk.
- Other: crackers, chocolate, fresh ginger, biscuits, seeds, peanuts, butter spreads (peanut butter, tahini), noodles, wraps, corn (for popcorn).

- Herbs (dried/powdered) that excite meals greatly: basil, oregano, dill, cinnamon, oregano, ginger, turmeric, paprika, curry, cayenne pepper, garlic black pepper, nutmeg, rosemary, chili powder.
- Oils /dressing/sauce ingredients: extra virgin olive oil, coconut oil, apple cider vinegar, balsamic vinegar, lemon juice, nutritional yeast.
- Baking essentials: Baking soda, sea salt, yeast, flour, and sweeteners. Prepare and learn to make your own bread.
- Extra excitement: cacao powder, vanilla, coconuts, coconut flour, coconut rasp.
- Drinks:
  - Coffee, tea, some beers in a secret spot for the halfway party.
  - Lemon juice or syrup can add excitement to water.
  - Rum or **Grog** for the halfway party!

ESTIMATES

How much do you need? Here are a few guidelines you can apply to calculate how much to stock up:

- You need to drink at least three litres of water each day (life at sea dehydrates!)
- Fruit: 1 piece/person/day (At least! More is better)
- Vegetables: something fresh with every mea.
- Pasta: 100 grammes (uncooked) per person per meal
- Lentils: 60 grammes (uncooked) per person per meal
- Rice: 90 grammes (uncooked) per person per meal
- Muesli/oats: 30 grammes per person (half a cup)

Provision the above amounts for your estimated sailing days, x1.5 for risk management. You need to ensure you have enough, but you also want to avoid having to throw away food.

One paprika, eight apples, loads of onions, onions, onions. We have made 1,400 miles. We have 800 miles to go. We try to average 140 miles a day—so that's six more days to go. With seven people. But we're *not* averaging 140. The wind is non-existent. We're currently going 3.5 knots, on engine. The **GPS** gives us an **ETA** of December 5, 7 pm. That is nine more days. With one paprika, eight apples, and loads and loads of onions. Of course, we have more food. Tinned stuff. And plenty of white pasta and rice. We'll be okay. It's difficult to provision for a trip like this. I have come to appreciate every bite of fresh fruit or vegetable—not just on board, but for the rest of my life!

Healthy choices

This is not a cooking book, but staying healthy at sea is so important for happiness and sanity. Here are a few more, healthy provisioning recommendations, based on my experience and health freak investigations. Buy nutrient dense food instead of the cheapest and/or fastest-boiling option. So, opt for whole grain pasta, rice, flour, and couscous. Nutrition dense foods won't spike your blood sugar levels like the white versions that are usually stripped from nutrition. They may be slightly more expensive, but are cost-efficient in other ways—you won't need to eat as much to feel satisfied, as well as feeling satisfied for longer, so you won't hit the snack cupboard or boil the kettle for a cup-a-soup!

- Stock up on ginger, garlic, turmeric and onions. These superfoods can help to combat (sea)sickness, are powerful infection killers if necessary, and they will last the whole crossing.
- Buy sea salt instead of the cheap sodium table salt. Sea salt has a high mineral content, which is great for keeping you powered when seasick.
- Get the higher quality *extra* virgin olive oil, which has healthier fats and antioxidants as the cheaper version that's mixed with processed oils. All processed oils don't contribute to your health.
- Sprout! And you can have the treat of fresh vegetables for the whole crossing. Sprouts are nutritional power plants: loaded with vitamins, minerals and enzymes, and it's fun to do! Lentils, chickpeas, flax, sesame, pumpkin, chia and sunflower are a few generally available seeds and beans that can be sprouted. Learn how to sprout in the 'fun in the galley' section.
- Stock up on an alternative to white sugar, like stevia, maple syrup, molasses, or brown sugar.
- Buy dried fruits for night snacking, instead of processed cookie crap and candies (that also come with loads of plastic wrappers that blow away). Even if it's just raisins: cheap and available in both Europe and Caribbean. Learn how to make energy balls.

- Dried vegetables are nutritional power houses that last months, if not years.
- Get plenty of dried herbs (herb suggestions above under food choices, quality and quantity). If they have been dried below 70 degrees, they contain almost as much nutrition as from fresh herbs. They also make cooking and eating much more exciting.
- Nuts (walnuts, almonds) and seeds (chia, flax, sunflower, hemp, pumpkin) are healthy, boost energy, and last long.
- Beans and peas are nutrition dense and cheap. If necessary, you can live on rice and lentils for weeks. Together they make a complete protein, it lasts, tastes delicious and is dead cheap. Lentils sprout easily so you can always make something fresh. Red lentils boil the quickest. Whatever bean or lentil type you use, soak them first for a few hours to maximise the nutrition powerhouse and reduce boiling time.

Party essentials

It could be a nice gesture to bring some 'luxury' food on board and hide it to surprise the crew at a special moment, for example the half-way milestone. Check if anyone is going to have their birthday on board and prepare something fun for that. Note that balloons are not a good idea for an ocean birthday or halfway party. The wind and the sun will make them snap, and they end up getting mixed into the plastic soup.

Up Spirits: the sailor and the rum

What's with sailors and rum? Back in the day, from a special barrel called the "Rum Tub", sailors of the navy received their daily ration of rum, known as a "tot" (about five tablespoons). Sailors' work was tough, so as support, they received a tot each day. "Up Spirits", between 11 am and noon, was tot time! On long voyages to and from the Caribbean, water got bad quickly, wine became vinegar, and beer was also spoiled after a week. Rum, on the other hand, is a liquid that lasts well for a long time! In the West Indies (the Caribbean), rum was already produced, so it was easy to provision. Over the years rations were cut. Eventually someone realised that it wasn't very wise to give spirits to working sailors and so the tot tradition was abolished. These days, sailors toast with a rum to a safe voyage, at the halfway point, and once arrived on the other side.

Provisioning in Las Palmas, Mindelo & the Caribbean

NOTES ON PROVISIONING IN LAS PALMAS (GRAN CANARIA)
- At Mercado Central in Las Palmas, they will pick the greenest fruits and veggies for you which will last the longest, and they will deliver your *compras* in carton boxes to the boat. My favourite stand: Antonio! Read more tips on Las Palmas.

NOTES ON PROVISIONING IN MINDELO (CAPE VERDE)
- Mindelo has a Central Market on the main street. The smaller market stables around town are cheaper.
- Most fruits and vegetable here are organic. Mangos, bananas, papaya, spicy oil, herbs, apples, maracuja (passionfruit), sweet potatoes, and tomatoes are available in abundance.
- Don't buy pre-packaged tea here. Most of the bags come individually wrapped in plastic. Delicious loose tea is available.
- Buy a bottle of the local **Grog** for the halfway party!

NOTES ON PROVISIONING IN THE CARIBBEAN
- The Caribbean islands are a heaven for spices. Stock up with nutmeg, cinnamon, ginger, turmeric, cacao.
- Farine (ground Cassava) is another fantastically versatile food to stock up with. You can have it like 'oats' for breakfast, make bread with it, or turn it into a hearty snack.
- Buy it if you see it. Some products are scarce or run out quickly so if you see something you want, don't assume you find it again. I've taken buses across islands to find a ripe banana, power adaptor or chocolate bar.

Hit the market
"Buenos dias, guapa!", Señor Pepe says while watching the TV from his home-trainer. He's wearing a T-shirt that says *'Aqui todo es muy bueno,'* meaning 'Everything here is very good.' Pepe moves from his home-trainer to the counter where his *'caña'* (glass of beer) is located. Before I order, I'm already offered a wild peach to try. 'How was the beach today?' he asks. I tell him about my day and order some seasonal fruit. Just enough for the day, so I can come back again tomorrow. He gives me some free *naranjas* (oranges), raises his beer and says *'Salud, hasta mañana*

Suzanna!' meaning "Cheers, see you tomorrow Suzanne!" This is what local grocery shopping is like in Spain. Isn't it fantastic!? Pepe made my day!

Seven reasons to shop locally

1. YOU MAKE THEIR DAY!

You can go to the big supermarket ends up? By buying locally, your money and appreciation goes to the local entrepreneur and stays in the family and the community, rather than paying for a second holiday home for Mr. Supermarket Owner. Local vendors mostly buy from local growers in the neighbourhood. This means more community support and less dependence on distant corporate chains and politics. It makes a place stronger in times of crisis.

Local market men delivering fresh goods.

2. IT'S AN EXPERIENCE

Engage the senses, experience the local scene, and you'll come home with a story! The chances are that you will be the one and only customer. The vendor doesn't get paid per hour, he or she gets paid by what you buy. They will do everything they can to make you happy and want you to come back! Have a chat, try some new foods and exchange cultures. It's all part of the fun!

3. IT HELPS TO MAINTAIN THE IDENTITY OF A PLACE

Every town has icons like Señor Pepe. Take Mr. Ice Cream around the corner, or the coconut man walking the beach every day. They form part of the identity of a place. By spending your money locally, you give back to the place you visit, and the money is reinvested into the destination. This is good for the travellers who will visit in the coming years, and good for future generations.

4. IT'S BETTER FOR THE ENVIRONMENT

Local vendors buy from their local farmer or friend, or even grow the food themselves. This means that little or no fuel is burned to get a meal to you. Not to mention less plastic, fewer chemicals, and less pollution. At the market in Las Palmas, they will pick the greenest fruits and veggies for you which will last the longest. They even come and bring it in carton boxes to the boat, without any plastic packaging. It's cheaper for you, you support the local entrepreneur, and reduce your plastic footprint.

Did you know that 90% of the world's goods are transferred by pollutive tanker ships? A large portion of this is unnecessary, and is driven by the demand of consumers who either don't know or don't care about the impact of imports/exports on the environment. We don't need to eat a papaya from Brazil if it's orange season in Spain. Which brings me to point five. . . .

5. FOOD IS FRESHER, TASTIER AND HEALTHIER

Okay, so maybe it would be nice to have mangos all year round, imported from Timbuktu. But the seasonal fruit from the neighbourhood is actually much healthier, and tastier too! Have you ever tried an orange straight from an orange tree? De-li-cious! And if you're in a faraway country, why not just try that weird looking veggie you see everywhere? It's in season; the locals are buying it, so you might just find a new favourite!

6. YOU KNOW WHERE THE FOOD COMES FROM

When you ask a Western kid these days where eggs come from, they are more likely to say 'the supermarket' instead of "a chicken", or "the farmer." The local vendor can tell you exactly where the food has come from, and probably with a fantastic story attached!

7. IT HELPS TO PRESERVE SPACES AND PLACES

Do you know those moments of happiness when looking at fields of sun-flowers, palmtrees, or green rice paddies? Let those moments serve as a reminder that these beautiful landscapes, managed by the local farmer, only survive when the farmer sells enough of what he's grown. Selling land for development shouldn't be the more tempting option. By making the food chain smaller, more money goes back to where the product comes from, stimulating local economies and reducing dependency on distant buyers.

The buying part has been done: let's bring it on!

How to store food?

Storage tricks that help preserve the food.

- Store fruits and vegetables in nets. Don't mix them. If possible, keep citrus fruits and apples together and the rest apart.
- Put fruits and veggies with a thicker peel below those with a thin peel.
- If you have green crops, like lettuce, put them in a bag and if possible in the fridge. It will keep them moist, and the green will thrive a little longer.
- Wash everything in a bucket with water + vinegar before bringing it on board to get rid of bugs and pesticides.
- Get rid of all paper and cardboard packaging that has been standing in a warehouse—this can be a source of bacteria, cockroaches and other unwanted inhabitants!
- You may want to make some nets in front of cupboard too, to prevent things from falling out when you open the cupboard.
- Store staple foods that are open in airtight boxes to keep moisture out.
- Rotate food that is ripe to the top and must be eaten soonest.
- Check daily for moist and rotten fruits or veggies. One rotten apple can spoil the rest!

8.3 SAFETY & RISK MANAGEMENT

Even in this era of satellite phones, safety and rescue technology, and communication systems, the nearest help can still be hundreds of miles away. What can happen? A lot! You can lose the rig, have a fire, get water in the boat, hit something, lose the rudder, rip the sails, break a leg, or in the worst case scenario, sink. Airplanes crash. So do cars. To be blunt, shit happens. The Atlantic has no reefs or rocks in the middle, so the risk factor of hitting something is extremely low. Still, you could hit another boat, a whale or a floating container. These are rare scenarios, but it could happen. That's why standing watch is so important.

It's extremely unlikely, but boats do sometimes sink. One of my fellow crew members was shipwrecked on a previous crew adventure. One of the boats that joined the ARC+, broke their mast on the way back and they had to abandon their ship. In the Azores, there was a boat on the dock getting repaired after it hit a whale. There are a few of these cases every year. Rescue services are phenomenal these days, but of course you need to rely on yourself. That's why it's so important that the boat is as safe and as prepared as it can be. And so are you!

How can you minimise risk and negative consequences as a crew member?

- Make sure that the boat you hop on has all the safety measures (using the checklists in Chapter 5)!
- Be sure that the ship has proper insurance and that you are not financially liable in the event of major damage or even worse, a sunken boat.
- Make sure that *you* have good travel and liability insurance.
- Have a backup plan, including an emergency budget to sustain yourself or to book a flight, should the trip not go as planned.
- Do your own research! Check, study, and be aware about the weather forecast, navigation plan, obstacles and chart.
- Calculate if there's enough water on board, and if a backup system is in place (such as a **water maker,** or two tanks, with one closed). Think about:
  - The number of crew, length of the passage, capacity of the water tank, estimated days of sailing + extra emergency days.

- - Each person needs *at least* three litres of water for *drinking only.*
- - Make sure there's a backup plan for contaminated tank water. If there's only one water tank, you need to have backup water, just in case the tank gets contaminated or salty.
- - Bring a filter water bottle for yourself so you can filter water at all times.
- - Learn the basics of how to use the radio. You can use the radio for a **Pan pan, Sécurité,** or Mayday call. Pan Pan is an emergency, but no life is endangered, Sécurité is a navigation warning (for example a container floating around), and Mayday is for when there's a life threatening situation on board. You can also get 'Pan Pan Medico' which will get the coast guard to call in a doctor so you can get advice for your problems or he/she can talk you through a procedure.
- Have someone (or a good book) on board with first aid knowledge.
- Make sure there is a well-equipped medical kit on board, including prescription drugs and pain relief.
- If no one on board has specific First Aid knowledge, is there a contact you can call with the **satellite phone** in the event of an emergency.
- Do you have a **life jacket** and safety line?
- Is your boat bed rocking-proof? Do you have a **lee cloth?** If not, make one. You won't be the first being thrown out of **bed.**
- Be and stay fit, so you can deal with any situation that crops up.
- Make sure the communication equipment has been tested.
- Save emergency numbers in the satellite phone and write them down and put them in a visible spot.
- Make sure to get a safety briefing on board before departure. Including:
- - Man Over Board **(MOB)** procedure.
- - Learn where all safety equipment is located (**Grab bag, flares,** life jackets, fire extinguishers, **life raft, MOB** gear, first aid kit)
- - Learn how the boat works as soon as possible. Walk all the lines. Observe, learn and memorise. If something happens to the skipper and/or other capable crew, someone's got to be able to take over.
- Know the passage plan as a crew member.

Things *will* happen. It's all part of the adventure. Hop on board with an 'it can be done' attitude, be inventive, alert and well-prepared, and you can tackle whatever situation comes up.

8.4 THE DAY YOU LEAVE

*"A ship in harbour is safe—but that is not
what ships are built for."*

—JOHN A SHEDD
(Writer)

So today is the day! You've been working towards the Atlantic crossing for weeks, months or even years—and today it's finally happening. It's time to unplug from the big hyperactive noisy world, and plug into the most magical place on the planet: the ocean! Enjoy the ride! You've worked hard for it.

Sea Ya—January 15, 2015

Life in Las Palmas has become too comfortable. It's time to turn the boat from a living boat into a sailboat. The boat is painted, washed, fixed, washed again, fixed a bit more. The steering wheel is put back on. Every square inch of the 44-feet boat has been stocked with food for four people for four weeks. We are like a cargo ship. Customs clearance, check! The dinghy has been pulled up. I've gone for a last run. Mum has been called. The batteries are charged. The GoPro is ready to roll. The water tanks are full. The forecast gives a 20 knot north east wind—perfect! We fuel up, and with our last euros, we buy an ice cream. All that's left to do now to is to throw off the stern lines and sail out!

A few tips before leaving

- Have a good breakfast and take your seasickness pill (a few hours before sailing out) if you're worried you might get seasick.
- Spend your coins! I've been carrying around euro coins for months. Unless you go to Martinique, Guadeloupe, St. Barts, or St. Martin (where they have euros), you won't be able to use them, so offload before leaving Europe. US and Eastern Caribbean Dollars are also not easy to change in Europe.

Sunrise in Las Palmas. Today we leave!

- Be prepared with a charged camera battery and sunscreen, and cap. Have it ready! Once you leave, your hands are needed on **deck.**
- Have your wet weather gear ready to grap, your bed ready to jump in, and your head torch charged. May you become seasick, which is likely the first day, you don't have to search.
- Has the weather forecast been checked!?
- Turn on an out-of-office auto reply on your email. Here's my example:

"Dear fan, I moved my office to a sailboat for the next few months. Responses may take longer than usual. Ahoy! Suzanne."

Ahoy!

On The Ocean

9

STORIES FROM THE OCEAN

The days pass happily with me
wherever my ship sails.

- JOSHUA SLOCUM
(Sailor & Writer)

YOU'RE OFF! WHAT'S LIFE ON THE OCEAN REALLY LIKE? What happens at night? How do you sleep? What do you do all day? Jump on board! This chapter features stories from the ocean.

9.1 SOUTHERN ROUTE STORIES (EAST TO WEST)

The Statistics

CROSSING #1 ON *SEA YA* (JANUARY–FEBRUARY 2015)
Las Palmas—Cape Verde: 850 miles
Cape Verde—Tobago: 2,262 miles
Sunrise & sunsets: 18
Windless days: 0.5
Rain: only on arrival day!
Highest wind-speed: 24 knots
Boat speed record: 11.4 knots
Fastest day: 160 nautical miles
Slowest day: 104 nautical miles
Boat damage: nothing major!
Tons of seaweed: Surprisingly, a lot
Days with dolphins: 1

Birds: every day! (Yes, even in the middle of the ocean!)
Other sailboats: only 1
Tankers seen: 8
Days throwing up: 1
Flying fish on board: 24
Open air cinema nights: 3
Number of times the boat rocked back and forth: 10,408,080
Bruises: 34
Shooting stars: More than wishes to make!
Falling pans: at least 4
Water temperature in Cape Verde: 25.5 degrees Celsius
Water temperature in the middle of the ocean: 32 degrees Celsius
Water temperature in Tobago: 32.1 degrees Celsius
Seconds of boredom: 0
Number of messages after 18 days of disconnection: INSANE

CROSSING #3 ON *EAU TOO* (NOVEMBER—DECEMBER 2016)
Fréjus (France)—Lanzarote—Las Palmas: 1,489 NM
Las Palmas—Cape Verde: 850 NM
Cape Verde—St. Lucia: 2,389 NM
Windless days: 10!
Rain: 1 massive **squall.** A few smaller squalls.
Highest wind-speed: 45 knots
Fastest day: 160 nautical miles
Slowest day: 100 nautical miles
Boat damage: Nothing major
Seaweed seen: zero
Days with dolphins: 10
Other sailboats: +90 (of which many were ARC+ boats) but also days without.
Tankers seen: 1
Thrown up: 3x
Flying fish on board: 10
Water temperature Cape Verde: 25 degrees Celsius
Water temperature in the middle of the ocean: 30 degrees Celsius
Water temperature St. Lucia: 29 degrees Celsius
Seconds of boredom: a few. We had so little wind!

Sailing from the Mediterranean into the Atlantic

SV *EAU TOO*—OCTOBER 17, 2016

I'm eight days at sea now. I open my eyes and see the reflection of water moving on the ceiling. I sit up (which is a luxury on board) and look outside. All I see is water. That's a change of scenery from the window of the **starboard stern** cabin. I always saw land when I woke up. We have made about a 1,000 miles from France now. Is it a new day? I check the time and it's 17.00. I feel like I've just experienced a few days since I was on **watch** from 9 pm–midnight, 3 am–6 am, and 10 am–2 pm, and there were so many happenings and incidents. All on a few square metres of the island called a sailing boat. With all the naps and watch-keeping shifts, rhythm on a boat is nothing like on land. It may sound tough but it takes a few days and then you're used to it.

Rewinding 11 hours. . . .

Early morning approaching Gibraltar

6 AM

I text my Tarifa friends with a photo of the chart plotter. The mobile 3G connection is working well. We're 17 miles away from Gibraltar. With an average speed of six knots we'll be passing the Strait in a few hours. My **watch** is finished so I crash to sleep. I'm on watch again at 10.00.

I hear a familiar sound. The sound of the easterly **levante** wind zoofing around. I hop out of bed, climb into the **cockpit** and catch the sunrise when I look over to portside. Looking **starboard** side, I see the rock of Gibraltar. I scan the horizon and there's dozens of tankers around, most of them **'not under command,'** and many leisure fishing boats. It's Sunday and there's a full moon. Full moon means more fish closer to the surface. It's awesome to see Gibraltar from a different perspective.

Usually I drive past it on the other side when I go to Tarifa to kitesurf and see my friends there.

I just came off **watch** two hours earlier but I'm too excited to go back to bed. We're sailing into another continent today *and* along Tarifa, which I've made basecamp over the last years. I already called my friends to get out there and wave from the land.

The rock of Gibraltar

We planned to be around here at exactly this time. And we are. Good navigation plan, skip! At 9.19 the tide changes and we want to go with it, since tides can be strong here. With the full moon the tidal differences and **current** will be strong. Our **COG** (Course Over Ground) is five degrees. We're super lucky with the weather. The forecast gives a mild **levante.** Last time I passed through it (story below), it was everything but mild. Apparently Levant ruled the whole summer, since my kitesurf friends could hardly kite due to the strong winds.

'All Ships, All Ships'. . . . Someone on the radio broadcasts about a boat with an estimated nine refugees floating around, if we can all look out for them. The weather is calm today, which is not that common for this zone. We, westerners making our sailing dreams happen, are not the only ones crossing the Strait of Gibraltar. It's also those that don't even have a passport risking their lives to survive. They make the same passage, the other way around, with a different boat, crew, destination, and

Sam and I on watch

purpose. There surely is no 'guide' for that crossing. This is a daily event here in the Strait and it breaks my heart. No numbers on refugees exist and only **Neptune** knows how many get taken by the **current.** Think about that.

9.30 AM
The wind speed metre is slowly going up. We're having around nine knots of wind now. With only the **headsail up**, a little bit of wind and current, we slowly glide towards Tarifa, running a boat speed of 3.5 knots. I'm on the helm now and zigzagging mainly between leisure Sunday fishing boats. On our **port side** one cargo vessel after the other is passing by, navigating through the **TSS** ('Traffic Separation Scheme'). Hundreds of them pass through here each day. On the **AIS,** we can see where they are going: Nicaragua, Mexico, Recife, Gran Canaria, Rotterdam. Our global sea transport system is fascinating, yet such a polluting element of our society. Not just the fuel but the noise does a lot of damage. Engine sounds reach much further underwater than via air. This noise stresses marine life and interferes with their acoustic signaling they use to communicate, locate prey and navigate (6). Another reason to go local and reduce transportation costs of our consumption.

Approaching Tarifa

11.30 AM

We have 12 knots of North East wind and the compass is pointing 83 **degrees** now. We slowly sail into the strait. From my obsessive kitesurf wind checking and analyzing back in the days, I know that around noon the **levante** wind usually picks up. I already see the kite surfers playing around at Balneario surf spot next to Las Paloma's Island, the most southern point of continental Europe. Like last time I crossed the 'Strait of Gib' from the other direction, I get on the phone with my friend Vince, who's walking the dog and waving. We locate a yellow buoy in front of us, indicating a hazard, and we have to pass it south. 16 knots of wind now.

1.20 pm

With a speed of 7.6 **SOG** we go across the Strait of Gibraltar. It's a bit quieter with the tankers now. It was super timing to do this passage on a Sunday! There seems to be less boats than usual. Great, because we have to somehow cross one of the busiest Traffic Separation Schemes in the world. The wind picks up and with 20–25 knots we cross the **TSS** to 'the other side.' It's like we're going through boiling water. Here is where the Mediterranean meets the Atlantic. There's no straight line separating the seas. With a different salinity, different layers mingle and create a wild water lane across the strait. Little Moroccan fishing boats show up. I can't believe the danger they put themselves in with all these tankers passing by on both sides. Tarifa gets smaller and smaller as the mosque of

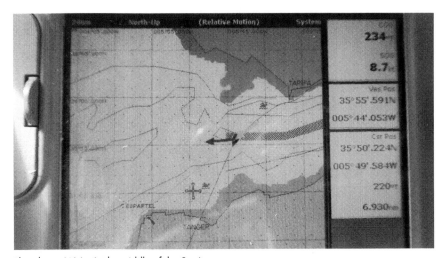

The plotter. We're in the middle of the Strait

Tangier becomes bigger on the horizon. With a separation of only 14 km, we have gone from Europe to Africa.

2 PM
I hand over the **helm** to the next watch. I take the best seat of the boat, the little corner seat at the **stern.** This restless soul finally finds the peace to sit down to enjoy the view of Morocco. Sam is putting her pirate socks on the **guardrail** to dry. George is talking Arabic on the phone. Carly is on 'mother watch', preparing foods. Bart is somewhere and Kirstin is asleep. Then I'm off for a snooze. Snooze number three? four? of today. I have no idea anymore.

5 PM
I wake up. I look outside and all I see is water.
I'm off to the **cockpit** to check out the Moroccan Coast. We have the Atlantic **swell** now meaning big long waves and a relatively non-rocky dinner outside. All together we have dinner and dolphins are stealing the show. We already got spoiled with dolphins on the **bow** but the show we receive now is unbelievable. I have never seen so many dolphins together. There's hundreds of them, jumping, playing and swimming towards our boat! What a day, what a day! This was such an exciting, lively and event-ful day! It makes you yearn for more. And there's so much more to come; it's just the beginning. Thank you *Eau Too* for having me as part of your

crew! I have to close the laptop now because in a few hours I'm on watch again and I need to take a rest. The exciting day isn't over yet!

9 PM

We have calm seas, the full moon in the sky and with Sam I chat about this memorable day.

In seven days, we sailed from Fréjus, France to Morocco. It was an eventful and beautiful first week at sea! Now in the Atlantic! To be continued. . . .

Canary Islands — Cape Verde — Caribbean

SV *Sea Ya*—January 15, 2015

DEPARTURE DAY

I give a kiss to the shore and we throw off the lines. The harbour of Las Palmas claxons us goodbye. It's a nice time to leave because now temperatures are dropping in the Canary Islands. Off we go: destination Cape Verde. Accompanied by new sailor friends in their dinghies, we leave the marina that has been my home for the last two months. It's a beautiful day. 25 degrees Celsius and 15 knots of wind from the north-east. We keep waving. Time to hoist the sails: the main, the **jib** and the **mizzen!** The marina gets smaller. Las Palmas gets smaller. I call Mum with my last bar of phone reception. I already start to feel meh. Seasickness, please don't kick in. I take my first water sample for the Microplastic

Leaving Las Palmas

project. I put on my life jacket, clip myself on with the safety line and with the blue bucket I scoop out ocean water into the sample bottle. I keep the blue bucket close to me, just in case. Eventually, Las Palmas is out of sight.

I realise we're not going to see any land at all for the next few days. A new and exciting experience! With sails up and a **SOG** of 7.2 knots, we're on our way to Cape Verde. I'm so happy to simply be breathing ocean air. Las Palmas is a great city but with city life comes polluted air. The difference is huge! Captain Rudy cooks our first meal in the rocking boat. We pull the flag down. On the horizon we have a beautiful sunset. The wind picks up when we 'turn around the corner' of Gran Canaria. I see the windmills making overtime. And damn, this boat rocks. Will it really be like this for the rest of the trip?

The night kicks in. There is no moon. It's pitch black. I go for a rest since I'll be on **watch** later. For a few hours I try to find a relaxing sleeping position. Not possible. But that's okay—I just lie there listening to the waves. As long as I keep my eyes closed, I won't feel sick. We are four on board. My watch-keeping shift is from 2am to 6am, the hardcore one! I'm two hours on with Rudy, then two hours with Goedele.

DAY 2—FIRST REAL DAY ON THE OCEAN

I get up at 1.45 am. The watch outfit I prepared is all over the place. It takes me a while to find everything and put it on. Ten minutes and ten bruises later I arrive in the **cockpit.** Rudy has made a tea. A great start to **watch!** I thought. . . . A few minutes later the fish are feasting on it, as well as the *nasi* I had earlier. Hello seasickness! Never mind—I know it will pass. Rudy gives me the blue bucket, a faithful friend to many Crew members before. Plankton lights up the water below; shooting stars fire through the night sky. It's all worth it. During my first night watch, I've seen two tankers. I haven't touched the helm. We **run** on autopilot. After watch, I crash to bed.

We are sailing **'goosewing'** or 'wing on wing', with both the **stay sail** and the **genoa** rolled out. It's a pretty sight. It's 23 degrees Celsius and the conditions really can't be greater. Except for my personal one. I still feel fuzzy. The temperature is fresh, but not cold.

DAY 3—LET'S STOP THE MEDICINE

This rocking of the boat puts my balance organ to the test. '*Dios mio,*' this boat rocks! Today I did not take a seasickness pill. Let's see how that goes. We have white caps on the water. The wind is blowing quite strong. We surf the waves. It's spectacular. I feel safe on this boat. The hull and masts are strong and well looked after.

The nights are as black as they can get. There is no moon and I cannot even differentiate the sea from the sky. The clouds disappear and there is the starry sky. I've never seen so many stars in my life! In the last few days I've seen more shooting stars than I had wishes to make. I'm looking at the brightest star in the sky. Through my galaxy scanning app I learn this is 'Sirius.' I'm scanning the stars and learning about the universe. The phone is on flight mode with the battery still half full after five days. I don't think that has ever happened before. I'm scanning Orion and learn where the name Orion comes from: the Greek hunter. The Big Dipper constellation is passing from east to west every night. Or are we on earth passing the Big Dipper from west to east? I have a lot of time to figure out and learn about the nature around us.

Time for a shift change. I wake up Noor and collapse into my bed, falling asleep immediately. I have already figured out the perfect sleeping position in a swinging boat: on the belly, with one leg up and pillows on each side. In this position, no waves can rouse me from my sleep.

DAY 4—BANGING SAILS

No second rounds for dinner today. There's spaghetti everywhere but in the pan. I watch the sunset between the two butterfly sails. It's 19.20 and only gets dark now. We're definitely moving on the map. The sails bang a lot. The captain doesn't like it! It damages the sails. The water is 23.3 degrees Celsius. I have a zillion bruises by now from navigating from cabin to **cockpit** and back. After three days at sea I have started to learn the booby-traps and the art of swaying with the boat. I have the sea legs on. I feel great!

DAY 5—BLUE MONDAY

I feel alive. I realise it's 'blue Monday' (3rd Monday of January—believed to be the most depressing day of the year).' It's blue for sure. The sky is blue, the ocean is blue, and my clothes are blue. I feel the happiest person on the most depressing day of the year. The water temperature is now 24.6 degrees Celsius. The air is warmer than in the Canaries. I don't need that sweater anymore. We're definitely **heading** to the tropics. On the horizon, we spot a boat! Exciting! This is the first vessel we've seen in three days. Rudy and Noor called them on the radio. It's another sailboat named *Kalibu,* also heading to Mindelo. During my watch we overtake her easily with our two head sails.

Noor comes green out of the **mess** after her cooking session. It is a rocky boat. She needs fresh air. Every day around this time we have dinner. It's the one moment of the day we are all together. Today we eat something simple. We (the girls) have given Rudy too much 'exotic stuff'. It's becoming too much for him. So it's plain old rice and ketchup for the captain. The girls slaughter a fresh Canary Island pineapple for a tasty touch. Rudy does the dishes today and comes back up with a tint of green in his face as well.

DAY 6—APPROACHING A NEW COUNTRY!

2 AM

"Wake up Suzie!" Noor wakes me up. It's time to start my night **watch.** I'm used to this rhythm by now. I had a few hours of sleep and have no

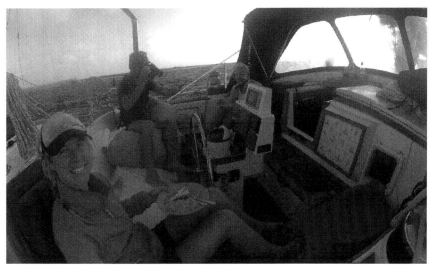

Rudy identifying what exotic stuff is on his plate today

problem to wake up. It's getting warmer now after a few freezing cold nights; I only need one sweater and pants today. I enter the cockpit. Noor goes to bed. The first two hours of my shift are with Rudy.

The night watch involves a lot of staring at butterfly shaped sails, the metres, the radar, and the compass ball. We are sailing with the compass at 220 degrees. At the moment we're 'only' going six knots. For five days we have had 18—25 knots of wind, straight from behind. It can't get much better than that! At one point we even reached a speed of 11.4 knots, when surfing a wave! Every day the numbers go up. We have travelled 760 nautical miles so far. The water temperature is now 24.5 degrees Celsius—an increase of 2.5 degrees since leaving Las Palmas. Tropics, here we come.

4 AM

Rudy jumps into bed and Goedele and I make up the next watch team. I hope she slept well. Last night she literally flew out of her bed when we surfed a wave! She and the wooden thingy 'preventing' her from flying out of bed, ended up in the **mess** of the boat. We have no boats on the horizon, **AIS,** or radar. I make some tea; I have already mastered the art of tea-making in a swinging boat—always a fun task! My sea legs are back, so I don't need seasickness pills anymore. This is my last night shift, for now. We should arrive in Mindelo, Cape Verde, tomorrow evening! With a warm tea in my hand, I watch the sails taking us over the ocean. I observe the tri-coloured head of the mast swaying from left to right, admire the bio-luminescent plankton, feel the ocean breeze on my face, and look around for shooting stars. It's a beautiful, peaceful, relaxed night. At this moment, I would be happy to just skip Cape Verde and keep going all the way to the other side of the Atlantic. I'm loving it!

At night watch

AROUND SUNSET

I see land!!! What a euphoric feeling to see land after 5.5 days of ocean. The sunset is spectacular. 20 more miles to go! I attempt to take a little siesta, but I'm too excited to fall asleep. Back to the **cockpit!** I want to experience every second of this approach.

00.40 AM

We have arrived in Mindelo, on the island of São Vicente in Cape Verde! It was quite a challenge to manoeuvre into the bay, the sky being pitch-black and the lights too dim. But we did it! We' gone like a rocket! It took us only 5.5 days from Las Palmas. That's fast. We ran an average of seven knots. We couldn't have better conditions. In the **pilot,** I read that it's 'day of the hero' in Cape Verde today. Perfect timing, right?! I feel like one! It's the first time I arrive to a country by boat. I cannot wait to touch shore and explore! This was 'just' a trial **run** to Cape Verde—an appetizer for the big pond.

Arrival in Cape Verde

After a good nights sleep, we wake up, have breakfast that doesn't spill. We put the plant outside and are off in search for customs and immigration.

Goedele has announced that offshore sailing is not for her, and she will leave the boat. A pity. The four of us have made a great team. Hopefully we can find a replacement crew member in Cape Verde!

MINDELO, CAPE VERDE

We stay a short week in Cape Verde. I go for kitesurfing, we dance on streets with Cape Verdean Jazz live music, and eat the local Cachupa.

We're one crew member down! Goedele decided the ocean crossing is not for her. With the three of us we make a good team but a fourth crew member would be nice! We try to find someone. We ask around, post an advertisement in Marina Mindelo on the bulletin board, and spread the word via my Facebook page and some Facebook groups. Locally there is only one dude around and he's looking for a ride to Brazil. Whereas in the Canary Islands dozens are looking for a boat, In Cape Verde there's no one. Three more boats here are looking for crew!

At the fuel dock in Mindelo: ready for the next leg!

With *Sea Ya* carried some goods from Spain to kiddos and old people in need in Cape Verde: clothes, books and pencils. We hope they can use it! Thank you, Rudy, for finding space on your boat!

JANUARY 28—NOW WE'RE REALLY OFF!

The boat is clean, new vitamins have been stocked from the local market, we are cleared out of customs, the **dinghy** is pulled up, the plants are put away, water tanks are full The *Sea Ya* is ready for the ocean! So are captain Rudy, Noor and I! We're going off island time. Gone with the wind! Caribbean here we come!

This time we set out to cross the big pond. It's somehow less exciting than leaving Las Palmas, but still special. We're only three now. We have filled the fuel tanks and stocked up on fresh bread and water. Some Swedish friends we met in Las Palmas blast a farewell horn. As we sail out, we wave over at some more sailing friends on their way in. The bay of Mindelo gets smaller and smaller. The view of São Vicente and Santo Antão is stunning. The islands get smaller and smaller. With 20 knots of wind and a speed over ground of 6.8 knots, we finally set off into the blue! This time it's for real. Rudy enters the coordinates: N 10° 40' 15.8412" W 61° 31' 16.3416". Destination Trinidad & Tobago! Woohoo.

DAY 4 OF THE BIG TRIP—REALITY KICKS IN!
I'm on a morning watch from 6am to 8am alone. It's my favourite time of the day. The sun is rising. There's no one else around. It's just me and that big sea. Around seven (boat time) it starts to become light. I have never seen so many shades of pink and orange in the sky. What a spectacle. It's real. I'm crossing the Atlantic.

DAY 5
Dolphin alert! "Suz, Suz! Wake up! There is a huge school of dolphins around the boat." What a wakeup call! I jump out of bed to meet my idols. They are little spotted dolphins, jumping in the waves, playing around and making the famous Flipper noise. It's around 10 am, my second start of today. I've only slept a little, but apparently, it's enough; I feel fresh and excited.

DAY 6

I play around with my action camera, read a book, try some yoga on a swinging boat, wash my feet in the ocean, clip my toe nails, 'run' a few rounds on the boat, take water samples, and do some breathing exercises to improve my freedive skills.

DAY 7

We have put up the storm sail in the main which helped the boat from swinging (a bit). Menu of today: Mashed potatoes boiled in seawater (which is de-li-cious!) and carrots!

DAY 8 — HALFWAY DAY!

1,070 miles, check! We celebrate with a shot of Grog! We have our first bin bag full of trash. We throw it in the **dinghy** that is pulled up at the **stern.** It stinks! We should have rinsed it better. One cargo ship on the horizon today. That's exciting! Captain allows to give my mum and dad a ring. That was a happy surprise! It's hot, the thermometre is showing 35 degrees Celsius. I try to write something but I can't. The boat is rocking. Not an ideal angle for writing. Maybe I'll just go for a snooze.

I LOST COUNT OF THE DAYS AND DATES NOW

We're all still happy, healthy and super tanned. We're going a steady 140 knots a day. If we go on like this, it will be another nine days of sailing.

We almost hit a weather station, water temperature is 29 degrees! So far, we have only seen some flying fish and one big seaweed parade. Again, a spectacular sunset.

FEBRUARY 10—MY BIRTHDAY

Sea Ya turned into a party boat today because it's my birthday! Fiesta time! I am spoiled with a brownie and a birthday song by my fellow crew members Noor and Rudy. They have decorated the boat and give me a crown to wear for the day. I have permission to call the parents with the **Satellite phone**. I can tell them I'm still alive and they can actually celebrate having me on this planet for 29 years. We have a visitor on my birthday: a tropical bird. Outside temperature: 29 degrees. Still another 480 miles till destination Tobago. The sunset today is absolutely spectacular. Again. We have dolphins jumping like the sea is a trampoline. What else to wish for?

Today I got to wear a crown

DAY 15—CLOCK & DESTINATION CHANGE

We change the clock. Every 15 **degrees' longitude** we change a time zone. We adjust the 'boat time' to not be jetlagged when we arrive. We 'planned' to go to Trinidad for Carnival. Today we decide to go to the little tropical sister, Tobago, first. White sand beaches, swimming, and coconuts are calling!

DAY 16—SWIMMING O'CLOCK

We now have half a day of almost no wind: *The* moment to jump into the ocean. The water is like tea, it's that warm (31.5 Celsius!) but still so refreshing after a week not showering and moving! Bikini days only from today. We're definitely approaching the tropics! At night it's just shorts and a t-shirt. Current fresh food status: We have two apples left, one eggplant, one red cabbage and one tomato.

DAY 18

For weeks, we think and chat about what we'll do when we arrive. Usually it's eating some sort of food. I've been talking about sipping a fresh coconut for 18 days now. Tomorrow is the day!

DAY 19—ARRIVAL DAY

February 16. 4AM boat time.
6AM local time?

Only when we approach the Caribbean we see the first sailing boat of the trip! He calls us on the radio. It's a solo sailor from Brazil and we are the first boat he sees after one month of sailing alone! That's how off the grid we can be as sailors. It's still dark but we have some lights on the horizon.

Approaching Tobago

For days, I've been trying to imagine what Tobago would be like. For months, I've been trying to imagine what the Caribbean are like! We have a cruise-ship on the **AIS,** and two small fishing boats on the horizon. While we get closer to Tobago, the sun rises and we get to see the island.

Happy, tanned, and tired we near the land.

The water is 30 degrees. I take a last water sample. I see palm tree beaches, loads of tropical birds. I smell greenery and burned trash. I hear cars and waves crashing into shore. We need to go to the main town of Scarborough first to check into the country. After 18 days we get the sails in. We anchor and shower underneath a **squall.** The boat is clean right away. We stay on board for a while. Then the cruise ship comes in mooring right next to us. Gosh, I'm happy I'm not on that thing. For 18 days, we haven't seen any other people and now I'm looking up to a floating city that has more people than the town we're anchored in. For some time, we just sit there and absorb the ambience. We're in the bay and we hear about ten music styles together. Tomorrow Carnival officially starts. The speakers seem to be working.

Time to meet some locals. We need to clear in the country. We get the **dinghy** in the water and paddle off to customs. We attach the dinghy to a fisherman dock next to a bright yellow painted boat saying: 'Why worry, men must live too.' I like that! From the dock I look at *Sea Ya,* right underneath the rainbow. We receive a friendly welcome by a fisherman. He helps us tying the dinghy to the dock.

Boat *Sea Ya* under the rainbow after we arrived from the Atlantic Ocean in Scarborough.

It's weird to step on land and walk again! This is what I missed most. Walking! Moving! Like hippies with dreadlocks, and way too tanned, we absorb the island vibe and dive into the bureaucratic procedure to check in the country. The customs and immigration procedure goes on **island**

time, manually with a pen and big red book. Nothing happens with a computer. Not often boats make their first landfall in Tobago. Many questions are asked but after about two hours we're good to go.

First things first: in search for a steak for captain Rudy, chocolate ice-cream for Noor and a coconut and salad for Suz! Eating fresh vegetables makes me feel like the richest person in the world. We're back in civilisation. Tomorrow Carnival starts. What a clash from the peaceful big blue ocean. We all can't wait to have a full night of sleep.

Exploration modus ON

We survived Carnival and are off now to check out the bays of Tobago. What a super chilled out friendly island!

Sea Ya in Tobago

Cheers to the adventure of a lifetime!

The *Sea Ya* party crew with a Carib beer on the beach in the laidback fishing town of Charlotteville, Tobago! Today I'll leave captain Rudy, Noor and boat *Sea Ya!* It was a memorable expedition. We've become like a little funny family in the last months. Now it's time for the next adventure. *Sea Ya* moves on to Trinidad this night. I'll spend some more time exploring, kitesurfing and freediving in Tobago! I'm not done with this paradise island yet!

9.2 NORTHERN ROUTE STORIES (WEST TO EAST)

The statistics

CROSSING #2 ON *CYCLOS II*
Antigua—Azores: 2,367 NM
Azores—Palma de Mallorca: 1,338 NM
Sunrises & sunsets: 10 + 11
Windless days: 0.5
Rain: +/- 40 **squalls** & 2 days of nothing but rain
Highest wind-speed: 48
Speed record: 16.8
Fastest day: 255 nautical miles
Slowest day: 150 nautical miles

Boat damage: Nothing major!
Days with dolphins: 5
Days seen whales: 5
Other sailboats: 15
Tankers seen: +20
Thrown up: 1
Shooting stars: Lost count
Falling pans: 0, we had a chef!
Water temperature Antigua: 28 degrees Celsius
Water temperature in the middle of the ocean: 24 degrees Celsius
Water temperature Palma de Mallorca: 22 degrees Celsius!
Seconds of boredom: 0

Antigua to the Azores

SV *Cyclos II* April 20, 2015.

1 WEEK AGO. . .

I land in Antigua where *Cyclos* is docked, as well as hundreds of other insanely beautiful yachts for the Antigua Classics. I've never seen such beautiful wooden boats. I don't think there is anything like it. I meet the crew. *Cyclos* is a privately-owned yacht with four permanent crew on board—Captain Zac from Canada, Kit from the UK, Belen from Spain, and Russell from Zambia. Then there is Arvid from Canada and Sam from New Zealand who will help to deliver the boat to Palma, Mallorca. Then there's me offering an extra hand on **deck.** It's a fun crew bunch!

The yacht is huge. She is a 90ft **ketch;** a two-master with the shorter mast, the **mizzen,** at the stern ahead of the wheel. Lots to learn on this boat with clipping **headsails** and no autopilot. There's plenty of hands-on sailing to be done. I'm the last crew member to join, and most of the preparations for this crossing are already done.

Randomly at the bar in Antigua (so maybe not so random), I bump into Rudy and Noor from *Sea Ya* who had sailed up from Tobago to here in the meantime. This crossing with *Cyclos* has a completely different setting than the sail with *Sea Ya*—the boat and crew are more than double the size, with a different route, different weather, different speed, different everything.

DEPARTURE DAY

We **rig** (prepare) the boat, buy a little bit more fresh food, and I say good-bye to Mum on the phone. At 3 pm sharp (as planned), we throw off the **bowlines** and we're off to Europe. First leg: 2.100 nautical miles to the Azores. Rudy and Noor make some noise waving us off from the *Sea Ya*.

Weather conditions are perfect. The sun is shining, 20 knots blowing (in the wrong direction, but that doesn't matter, for now). We just have to go around the island. We hoist the **mainsail, headsail** and soon we average around ten knots over ground during the first hours of sail. I have never experienced an average speed of ten knots before. Zac gets out the rum. We toast to **Neptune,** the god of the sea. The rum goes around and everyone says a few words ended by a shot for Neptune in the sea, and a shot for ourselves. May it be a fun and safe journey! We're going like a rocket. Antigua disappears from the horizon at sunset.

DAY 1

I shouldn't have gone to that rum punch party. . . I suffer from sea-sickniss. No worries though, I know it will pass after a day or two. Enough stars are shooting at night to wish it away! The night sky is as clear as can be. Speedy sailing today! We reach 13.5 knots **SOG** at night. It feels *so* good to be out at sea again.

Sailing on *Cyclos*

DAY 2—WORK TO DO!

We have a situation. Every hour we check the metrics—the temperature of the drive shaft has become way too hot, and the pump of the generator is having issues. Luckily, we have lots of engineering knowledge and experience on board and the guys are on the case. With this situation, another situation is discovered, and the rest of the morning we're rinsing and drying up spare parts that were stored below the beds and got soaked in seawater. Sam jumps into the ocean to check if anything unusual can be seen underneath the yacht. Nothing. We move on, keep a closer eye on all the indicators, and make plans to stop for an extra day or two in the Azores to hopefully solve the problem. Luckily we're a sailing vessel and not a motor boat. Whatever technology fails, the sails will get there eventually.

DAY 3—RAIN

We have another situation. Goodbye **trade winds.** Hello rain! The **foul weather sail outfits** are on. The wind is up and down. The sails are up and down. At least we're moving, and in the right direction. It's been a long time since I've experienced this kind of weather.

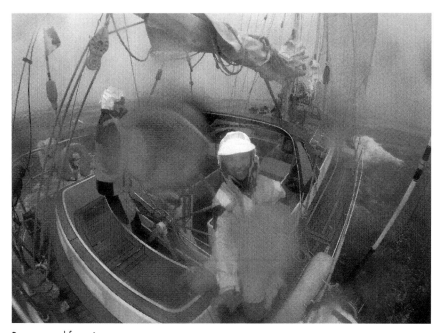

Be prepared for rain

DAY 4—1,000 MILES!

A bright light shines right into my cabin. It's the deck light shining through the hatch above my **bunk.** It's around four in the morning and I start my watch-keeping shift. We're taking three-hour shifts, rotating every 1.5 hours so you get to see a new face occasionally. After the three hours, you have six hours off. It's a nice scheme and works out well. It's sail changing time. The **genoa,** or '*Jenny*' gets changed for the smaller **stay sail,** and we're going to motor sail. It took me a while to learn the names of the different **headsails.** By now I know. We also have a third headsail, 'the **yankee.**'

It's raining cats and dogs. It's raining now for 24 hours straight. Even the experienced sailors have never experienced rain for this long. I jump into my yellow sail outfit, and head up to get soaked. Again. After 1.5 hours, Captain Zac is off and Sam joins for the second half of my watch. It stops raining (as usual, just when Zac goes off watch). I'm cold to the bone. Two days ago we were sunburnt and sweating out of our beds. Now we're drinking hot chocolate drinks in the cockpit.

Later today we move the clock forward by an hour, and celebrate the 1.000-mile point with a beer!

DAY 5—BOAT CLEAN-UP & THEME PARTY.

The boat needs a good clean—after five days at sea with seven people and lots of rain. . . . You can imagine what it looks and smells like. Then for the rest of the day we are busy turning *Cyclos* into a party boat! Today we throw a halfway party to celebrate being halfway into the first half of the trip. The theme: dress up as your favourite actor/singer. I'm dressed up as Jacques Cousteau and wear a moustache. We thank **Neptune** again, have a shot of rum, a Carib beer and delicious pizza, sandwiches and apple pie made by Belen. We're filming this trip. Belen made an awesome trailer of the footage so far. The premiere is shown at the halfway/halfway party. After about an hour everyone is already hungover from the one beer and crashes into bed. This is partying at sea! It's a calm night. Best night (read: few hours) of sleep I've had since we left.

DAY 6—KONINGSDAG!

Today we all wear something orange—at least that's what I'm trying to get everyone to do! After all it's 'Koningsdag' (King's Day) in The Netherlands. All sails are up. We're running 13.4 knots. We celebrate all this excitement with the last seven beers on board. A memorable sailing day! Everyone is happy.

ONE WEEK AT SEA

Last morning of wearing shorts. The hats, gloves, socks and shoes come out of the (disastrously messy) closet. We decided to start using the coffee grinder (manual workout **winch** machine) instead of the electric push button **winch.** We're getting fat. Let's change that into getting fit! From now on, Belen and I built in a daily yoga/pilates/workout routine. All three sails are up. In the last 24 hours we've made 255 miles! That's a new record.

DAY 8—BEATING THE SPEED RECORD

I beat the speed record making 14.5 knots over ground. We hand-steer only on the *Cyclos II;* there

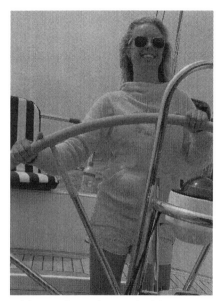

Celebrating the Dutch King's birthday

The Stats

is no autopilot. The feeling of helming a 90ft sailboat with all sails up in 20 knots of wind is definitely the highlight of this trip. My speed record doesn't last for long—Zac beats me with 15.7 and later Kit with 16.8 knots over ground! For the first time this year, I sleep with a blanket.

All sails up!

DAY 9—JIBING & JUMPING DOLPHINS

Jibe time! Now that's exciting. That hasn't happened in a few days. Our course is too far south so we put the boom in, move the sails to the other side, and go 40 **degrees** straight to destination Azores. We have dolphins jumping around us!

LAND IN SIGHT!

We still have dolphins leaping around us in the water. It looks like they are guiding us to the land. We **jibe** again. We're all busy on **deck** when Russel asks "Did anyone see that tanker on the **starboard** side?" Holy moly! Out of the mist there is a big tanker showing up. TACK! NOW!

Rule number one: Always look around you no matter where you are or what you're doing! There can be no boats for days and weeks, and suddenly you are about to hit one.

It's 5 am, boat time. We have no idea what the local time is. It's misty and rainy. On a clear day we should have seen land already, but nothing to see so far. After nine days of fishing, Sam caught a fish. It's yellow fin tuna for lunch. We're all a bit restless, tired, soaked, and, last but not least, excited, because today is the day we arrive in new territories.

Suddenly there's 'land ahoy', and we have arrived in the Azores! Hello Europe!

Looking for land

IN THE AZORES

We're now docked in Horta, Faial. It's green and blooming. Peter's Sports Bar is the place to be, the most popular stop for the majority of sailors crossing the Atlantic. Tomorrow, the spare parts will arrive and it looks like we'll be leaving a few days later on Wednesday.

We go to the bar, fix things, wash, go to the bar, stock up, explore Faial, go to the bar, and we celebrate that we made it halfway. It's great, strange, and cheap to be in Europe again. Today I dove underneath the yacht to check out the situation below. Freezing cold, but so nice to be in the water again.

The next leg is from the Azores to Palma de Mallorca, Spain. 1,100 miles to go! We're all getting ready and are excited to set off sailing.

Sailing back into Gibraltar

SV *Cyclos II*

A lighthouse. Beeping phones. Airplane stripes. Fishing boats. The smell of pine trees! That pine tree fragrance is what strikes me the most after days of breathing ocean air. We are approaching Cabo Roca in Portugal, the most western point of mainland Europe. It's the start of the most exciting and challenging part of the passage: the Strait of Gibraltar!

It's 10.30 on Sunday evening. Day five after leaving Horta, Azores. I have my three-hour watch with Captain Zac and Sammy Zig-Zag. We have more and more booby-traps to avoid now. We have four sails up. What a nice sail today.

As we get closer to land, the wind shifts and soon we'll have to drop some sails. After my watch, I, Snoozy Suzy (one of my nicknames) am going for siesta number four of the day. As usual, I crash asleep right away. I think that's what a swinging boat and salty fresh air does to you. When I start my next watch at 4.30 am, we have passed most of the coast of Portugal. We have an eventful day ahead of us!

A strong **levante** (eastern) wind is forecasted for the next few days. Captain Zac considered stopping and waiting in Portimão, but it seems safe enough to just go and conquer the elements. *Cyclos* and her crew can handle it! We received a request from another yacht to tow them. They left the Azores on the same day as we did, but they are having engine problems. With no wind (yet) they are just floating around. Since the boat is about the same size as *Cyclos*, it's not responsible for us to tow them, but we lend them a hand by sending over Russel, our top engineer, to check out the engine situation. They are only ten nautical miles away from us. Once there, I take advantage of the boat being still for a moment, and jump into the sea. Shocking freezing cold! I can barely breath, let alone swim. But good to have the blood fully pumping around again after mostly sitting on my ass for almost a week. We take off, feeling sorry for these guys. They'll need to sail into Cadiz to get the engine fixed. Soon after we wave goodbye to them, we rip a loop of our **mainsail.** We put a **reef** in the mainsail and continue. Not a boring day so far, and it only gets more exciting!

We're sailing close to Cadiz now. It's starting. The **levante** wind kicks in. This is the wind I lived for when I was kitesurfing in Tarifa. Tarifa is the southernmost point of mainland Europe and only 14km from Africa. It's famous for its wind. Strong, warm, pressing Eastern Sahara wind funnels through the strait, reaching up 50 knots. We are going straight into it. Against the wind, against the waves. Waves are around two metres now and become bigger every hour. It's one big rollercoaster ride. We have another colourful sunset spectacle behind us. Time to be alert for the fishing boats which are floating around the area. We can see the lighthouse of Cape Trafalgar. This is where Tarifeñas (the people from Tarifa) go kitesurfing if the wind in Tarifa is too strong. It's cool to see Costa de la Luz from a different perspective. I visited most of these lighthouses on land;

now I'm using them as a reference point to try to figure out where the hell we are. It's dark now.

Siesta time for Snoozy Suzy. With the banging on the waves, it's impossible to sleep in the forepeak where my **bunk** is. Instead, I build a bunker of pillows on the sofa and crash out asleep to be (sort of) fresh again when my next watch starts. Who knows what will happen in the meantime. The wind is whooshing outside, and the boat is making noises I haven't heard before in these 20-something days I've been sailing on *Cyclos*. What a super boat being able to handle all this. My friend Vince calls me and wonders when she should go out and wave from the beach in Tarifa. It looks like we'll pass by Tarifa around midnight. Russel wakes me up when are approaching Tarifa. I want to see this of course! The weather is insane. Arvid is steering. The wind is up to 40 knots. Our course over ground (COG) is 95 **degrees** but we have to steer 75 to actually stay on course. Imagine how strong the **current** is! It's nuts out there. It's weird to be so close to home but still so far away. We focus, in silence, and get through it. We pass the corner of Tarifa and the weather calms down in no time. We're out of the wind funnel. I go down to try to make teas and coffees. Everyone is soaking wet. My watch is about to start at 1.30 am. Just one nautical mile past Tarifa the sea is as smooth as glass. But we need to stay focused for the next booby-trap: Gibraltar and its traffic jam of boats.

Sammy Zig-Zag, with whom I've stood 50 watches by now, has taught me about the lights of boats at night and what the different combinations mean. Two red lights on top of each other is a boat **'not under command.'** "Basically they have all taken off and gone to bed.", he says. Many boats seem to use this tactic so they are first in order of preference—everyone has to give way to them. So we're zigzagging between these cargo ships. It's calm. I hear the spraying of dolphins. We have some company around the boat again. A huge shooting star flies overhead. The biggest I've seen this trip! My watch ends at 4.30 am and I 'take off and go to bed' just before sunrise. I'm exhausted and can't stay up to watch it. Mañana. . . .

We celebrate the exciting passage with two beers the next day, with the snow-peaked Sierra Nevada in the background. We turn *Cyclos II* inside out to dry from the Strait adventure. A few more days on this lake called Mediterranean, and then Palma de Mallorca!

10

LIFE AT SEA, HAPPENINGS & SITUATIONS

"The problem is not the problem. The problem is your attitude about the problem."

— JACK SPARROW
(Captain of the Black Pearl in the movie
Pirates of the Caribbean)

"**WE HAVE A SITUATION!**" You'll hear this on every boat, multiple times, if not daily. Usually so much happens in a day that it feels like three days are squeezed into one. You might think it's a long repetitive chain of the same days, but no two days are ever the same!

This chapter talks about different parts of life on the ocean. What does it involve to be 'on watch'? What happens at sea? How to you deal with people, cooking, dinner, dishes, showering, toilets, weather, sleep, the galaxy, laziness, boredom, swimming, communication, power, water, waste, and unexpected situations? Find out the good and the bad!

10.1 WATCH

I remember when I started to look for a boat to cross the Atlantic, I kept reading about the task of being 'on **watch**.' Is this like sitting up in the mast watching out for icebergs? What does it mean to be on watch? What is expected from you? What is it like?

Someone is pinching me. 'Suzanne Suzanne' Watch time! Wow, I come out of a deep sleep. It takes me some moments to realise where I am and what's happening. I'm going from left to right in my bed. It's night, and I hear water sounds. Right, I'm in the middle of the Atlantic, and at 3 AM I'm next on watch. I have 15 minutes to get ready. And I have not finished sleeping. I'm exploring the bed with my hands to find where the head-torch has ended up this snoozing session. I perform acrobatic skills to get over Kerstin who is crashed between me and the bed exit. Oh yeah! I manage not to put my feet in her face this time. I step on the floor and get thrown against the wall by the rocking of the boat. Shit, I hope I didn't wake up Sam and Steve who are attempting sleep in the next cabin.

I put the red light on of my torch and make a bathroom stop. With one foot in one corner, and the other one in the opposite, and while leaning against the wall, I smash three drops of water in my face to wake up. I wipe my face with the towel that is in use now for a week and has been more on the floor than on the hook. I can't be bothered. All right, one step closer to being ready for watch. Before I went for my snooze, I had put my wet weather gear ready on the hook so I wouldn't wake Kerstin up. The hook is empty; the floor is full. I get down on my knees and try to collect my gear. I explore the floor for my pants, sweater, jacket, socks, hat and life jacket. I think I have all the items. Next challenge: put it all on without waking up others and getting too many new bruises. With my oversized **foul weather gear**, three-kilo **life jacket** on my shoulders, and torch on my forehead I feel ready to go to the moon. The previous watch boiled water in the kettle. I make some tea. 15 minutes and six new bruises later, I arrive in the cockpit.

'Wind is around 15 knots. There is one boat at three o'clock. Clear skies. Many shooting stars. That's it.' The previous watch briefed and they're off to bed. I make another tea because the one I made fell over.

This is the start of **the watch.**

When on **watch** you're in charge of the boat so others can have a rest. Afterall, the boat is sailing continuously day and night.

Once on watch . . .

SV *Eau Too:* Suzy Zig-Zag at the helm

From Cape Verde to St. Lucia we basically need to turn left once out of port and keep a course of 280 **degrees** for 2,100 nautical miles. Thank god we have Bob. Since we're talking about the autopilot a lot, it has been given a name. The name is Bob. Bob sometimes needs a break too, and he's pretty noisy anyway. So I'll hand steer and give the fellow crew members some peace in their cabin. On the GPS I can see a straight line to the destination. By steering just a few degrees north, I suddenly find myself heading toward the Bahamas. I adjust a little bit towards French Guyana. Now we're aiming for St. Lucia.

It's cloudy, and we don't have a compass light. Usually, I pick a star to navigate to, to stay on course. But not now; it's cloudy. The moon hasn't risen yet, and it's pitch black. I try to feel the wind and not look at the instruments too much. Their bright lights hurt my eyes and blind me from seeing anything else. When the wind blows along my right ear, it means I'm on the right angle.

We have both **headsails** up: the **genoa** on portside and a **poled staysail** on **starboard**. We have around 15 knots of wind, going a steady 6.5 knots. I scan the horizon for any boats. Nothing to see. I check the radar for **squalls** and boats. I'm not looking to avoid land or **reefs**—we're in the middle of the ocean. Everything seems alright. I breathe the ocean air and start to feel awake. Steering helps with waking up, instead of putting Bob to work. Two hours and 45 minutes later, it's time to wake up the next watch! I make a log, write down the coordinates, **SOG**, check the barometre, wind speed, and add any comments from my watch.

Watch can be boring. Watch can be exciting. Whatever the situation, take this job seriously- everyone's lives depend on you!

What makes a good watch keeper?

- You show up to your shift on time in the proper outfit.
- You don't bring out the entertainment set to make your watch more comfortable—it distracts you from the task.
- You scan the horizon every ten minutes for boats, obstacles, **squalls,** lights, and at a certain point, land. Anticipate accordingly.
- You stay on course and trim the sails (if the captain has approved this as a watch task).

- You keep an eye on wind speed, wind direction, gusts and weather changes, and act accordingly.
- You make a log in the logbook during and/or after your watch.
- You brief the next watch on the weather, wind, any happenings, concerns, other boats nearby, the engine situation, and any other useful information to keep the boat and crew safe.
- You notify and/or wake up the captain when you think it's necessary. Depending on your capabilities as well as the captain's commands, this could include:
  - Any concern or uncertainty in relation to the safety of the boat and crew.
  - Any big change in the barometer.
  - You feel sick and don't feel competent to stand watch.
  - Wind changes of more than 5 knots. Changes in wind direction.
  - Before making sail changes or big course changes (more than 15 **degrees**).
  - Any other changes in weather or situation that the captain should know about. He or she is the one responsible in the end!
- You never ever go to bed before the other watch has arrived! I have heard this happening and is not OK. What if the next watch falls back asleep again? What about a debrief? Make sure you don't fall asleep during your watch! Get up, steer, make tea, have a snack. Do whatever to stay alert.
- Boil the kettle for the next watch. It's great to start a watch with tea or coffee.
- You don't get too comfortable, or you might fall asleep.

On Sea Ya, we had a bean bag, which was far too comfy! I just fell asleep in that thing, which is irresponsible.

- At all times, keep a weather eye open!
- Tread lightly, avoid waking anyone.

Watch handover: "It has been calm. The wind has picked up a bit. We may as well put the **genoa** fully out now. Just keep an eye out on the dark clouds behind us." I'm next on watch. I check the wind metre and see it going up to 24 knots. I turn on the radar and see *way* too many colours on the screen. That means obstacles. In this case, rain! Then it starts raining. We have all the sails up and need to put them away *now*. "We need more hands on **deck**!" I wake up the rest of the crew. "We need to put the sails away *now* because of a **squall**." Ten minutes later . . . Well, we have our shower we've all been longing for. Buckets fall out of the sky, and we're all soaking wet. This was our first squall.

Watch systems

The watch system can be tackled in many ways. It depends on the boat, crew size, skills, and captain's preference. Here's how we did it on each boat:

ON *SEA YA:*

(Canary Islands–Cape Verde: four crew)
- No watch schedule during the day.
- Watch in pairs between 20:00 and 8:00.
- Everyone did four hours of watch in a row.
- My watch was from 2:00–6:00—Two hours with Goedele and two hours with Rudy.
- This was tough! Especially because of the hours in the middle of the night, every day.
- We only used the autopilot.

(Cape Verde–Tobago: three crew)
- No watch schedule during the day.
- Solo watches at night.
- Everyone did four hours.
- My watch was from 8 pm–midnight, and then at 8 in the morning again.
- This was a-ma-zing!
- Solo night watches are special, but you need to be able to trust yourself and the crew 100%. No one will notice if you fall overboard. No one will notice if you fall asleep during your watch, until you hit something!

ON *CYCLOS II*

(Antigua–Azores–Palma: seven crew, six watch keepers/one chef)

- 24-hour watch-schedule
- Watch in pairs: one watch leader, one watch keeper
- Three hours on, six hours off
- Two rotation schemes of three people, so after 1.5 hours on watch you get to talk to a new face.
- No autopilot, only hand steering.
- With this scheme, you have watch and rest shifts at different hours every day
- Tough in the beginning. Nice after a few days since you get to experience different parts of the day.

ON *EAU TOO*

(Canary Islands–Saint Lucia: seven crew, six watch-keepers)

- Special system!
- Every day one person was on 'mother watch'—taking care of cleaning the **galley** and the food for the day. The mother watch did not participate in watch keeping that day, and gets a full night of sleep. Those who are on watch don't have to do anything in the cooking and cleaning department.
- The captain did not participate in mother watch.
- During the day we had two-hour solo watches. At night three hour watches in pairs. Always different combinations, so you get to talk to many faces.
- Every day our watch hours were different, which I personally like because you get to experience different parts of the day.

Watch Take-aways

- The mother watch system is really nice if your crew number allows it. It gives you a break from watch-keeping and a full night of sleep. As a watch-keeper, you don't have to think about cooking or cleaning for a few days until you are on mother watch again. You can just relax after your watch. Being on mother watch was fun too because you can fully dedicate to that job.

- See how your watch system goes and if you think you can optimise it, speak up! The earlier in the journey, the better.

Not everyone was happy with the watch system between Las Palmas and Cape Verde. I sat down for one morning to redo the watch-puzzle with seven crew and the mother-watch system. It took a while, but it resulted in a happy rest of the journey.

10.2 SEASICKNESS

Seasickness happens when the body and brain fall out of synch, and the brain decides your system needs to be flushed out. In France, they say seasickness is triggered by the three F's (*faim, froid, fatigue*)—hunger, cold, tiredness. Stay ahead of that! Hopefully, you prepared for seasickness.

How to deal with seasickness, once at sea?
AT ALL TIMES: Stay hydrated!
THE FIRST DAYS: Have easily digestible meals, with fruits and vegetables, during the first day or two at sea.

When you start to feel seasick (early symptoms: yawning, sweating, a little headache):

- Don't go below **deck.**
- If you feel like drinking or eating, have something before or at the beginning of your watch. If you eat or drink right before going into bed, throwing up is almost guaranteed!
- Add a mineral and vitamin-rich solution (like electrolyte sachets) to your water to make sure your body gets what it needs.
- Eat cookies, ginger candy or bananas.
- Take the **helm.**
- Watch the horizon, if near land, watching the coastlines helps even more.

WHEN YOU ARE SEASICK:

- Be aware of the wind direction, and throw up on the **leeward** side! You will only forget this once. Be attached with a lifeline or have someone holding you. If that's not an option, get a bucket.
- Stay in the cockpit, lay in bed with your eyes closed, or take the helm.
- Keep drinking small sips and eating small snacks to stay hydrated and energised.
- Lick the sea salt from your skin! It's full of minerals!
- Stay involved. Though you most feel like it, going to bed and staying there forever is not the quickest solution.

WHEN YOUR FELLOW CREW IS SEASICK:

- Help them get over it. Provide water, biscuits, and don't leave them alone for too long.
- Don't let someone who feels seasick cook, wash dishes or clean the toilet. Time below **deck** should be minimised.
- Don't let them stay in bed for days. They may feel better, but it won't help them get over it quickly either.
- Don't make fun of them *too* much.

Remember: it *will pass*.

I almost always become seasick my first day at sea and I still happily jump on board. It's so worth it!

10.3 PEOPLE HABITS & HURDLES

"The cure for anything is salt water:
sweat, tears or the sea."

—ISAK DINESEN
(Writer)

The social life and dynamics on board can make or break the experience. You're in a tiny space, for a long time, with the same people. Everyone has different habits, norms, values, opinions, behaviour, music tastes, and food preferences. An Atlantic crossing is basically a big social experiment. You really get to know yourself and your fellow crew members. That means that sometimes you have dinner with Rammstein in the background, or some days you'll get food that you would rather throw overboard. It's all about accepting other people for who they are, without making too much of a fuss. They say the boats get one inch shorter every day, so don't rock the boat too much!

Crew behaviour

- Act wise, friendly and communicate like family. Avoid problems and irritations by a few common sense guidelines when living together on a boat:
- Be clear, concise and precise in communication on board. Understand each other's terminology, and agree upon wording at the beginning of the trip. Especially when there are different nationalities on board and when it comes to sailing pay extra attention to this to avoid miscommunication. Understand what to actually do when the captain says things like 'let off', 'undo', 'slack', 'more main,' 'less halyard.
- Stay positive and calm in every situation. Communicate and solve any disagreements right away.
- If you don't like something, change it. If you can't change it, accept it and deal with it! Stop nagging, complaining or worrying about it. This is a waste of everyone's energy, including yours.
- Don't touch or use anything until the captain has explained to you how things work. When in doubt, ask.
- Don't invite your friends on board, without permission from the captain.
- Don't invite yourself on other boats. Always ask permission.
- Know the shoe policy. This is different on every boat. When in doubt, take them off.
- Keep your stuff with you or in your cabin. Boats can get messy super quickly.

- Stay clean, brush your teeth, and clean up after yourself.
- Never ever fall overboard.
- Treat every drop of water like gold.
- Be aware of the wind direction when smoking.
- Ask fellow crew if they are happy with music or you playing the ukulele.
- Ask for preferences when it comes to cooking, music, and sharing a cabin.
- Duties like cooking, dish washing, and cleaning are generally shared amongst all crew, unless discussed otherwise. It's normal for captains to not to participate in this, they already have responsibility enough.
- Adapt.
- Smile.

What people situations did the surveyed crew have?

"I found the psychological aspect of the trip quite interesting. The boat is a bit of a floating Big Brother house, and I'm surprised nobody ever made a reality show about this. My roommate got into a relationship with one of the girls aboard, and during the passage, they broke up again, after which they both said they couldn't wait to leave the boat (at least I ended up with a private room for some of the trip). The guy in question also ran out of cigarettes a few days before we reached the Caribbean, which wasn't too good for the atmosphere aboard. It just influenced the general atmosphere."

"Some people become sensitive after about a week on the boat. I had a minor conflict with one of the crew members; he got verbally and physically aggressive towards me due to a neglectable issue which was blown up due to his unhealthy approach to the conflict. We did not talk to each other until end of the trip except for necessary communication during manoeuvres. This conflict made my trip less enjoyable, and I mentally tried to forget about it."

"We started to have social tension towards the end. One crew member decided to leave before his intended destination, and I also seriously considered it."

"There were some issues with a clash of cultures and expectations on the boat and people ate very differently which was hard sometimes."

"We pushed off one crew member at Bermuda because he wasn't vital enough."

"One captain wanted to sleep with me, and I had serious problems with him."

"Captain didn't know anything about sailing. His wife, who was also part of the crew got pregnant. They didn't seem so happy about it, which had an effect on the atmosphere on boat. On top of that, they didn't wash themselves at all, so the boat stank as bad as they did. Overall, the experience of crossing was amazing, yet it would have been so much better if I just did it with the right people.

"The most difficult part was self-control. With four people and a lot of differences living together was really difficult!"

Increase the happiness on board

A few suggestions to keep good vibes:

- Throw a halfway party!
  - Make it a theme party.
  - Stock up with some exciting food just for this occasion (chocolate, baking stuff, crisps, popcorn).
- Create an arrival time competition, where everyone has to guess the arrival time at the beginning. You write this down on a piece of paper and put it somewhere on the wall. This results in some excitement during the whole passage to see who is closest to the ETA. The winner gets a prize. You have plenty of days to create a prize!
- A special event might be happening during your crossing, like Thanksgiving, Halloween, Sinterklaas, Christmas, New Year's Eve, Carnival, St. Patrick's Day, or King's Day. Make it an exciting event on board! For example, on *Eau Too* while we were out at sea it was 'Sinterklaas'. This is a Dutch holiday where 'Sinterklaas' tells poems and gives presents. I played Sinterklaas on board, wrote poems and organised a treasure hunt. This certainly put some smiles on some faces that were getting bored because of the lack of wind.

- Set up a daily workout parkour.
- Make bread, invent energy balls, and create excitement for taste buds.
- Throw a random dancing party! Every day.
- Shoot a video with your crew.
- Play games, have movie nights, tell stories!
- What can keep the moral high is a daily meeting at a set time, for example with dinner when everyone is up. This doesn't have to be long. It is good to talk through what's happening with the weather, boat, food, waste, and fun things. It's an opportunity for everyone to have a say and it can avoid tension building up. Here's an example of what we chatted through on *Eau Too*.

Crew meeting minutes *Eau Too*
Day 13: Cape Verde—Saint Lucia

CAPTAIN:
- Miles covered last 24 hours: 120
- Average three knots
- Course to steer in the **logbook:** 72 **degrees**
- Weather forecast: Similar—no wind
- PredictWind suggests it's coming easterly. Tomorrow's wind comes around east south east.
- Jobs: The main dynamo strap is broken. Can someone bring it in and put a shackle on it, and bring it back out? We'll also have to oil it. As well as the genoas furling. The sounds drive us nuts.

GEORGE:
- On the **SSB radio** this morning:
  - Someone lost the main and only has 60 litres of fuel left
  - We dropped down on the list. We're #13 in class A of the 27 boats.
  - We're #25 of all boats. We're right in the pack, more inside than yesterday.
  - **Water maker** is topped up.
- The crack on the screen is advancing. We need to keep an eye on that.

SAM (WHO OVERSEES THE FOOD SITUATION)
- Captain: "Galley? How we're doing on the food." Sam: "There are tomatoes that need to be eaten. Only eat the snacks from the snack box, please!"

SUZ (I MADE MYSELF IN CHARGE OF THE WASTE & RECYCLING):

- Captain: "Rubbish?" Suz: "Make sure to put the recyclable material in the recycle bin and not the waste bin. Rinse the recyclables, otherwise it gets stinky. We also recycle cans"

CAPTAIN: "ANYTHING ELSE?"'

Not much to mention during this meeting. But it's a nice moment together to make sure everyone is on the same page.

~~~~~~

10.4   FUN IN THE GALLEY

Cooking

It's your turn in the **galley!** You've been contemplating the whole previous night watch what you're going to make. You want to make something special. Well, it blows 25 knots, waves are coming in at the wrong angle, so good luck with making that curry from scratch that you have been planning. On to Plan B!

Cooking on a boat is nothing like cooking in the 'real' world; you need to be innovative and creative, yet simple. You have to pick the right ingredients to use at the right time. You have to think about what foods will still last for a while and what won't. Perhaps there's hardly any food left. You've got to 'row with the paddles that you have,' as we say in Dutch. Then the challenge is to make something exciting anyway. Perhaps you don't have a working fridge. You must be conscious about preserving food. All this, on an angle, if

When going for seconds. . . .

you're lucky. Especially when you go from east to west, the boat never stops rocking, and nothing stays in place. You just have to hope that a big wave doesn't hit, and that the person behind the helm is alert. You have to hope that the sails aren't being changed, which may result in you cleaning the **galley** floor and having crackers for dinner. Somehow your taste buds also act differently on the ocean. Enjoy the challenge of making cooking and eating at sea a fiesta!

A few ideas to make food on board exciting

- Make your own bread, granola, cookies, yoghurt, and chocolate! Experiment. It's easier than you think. And loads of fun!
- Sprout seeds (alfalfa, broccoli, radish, kale) or sprout some grains or beans (for example, lentils). This way you can have some crispy fresh nutrition bomb at any stage of the journey.
- Cook with +/– 30% salt water. This contains loads of minerals, and saves some precious tank water.
- Use loads and loads of herbs. Food somehow seems less flavoursome at sea. Tip: Create one spice mix at the beginning of the trip, so you don't need to get all the herbs out on every cooking session. My 8-spice favourite that does well in many meals: sea salt, turmeric, oregano, thyme, paprika, garlic (powder), black pepper, dried onion.
- Experiment and unleash the master chef in you. You'll have loads of time in the **galley to practise.**

Here are a few winners that are fun and easy to make and bring smiles on people's faces. They do need some experimentation to master it. That said, it can't really go wrong either.

Recipes

~ *Bread 'Artisanal Atlántico'* ~

INGREDIENTS
- Flour (4–6 cups)
- Water (1–2 cups, preferably warm)
- Yeast (1–2 table spoons)
- Salt (1–2 table spoons)
- Other essentials: Hands, an oven, and practice.

Bread excitement on board

THE STEPS

1. Mix and knead the four ingredients until the dough it's not wet and sticky but not dry either. Better too little than too much flour.
2. Let it sit in a hot place for 2–4 hours on the tray you'll put in the oven. You can simply put the dough on oven paper (a baking form also work). Bonus tip: if you have an engine room with space, put it there—warm and dry and your dough will grow in no time). This is when the fermenting and rising takes places.
3. Put the mass, that should have grown, in a hot oven.

Ingredient amounts and results depend on humidity, temperature, you kneading, swell, and the number of times you practice.

TIP 1: When provisioning in the Caribbean it's nice and healthy to make bread from Cassava flour (called Farine in the islands)
TIP 2: Add some spices like oregano, garlic, and onion to make it savoury. Or add coconut, cinnamon, and/or raisins, and brown sugar to make it a sweet treat.

~ Sailing Sprouts ~

Sprouts are super healthy living foods. The process of seeing the progression of seeds growing into little plants is fun. The result simply gives you superpowers.

INGREDIENTS
- Seeds/beans of any kind
- Water
  Other essentials: a jar or bowl

STEPS
1. Soak the seeds/beans overnight.
2. Rinse well. Add a little bit of water and let it sit.
3. Every day. Rinse and repeat. Watch your superfoods grow! Within three days you can have edible sprouts. Sprout a few days longer for more volume.

~ Super Power Balls ~

INGREDIENTS
(Pick 4–6 including something sweet and sticky):
Oats, dates, nuts (any—grounded), flaxseeds, raisins, coconut oil, molasses, cacao, chia seeds, cassava flour, coconut flour, coconut rasp, lemon zest, banana, peanut butter. Spices like cinnamon, nutmeg, vanilla, and sea salt.

The act: Smash, mix and match 4–6 ingredients (try and invent) all into a dough. Make balls. When possible put it in the fridge to harden it. A great snack for any time during watch! No gas needed. My favourite: dates, nuts, coconut rasp, cinnamon, and sea salt.

Find more sailing friendly recipe- ideas that generally puts a smile on everyone's face and are gluten free, vegan & healthy *Oceannomad.co/resources*.

Dinner

The sound of someone saying, 'Dinner is ready,' puts smiles on every face. Dinner is a highlight! Dozens of times lunch or dinner have been accompanied by dolphins. It's one of those highlights on the journey and a reminder and extra motivation for why we have to take care of this precious ocean.

Have dinner at a moment when you're often are all up and another day at sea is coming to an end. When **heading** west, you follow the sun and are treated with a spectacular sunset in front of the boat daily. Unless you're off course . . . On every boat, we had dinner around 5 pm when it's still light, and we could do the dishes before dark.

Dishes

Then comes the most exciting part: doing dishes! I still have to meet the first person that likes doing dishes on board. If you're cooking and someone else is on the dish washing team, it's nice to have cleaned your cooking mess as much as you can.

Dish washing procedures are different on every boat. Since fresh water is limited, most likely you'll have to take a bucket from the sea. Never ever let the tap run, not even five seconds. You have to be very economical with the resources on board.

W e take a bucket from the sea. I have mastered the technique by now of getting a bucket of water from a sailing ship. Trying to bring it safely into the **galley** without getting a new bruise is a whole other challenge. You put your feet in opposite corners of the galley, so you don't fall. We wash the dishes in salt water and rinse with a couple of drops of fresh water. We have one tea towel that I'm surprised hasn't walked away by itself yet. We're definitely building up a strong immune system on this trip. If you're not quick enough with doing the dishes and putting them away, you have to get them out of the bin and start all over again. The boat really does not stop rocking . . .

Time to do the dishes

On *Eau Too* hygiene standards were better monitored. 'Name the five usages for a tea towel?' the captain asks. "Dishes, dishes, dishes, dishes, dishes—and nothing else. Not your hands, not the galley, the tea towel is to be used for nothing but drying the dishes."

If one person is sick and dries his or her hand with a tea towel, the whole boat can get sick. Use them for dishes only. While personally, I didn't experience any people being sick on boats besides seasickness. I've heard others that had to do +24-hour watch shifts because all fellow crew got a bug. Keep the hygiene standards high!

10.5 SLEEP

'm off watch. Time to live up to my nickname 'Snoozy Suzy.' I'm too lazy to brush my teeth. With my garlic/onion breath, which we're eating daily by now since that's the only fresh stuff we still have in abundance, I fall into bed. It's so hot, maybe 35 degrees (Celsius). The designer of this boat definitely did not cross an ocean before. We can't open the hatches. Not even on the calmest day. They are built in too close to the waterline. We do have a little fan. Time to turn that on. I go from left to right to left to right. It's hard to relax my muscles with all this movement that never stops. I need to change strategy. With my sticky sweaty body, I twist 90 degrees in the bed. This way it's only my stomach in my throat with every rock of the wave. My lower legs bang a bit outside the bed. That's an okay compromise. The current watch keeper seems lazy today; I can hear the wheezing sound of the autopilot perfectly in my cabin. As well as the gurgling sound of the **bilge** pump getting rid of some water. I can also hear the wind whooshing, which I like. I hear water slapping against the hull. The squeaking of the boom. The backing sound of the sails (the worst sound for a captain to hear—this can mean damage for the sails). The wind generator. Someone is putting the kettle on. The first few days on board, every sound is new and unfamiliar—but you get used to them. Then, when the food stock reduces, you start to hear new sounds, signalling the start of ongoing Tetris games with the pots, pans, fridge and foods, to avoid them from rolling and keeping you awake. Now, every three seconds there is a tick . . . tick . . .tick . . .tick . . . It takes me a minute to figure out the source. Okay. Let's get up. The ticking comes from my clothes banging against the wall. I might as well throw them on the floor since that where they will fall eventually anyway. Next strategy. Let's find some earplugs. I. need. to. sleep. I explore the bed for my earplugs. I find one and try sleeping on my side with one ear on the pillow.

What are the sleeping arrangements like on a boat?

- On every boat the sleeping arrangements are different. Normally, there is a bunk for you, and you'd have to share a cabin (with someone of the same sex). If you have your own cabin, you may not complain.

- It's not normal to share a cabin with the opposite sex due to 'limited space.'
- Stern bunks are less bumpy but often noisier since these are often below the cockpit. Sofas are also often used as crash places since they are comfortable, and from there it's easiest to hear what's going on.
- Since there is always someone on watch, rotation sometimes happens too.
- With watch schedules, you'll most likely have a few little sleeps each day as opposed to a full night of sleep. Don't worry, your body will get used to this quickly at sea.

Tips for sleeping

- Opt for the smaller bed. The smaller the bed, the better you will sleep because you will be 'stuck'. In a bigger bed, you'll just be rolling.
- Make a **'lee cloth'** if there isn't one already. This is basically a net or cloth next to your bed to prevent you from falling out.
- Get earplugs. Earplugs can help to dampen the noises on the boat. Be sure only to wear them when appropriate. It's important to be able to hear what's going on, especially if you are on standby. Judge for yourself in which situation you can wear earplugs. If on your boat you do solo night watches, it's not responsible to wear them. You need to be able to hear a call for 'help.' Keep them with you in a little box after using them. Obviously, I didn't. I ended up finding earplugs in my hair, in the bed, on the floor, in our pockets, between the cushions, even in the **grey tank!**
- Many pillows are useful to build bunkers and get a restful sleep.
- A sleeping mask that covers your eyes can also help you get a good rest; you won't be woken up by daylight, or fellow crew turning on the light.
- Sleep when you can to stay fit. You never know when the next situation will come up and how severe it will be.
- Try different strategies, angles and pillow combinations! Sleep is important.
- The 'mid-ship' sofa in the mess often provides the best snoozes!

This is how Snoozy Suzy lived up to her name:

- On *The Bounty,* I was expected to share the cabin with the captain, since I was not a 'passenger', but crew. I didn't like this, but I thought that's just how it is on a boat. I now know that this is not normal and would never agree to this again. It's quite common that sleazy captains look for something extra from girl sailors. This was thankfully not the case here, but still, I felt uncomfortable sleeping next to a big snoring stranger of the opposite sex in a tiny cabin.

- On *Sea Ya,* I had a nice spacious bed at the **stern** of the boat. It is less rocky than the bow but that side is usually noisier—you can hear everything that's going on in the cockpit. Goedele had the bow bed and she literally got thrown out of her bed into the **galley** by a wave. It's actually nice if the bed is small, otherwise you'll just be rolling around in it.

- On *Cyclos II,* I was in the top bunk, hoping every day that the angle would be on the **starboard** side so I wouldn't fall out of bed. If the situation wasn't promising for a good few hours of sleep, I just built a bunker of pillows on the sofa and crashed there instead.

- On *Eau Too,* Kerstin and I shared a double bed. A few times per day we swapped corners, depending on who was on watch and when. After a wave launched Kerstin out of bed, we changed our strategy and also rotated in angles of 90 degrees, depending the angle of the waves.

Sharing a Cabin

We have a situation. We cannot see the floor anymore. A bomb has exploded in the girl's cabin of *Eau Too,* aka the Children's Room as the captain likes to call it. We, the 'children', call it the chill zone. When things get tense on the boat, which it does sometimes, we go into the chill zone. It's a disaster. No one really seems to bother. Next to the bed we have a railing where we can put books. Now there's earplugs, a water bottle, sunglasses, chargers, cables, socks, sleeping mask, and more earplugs. When you open the cupboard, you have to either raise your hands or duck dive. 90% of the time, something falls out of there. The "have you seen my . . .—(water bottle/earplugs/cap) question?" is routine. This chill zone is an extreme luxury on board. We can sit up straight here. On crossing #1 and #2, I could not sit up straight in my bed. I'm trying a few sitting yoga positions and progress from feeling like a Playmobil poppet to a Barbie, which is slightly more bendable.

10.6 THE HEADS

What is the toilet situation like? Toilets are called **heads** on board. If
you're lucky, you have an electric button to flush. Most boats just have a
pump system and need some manual work to flush. Toilets are flushed
with seawater so don't worry about wasting fresh water here.

The toilet experience gets an extra exciting dimension at night. If you
go in the dark or just with your torch, you may see fluorescence from
plankton when pumping up seawater. Disco in the toilet!

Never drop anything else in the toilet than what comes out of your
body! No paper, chemicals, and definitely no tampons.

10.7 NIGHT TIME

The boat will sail day and night to go the other side. There's no anchorage
in the middle of the Atlantic. With no light pollution the view of the
Galaxy is like you've never seen before. There is no way to describe what
it feels like seeing millions of stars, the milky way, and more shooting
stars than wishes to be made. You will watch this show almost every
single day. You have to experience this. Having all these stars and planets
above you, while you're in the middle of the ocean, on a 14m sailboat,
makes you feel special, small and big at the same time. It puts everything
in perspective.

As you keep the same course (more or less), you see the same patterns
and really get to learn about the stars, planets and constellations. With
an ocean passage usually lasting around three weeks, you almost see
the full moon cycle. On the days when there is no moon, when it's pitch
black and you can't even see the difference between the sea and the sky,
the starry night sky is breathtaking. On these days, the bio-luminescent
plankton lighting up from the movement of the waves (or dolphins) is
just spectacular. On one night watch dolphins surrounded by a pod of
dolphins. We saw them swimming like green torpedoes underwater, lit
up by the plankton.

When there's a full moon and the moon reflects on the ocean, you
don't even need a light to read a book. The only way to capture this magic
is by experiencing it!

When the night kicks in, it's time to turn on the instruments and appropriate navigation lights. Be mindful at night with using lights and especially white light. Bright lights blind you and fellow crew, and it affects your sleep rhythm. It's useful to have a head torch with a red 'night watch' option.

10.8 LAZINESS & EXERCISE

I crash on a cushion in the cockpit. My head is 'resting' on an uncomfortable plastic back seat and I stare straight out at the horizon. I see the sun glittering on the water. I see the blue sky and scattered fluffy clouds. I see glitters again. And the clouds again. Glitters again. Clouds again. Repeat x87. I'm not moving my head or eyes. The rocking of the boat gives me a new view every few seconds. There's not a single airplane stripe in the sky. It's beautiful. Ah, and there's the glittering water again. And the sky again. And the sea again . . . I feel like a wet towel, or a 'smashed banana' as one hitch-sailor perfectly described it! I'm moving so little and eating so much white bread, pasta and crap I usually don't eat. It's alright for a few weeks. But after the sugar rush, it just makes me tired. I won't starve, but it makes me appreciate even more the value of good pure food.

How can you manage to work out on board? Well, you can't. I tried yoga, push-ups, wall sits and a few more manoeuvres. You just keep falling over. Changing sails is great exercise, but during an ocean crossing you probably won't change the sails much. *But,* you are training your core. The constant rocking motion keeps you (unconsciously) adjusting and balancing your body, especially in your bed. You really feel those core muscles after a few days.

The view

One of those few times changing sails

The watch is boring. And I need to move. The wind is inconsistent so I have to stay alert. To bring some excitement and movement to my watch, I create a choreography written by the speed of the wind. With every change in knots, I create a dance move. With the wind going up and down, it's quite a dance! And entertaining for the rest of the crew. I think it's about time we arrive soon . . . I'm getting a bit kookoooooh.

Tips against feeling like a 'smashed banana'

Attempting Boat Yoga

- Move, move, move.
- Don't just use the autopilot when you're on watch. Stand up, feel the boat and stay awake.
- If possible, dip your feet in the sea water on the **stern** of the boat. It balances the ions in your body! On *Sea Ya*, I was able to sit on the platform at the stern of the boat to wash my feet and simply just touch the water. This was a highlight of my day.

- (Try to) stretch!
- Breathing exercises are great to keep you sane as well. Pure air for three weeks is priceless.
- Train your balance and try standing behind the wheel without holding on to it. You train your whole core with this. Don't go off course!
- Don't eat too much crap.
- Suggest a swim to the captain. Up next!

10.9 SWIMMING IN THE OCEAN

'm testing the waters . . . figuratively . . . Because I want to test them literally! Weeks of staring at water make me want to jump into it so badly! "Captain, how do you feel about going for a swim at some point? We've had a few days with little wind now." Steve: "Let me think about it . . ." At lunch time "So who would like to go for a swim today?" At 2.30 pm, we stop the boat for a swim. We put the lines out with a fender so we can grab it and won't get lost. I jump from the **bow** into the 4,000-metre deep ocean. Yahooooooo! And I jump again. The water is like tea it's so warm (31.5 Celsius!) but still soooo refreshing after a week not showering and moving! I put on my freediving mask and check out the situation below the surface. The ocean is so clear and blue. Nothing to see though besides the butts of fellow crew. There is a bit of a **current,** but not as much as I expected. This makes me feel GREAT. This was exactly what we needed after days of rocking and little wind. Don't be afraid of sharks when jumping in. They are not after you but after the weakened fish to keep the ecosystem in balance. So we better stay friends with them. Be more afraid of losing the boat, or your swimming wear!

Take the opportunity to jump into the big blue if you can and have permission to do so! It's refreshing, liberating and will bring joy on board on a little wind day. A few considerations:

- You can only do this if there is hardly any wind and swell!
- Only jump in with permission from the captain, and after the boat has stopped completely.
- Hook yourself onto a line. Even though it might seem like the boat is still—it's not. There are **currents**. You don't want to get lost at sea.

- I guess you don't want to show your private parts to fellow crew, so tighten your bikini or shorts!

10.10 BOREDOM

An *average* day on the ocean looks something like this: 2% cleaning, 5 % **helming,** 5% fixing something, 10% autopilot, 30% sleeping, 10% fun in the **galley,** 5% sailing action, 3% eating, and 30% chillaxing.

Though on average, there is no average. You can be fixing something the whole day, cleaning up a disaster half the day, while other days you're chilling and read two books.

Some find an ocean crossing boring. Depending on the weather, it can be indeed quite a monotonous ride.

Approaching the Atlantic from the Mediterenean. Calm seas. Chill day.

Eau Too—This crossing has little wind and we tried many different sail set ups. Instead of the **stay sail** we get the **genoa** out on the **pole.** This is a bigger sail. Doesn't really work. The wind dropped and we're rocking all over the place. We put the sails down and turn on the engine. We are in the super luxurious position that we have 2,000 litres of fuel. We're seriously 'motoring across the whole Atlantic.

You may have perfect sailing conditions. You may have not. You'll likely have a lot a chillaxing time. It's up to you what to do with it. I didn't get bored one single second. And the days flew by in no time. Really? Really! What do you do the whole day? Watching the butterfly shaped sails, looking at the waves, the seaweed, reading, stretching, learning, eating, drinking, making food, making drinks, watching sunrises, watching sunsets, sleeping, napping, reading books, watching dolphins, taking water samples, taking photos and videos, calculating **ETA's,** and again and again, more napping, counting flying fish, chatting with the crew about life, watching the stars, making wishes after seeing shooting stars, watching the clouds, listening to podcasts and just thinking about life. But mostly you just ARE. That's what I love most. When else do you take the time to read those books, to appreciate fresh air, or watch that sunrise?

There's a lot of observing each day. Looking at the compass, looking at the numbers. How fast are we going? How many miles did we make today? How many more miles until we're halfway? The numbers all go up. Seawater temperature goes up and up and up.

Exciting moments are those when you see another boat. During the crossing with *Sea Ya,* we saw two other sailboats, both on our last days before arrival in Cape Verde and Tobago. We've seen a few cargo vessels. We have also had one full week without seeing any other civilisation. With *Eau Too* and the ARC+ we saw more boats but we also had days in a row without seeing any. On *Cyclos II* we didn't see many sailing boats. We did see many tankers, and almost hit one on a foggy day!

Apart from boats, there are the uncommon sightings that can make the day memorable. We've seen a floating weather station (thankfully it was daylight!), one big **sargassum parade,** plastic, many flying fish, and on my birthday we had dolphins jumping on the horizon. We also had a few birds boarding the boat.

Last crossing, we had many days with very little wind. Nothing can be changed about the weather. You just need to deal with it. How often in life do you have the luxury of pure air, ocean view and no agenda, for weeks in a row? It's the best situation to find that true peace of mind. The constant wind blowing in your face. The salty skin. The inner feelings are transformative. You'll feel relaxed out here. You don't have any appointments; places to go. You have no idea what time it is, or even what day. No one cares how you look. You'll have so much space in your head to think and gain fresh perspectives.

I'm not saying it's easy! I'm one of the most restless souls out there. All year round I have a crazy monkey mind thinking about life, business

Sargassum parade

ideas, what's next, etc. On the ocean, I have the time to reflect and think deeply about life and what truly matters. Because no one, no thing, no noise, no emails, no social media feed, distracts the thinking.

Suggestions for when you're bored:

- Learn to master some knots!
- Define your life goals for the next year, 5 years, 10 years. Think about the why and make them actionable.
- Bring a mini projector and watch films on the sails.
- Read, write, listen to music, podcasts, listen and share stories with fellow crew.
- Just sit, stare and observe. The most difficult, though rewarding investment of time.

Initially the hardest but gradually the most rewarding time you spend on board is the time spent simply doing and thinking about . . . nothing. That said . . . It's pretty much guaranteed you will have plenty of situations to tackle, so you'll actually be happy if you have time for a moment of 'boredom'! Which brings us to the next part.

10.11 EXPECT THE UNEXPECTED

"A smooth sail never made a skilled sailor."

—FRANKLIN D. ROOSEVELT
(32nd President of the United States)

Almost every day something will happen or needs to be taking care of. Like a blocked toilet, broken lines, broken sails, finger in the **winch,** too much water in the boat, rinsing spare parts for two days with fresh water because we had too much salt water in the boat, leaks, things flying through the boat because it's rocking (pot, pans, cutlery, cups, teas, food, ventilators, tools).

Our bathroom stinks. Bigtime. Not because we ate something wrong. In the humidity, something is brewing and we've got to get to the bottom of it. Literally. I stick my nose in every corner of the bathroom. Girls team in action. Kerstin gets the torch. I get the screwdriver. I take a deep breath, hold it and open up the wooden floor to check whatever is underneath. Oh-my-freaking-God . . . I see things moving. There are bugs. Things crawling. I look around and they are everywhere. Thousands! We have a situation. In the meantime, . . . The. boat. does. not. stop. rocking.

We must clean this now! We need to put a severe amount of water through those pipes. We get the buckets, seawater, and a brush from the cockpit. The rocking of the boat makes the bathroom door bang against the wall. We had put a hook in there before to stop the banging. That lasted about a day until the half the wall came out. Now we 'just' hold the door. With one hand I open the wooden floor. With the other hand I hold the brush and scrub. The smell is unbearable. In the mess the thermometre shows 33 degrees Celsius. When going into the bathroom, I think you can easily add ten degrees. We can't open the hatch here. It's too close to the waterline. It's a sauna. In the meantime, . . . The. boat. does. not. stop. rocking.

What cleaning shizzle do we use? Bleach is the only option we have (we thought!—Vinegar and baking soda could have solved it too). This is not ocean friendly. What to do? Okay, bleach it is. Shit, we should have prepared better. I take off my clothes. I'm wearing shorts that Mum made. I don't want them ruined with white dots. So I just put my white dotted bikini on. I put on pink gloves. God knows what had been in there before. But it's better than getting bleach into the wound I just created on my finger by getting my fingers on the **winch.** BANG, the wooden floor crashed against the door. "Can we please not move the boat for a minute"!? Hmm doesn't work. Wishful thinking. We also check the grey-water tank. We think the source of the smell might be in there. It seems so and the bleach has its effect. We **bilge**-pump the shizzle out to sea, and pollute the ocean by doing so (Not ok— next time we know better). Situation 'bugs in the bathroom' under control for now. It's still a mystery how that started. I have no idea what kind of bugs these were, how they got on board, and what fed them to multiply.

~~~~~~~~~~~~~~~~~~~~~~~

What unexpected situations did hitch-sailors experience?

*"I had a flying fish in my **bunk**."*

"Spectacular amounts of nothing. We saw one boat in 22 days."

"Man overboard!" (& recovered!)

"Small fire!" (controlled)

"We hit an unidentified object, no water in the boat, but it was frightening."

*"Boat filled with water during an unexpected wave from **port side**."*

"We ran out of gas. So we had to cook on the barbeque."

What kind of things break during the crossing? On the adventures I was on, we broke little. We had situations like a line in the propeller, a broken generator, water in the boat but nothing major that caused huge delay, danger or damage. I asked the hitch-sailors what happened on their journeys:

"We broke a sail and a hublot during a storm."

"Crew member broke his leg!.

"The toilet got blocked but it was fixed after a couple of attempts at de-installing and cleaning the pipes."

"All the sails broke, except for one."

"The generator stopped working but it was fixed promptly thanks to having spare parts on board."

*"We lost our **spinnaker** in a **squall** a few days into the crossing from Cape Verde to St Lucia and had an unintentional gybe.*

"The water pump broke and we got it fixed."

"Rough and stormy ride between The Canaries and Cape Verde with a broken boom and a broken foresail."

*"We broke the spreader causing **rig** failure, Thankfully the rig stayed up and we made it back to the Caribbean without losing the mast."*

"We broke the engine."

*"We lost the steering 9 times, ripped the **genoa** twice, two water leaks, and the generator stopped working."*

*"Engine cooling fractured resulting in two feet deep of Atlantic water in the cabin. We resolved it with **seacock** bungs, manual pumping, and the engineer made an alternate cooling system."*

"We ripped a sail and fixed it."

"We ripped a genoa" And almost poisoned ourselves with tuna we kept in the fridge for too long."

"All the electrics stopped working for a few hours."

*"We had a sail torn. The **spinnaker** knotted in the fore stay which was a huge fight into the night to get it out.*

You see, it's definitely not boring! It's being inventive, adaptable, flexible. It's going from one situation into another. An ocean crossing turns you into a handyman, engineer, sailor, cook, cleaner, inventor, plumber, electrician, acrobat, and monk.

10.12 SAFETY AT SEA

What can you do on the ocean as a crew member to stay safe?

- Carry a knife.

- Guys, don't pee overboard! This is how people get lost at sea. If you really have no other option, put a **life jacket** on, secure yourself, and make sure someone else is on **deck.**
- At night: wear your life jacket, stay clipped on, and don't go out on the front deck alone. Better, don't go out on the front deck at night at all, unless it can't wait.
- Wear shoes and gloves to avoid getting nasty cuts. I always thought gloves were nonsense until I my finger got stuck between the **winch** and **jib sheet.**
- Know the boat, potential liabilities and do what you can to stay ahead of a real problem.
- If not initiated by the captain, initiate daily checks of the **rigging, guardrails, bilges,** and engine.
- Rest when you can, so you're fit when you're needed.
- Make sure no one gets drunk (or even drinks alcohol!). Consuming alcohol at sea is risky, irresponsible, and dangerous.

*Hitch-sailor "We had 60 knots of wind. The captain starts **reefing** the **mainsail** in mast, which should've been done way before. He didn't secure the main **sheet** properly, suddenly we have the whole main out. It was quite epic to reef the main in the roughest sea conditions I've ever seen. But we managed and the storm passed."*

10.13 LIMITED RESOURCES

When you're on a boat, you will come to appreciate the scarcity and value of power and water.

Power

Today's boats are stuffed with devices that need energy: navigation equipment, lights, radar, radios, autopilot, **water maker,** fridge, freezer, fans, and then there are crew phones and tablets. This all adds up. To generate power, boats have solar panels, wind-, hydro- and/or diesel-powered generators.

O n each boat I've been on for the Atlantic crossing we had solar panels. Still many boats don't. *Sea Ya* and *Eau Too* also had a wind generator. The *Eau Too* had two diesel generators. Still, on each boat we ran the noisy generator almost every day. It was mostly needed to run the **water maker** (which we had on *Eau Too*), power the fridge and navigation equipment that all demand a fair bit of energy. This was also the moment I was able to charge my laptop.

POWER SAVING TIPS
- Only turn on lights when necessary.
- Ask before charging anything.
- Steer instead of using the autopilot all the time. It's part of the fun!
- Keep the fridge full. It'll keep it steady and cool.

Water

Water is a limited resource on board. It's to be used wisely and sparingly. Our perception of the value of water is mostly based on pricing and availability. Your perception will be changed forever once you've done a crossing where every drop is to be treated like gold.

Here are some 'fun facts' about water usage:
- A regular shower (e.g. on land) uses 5–10 litres of water per minute
- Every toilet flush: 6–22 litres
- For general health, 50 litres per person per day is the norm (on land). Minimum recommended is 30 litres (5 litres for cooking and drinking, 25 litres for hygiene)- having access to 15 litres or less is considered an emergency.

Forget about all of the above when you're crossing the Atlantic. You'll only have a few drops! Water on board is most needed for drinking, and some for cooking, dishes, cleaning, and washing clothes.

WATER USAGE

A 40–44 ft. boat, has a 400-liter water tank capacity on average, usually divided over two water tanks. Some boats have way more capacity (the big guys), some less (for example racing boats). Some boats have a salt water tap. Some boats have a **water maker.** Some boats don't allow

Imagine all this being dumped in the Caribbean

any shower, some allow a shower every day and top up the water with a **water maker.** The greatest resource that all boats have, is a big pool of salt water around the boat. Salt water can be used for washing clothes, brushing teeth, doing dishes, cleaning the cockpit, showering,

DRINKING WATER

Above all, you want to be sure to have enough drinking water on board, and have a back-up system in place may a tank get contaminated. The amount of plastic can really add up if you just buy bottled water as a back-up. Water bottles are one of the biggest ocean polluters and unwanted in the Caribbean. If every boat that crosses the Atlantic stocks up 100 litres bottled water (1,5-liter bottles). That's 93.750 (1,500 x (100:1.5)) disposable plastic items brought over to the other side where waste disposal and recycling facilities are practically non-existent. As ocean lovers, we can do better than this.

As alternatives solutions to 1,5-liter water bottle back up, consider:
- Placing a filter on the tap, so tank water is perfectly drinkable.
- Source water with reusable jerry cans or foldable water containers (that you can more easily store). You can also place a filter on these or obtain one filter water bottle for each crew member for easy and safe refills.

- Can't find a jerry can or water container? If you need to buy bottled water, choose the 20-liter bottles with a pump. As opposed to six-packs of 1.5-liter bottles with an extra plastic wrapper around it. In the Caribbean, these circulate for recycling.
- Catch rainwater.

On *Sea Ya* the water tank was 400 litres (an average size tank for a 44ft boat). I took three 'showers' in 18 days (read: put a few drops of water on my head from the tap!). It might sound gross but it's fine on a boat. At a certain point you really don't care anymore. Of course you still wash yourself. There's a basin around you. Take a bucket of salt water to scrub yourself, and then rinse off with a few drops of fresh water. Or just stay salty. Also a small hand towel and a bottle of water do the job.

On *Eau Too* and *Cyclos II* we had the luxury of 2,000-liter tanks and water makers! This is a huge luxury and not the norm. We were able to take showers whenever we wanted—but of course we still had to remain water-conscious.

In the *Caribbean I* was on a boat and with six crew and a 200-liter tank. We did not take any showers at all for a few weeks. We did have salty showers in the sea . . .

WATER-SAVING TIPS
- Take a bucket and wash yourself with sea water. Or get a crew member to throw a bucket of water at you. Works great! Just accept the salty feeling.
- Doing dishes on board usually uses most of the water resources. Master the dishes technique.
  - Wash with sea water! Rinse the salt crystals in a bucket with a layer of fresh water. Some boats have a salt water tap. Every boat has a bucket.
  - When in the marina you might not want to use the sea water pump (dirty!).
- Turning the tap off when brushing your teeth and soaping yourself is a must. It saves huge amounts of water.
- Cook in sea water! It's delicious and full of healthy minerals from the purest source. Although unless you like super-salty, you should dilute

it. I find 30% seawater 70% fresh water to be a good ratio. Don't be afraid of bacteria, on the boats I've been on no one ever got sick on board, only excited because the food tasted great.

- Keep the hygiene high but you really don't need to shower or wash your hair every other day. If you do, there is an ocean of water around you.

10.14 WASTE MANAGEMENT AT SEA

How to dispose of waste at sea? Can you throw tins and glass into the deep? What is recyclable? How to dispose our waste on the other side. For sure, the intentions of the sailors are to take the best care of the environment. We all love the ocean, and we like to keep it healthy. We also love visiting islands and other destinations where waste management facilities may be non-existent. We also like to be practical.

So how to deal with waste? With conscious provisioning, you have already reduced your negative impact tremendously. But now you're out there on the ocean. How to manage the waste you are creating?

What can go overboard?

- **ORGANICS (FOOD)** can go overboard once you're beyond 12 miles off the coast.
- **NOTHING ELSE** but coconut shells and (untreated!) wood items go overboard.
- **GLASS?** No. It sinks, but never ever disappears. It may be made from sand, but it is still a man-made product that does not form naturally. Most glass has two extra chemical coatings for functionality and to prevent premature breakage. 50%–80% of glass is recyclable, so keep your glass waste for this. Recycling saves a lot of resources and raw materials as opposed to making glass from scratch. Jars can be great for staple foods, herbs, spices, oats, suger, sprouting, spreads and all sorts of storage.

CANS? No. Nearly all cans (aluminium and tin) are printed with ink and are coated with a type of plastic on the inside for food and drink preservation. This is also an easy material to recycle—it doesn't take many resources to process aluminium into new cans, containers, or maybe even a boat! It does take a lot of resources to extract new raw materials from the earth.

CIGARETTES? No. They are loaded with toxic chemicals. Compounds leaching from cigarette butts are loaded with substances, including arsenic, nicotine, and heavy metals. This poses a huge risk to marine life. Not only that. Most filters are made from plastic (7). Some filters may be biodegradable.

PLASTIC? No. It never ever disappears. Read more on the plastic challenge.

CHEWING GUM? No. This is a type of plastic.

CARDBOARD AND PAPER TOWELS? If it's untreated paper, then it's ok to throw overboard. If it's white or has any sort of ink on it, it's not ok! Almost all paper and cardboard is treated (with ink, UV coating, foils, glues, **polymers**). White paper towels are treated with chlorine which is a dangerous toxic for your own and the ocean's health. It should not go overboard. Cardboard usually has ink on it, which is a kind of plastic. This includes the label of a teabag, which is full of ink.

Many **pilots,** guide books, articles and sailor forums say that tins and glass jars can go overboard in deep seas. After all, they sink and are made from natural materials, right? Accordingly, many sailors do this. However, these articles are usually written from a practical perspective, not from an environmental one. Re-using and recycling can be very practical on board too! Bottles and tins have been found in the deepest ocean trenches with the brand names and logos still readable. Considering the critical state the ocean is in, every item that does not come from the sea should not be tossed in. Glass and tins are much more valuable on land than at the bottom of the sea. Recycling uses fewer resources than extracting new materials from the ground. These materials simply do not belong in the ocean. The ocean is not a dumping ground. If you wouldn't eat it or put it on your skin, why should the living organisms in the sea have to deal with it? Your waste might sink into the deep, but it won't be gone.

No glass, no cans, no cardboard, no cigarettes and no paper should go overboard. And definitely no plastic! Never throw anything overboard that doesn't decompose quickly in water. Even fruit peels can take years to biodegrade at sea. They are valuable at land as compost. Do the best you can to close the loop and contribute to the **circular economy.**

How to process waste on board?

- Set up a system of three buckets or containers in the galley:
  - One for organic waste. Several times a day you can throw it over-board (**leeward!** ;))
  - A bag or basket for (rinsed) recyclables (cans, plastic, jars, bottles)
  - Other waste. If you manage your waste well, this will be the last bucket to fill up! Bonus points if it doesn't fill up at all!
- Rinse waste (salt water does the job) to avoid smells and the introduc-tion of invasive species when disposing in a new destination. Meat, cheese and dairy packaging, in particular, should be rinsed thoroughly.
- Once the recycle bin is full, move it out of the **galley** and into a storage compartment. It helps to separate plastic, tins, cardboard and glass right away into different bags to make disposing easy on the other side. Crush the tins and bottles to save space if you need to.
- For the smokers, make an ashtray (you can simply tape a bottle to the boat). Cigarette butts can be tossed in there. Or 'just' make the cross-ing your quit smoking milestone!
- Cut non-recyclable plastic (film, bags and thin wrappers) into small pieces to reduce the volume. Though in general, if you have space to get it on board, you have space to store it until you can dispose of it properly.
- Have all organics dumped overboard at least 12 miles before arriving at land. You don't want to bring anything invasive into an island. It can impact the whole ecosystem.

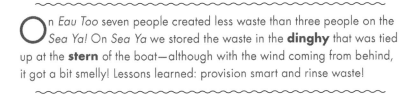

On *Eau Too* seven people created less waste than three people on the *Sea Ya!* On *Sea Ya* we stored the waste in the **dinghy** that was tied up at the **stern** of the boat—although with the wind coming from behind, it got a bit smelly! Lessons learned: provision smart and rinse waste!

Navigate to the "On The Other Side" section for more information on how to dispose of your remaining waste once you arrive at your destination.

On The Other Side

11

LANDING AND LEAVING

"I get up every morning determined to both
change the world and have one hell of a good time.
Sometimes this makes planning my day difficult."

— E.B. WHITE
(Writer)

ARRIVING BY BOAT IN NEW TERRITORY is one of the most exciting parts of sailing! What's next? Can you just leave the boat? How to dispose of waste? Is it easy to find another boat to the next destination? Or a job?

11.1 ARRIVAL: COCONUT O' CLOCK

Woohoo! You have arrived! The captain has to go to customs and immigration to clear in. Sometimes crew has to join. Finally, you can have that coconut, jump in the sea (if you haven't done so halfway), and go for a ten-mile (instead of ten feet) hike! Let the exploration begin! The world will be under your feet again, and you're about to be on your own.

> **DON'T:** Connect to the WiFi just yet. The amount of messages and news stories that pile up can be horrendous. Enjoy the arrival day. I repeat, *do not* connect to the WiFi! Just give your family a call to let them know you are safe and start to absorb land life.

Navigational Hazard! There's something about sailors and bars. On many boats, the first discovery that sailors are after on arrival is looking for the bar. Most boats are a 'dry boat', meaning no alcohol at sea. The missed-out alcohol seems to get balanced as soon as possible again once on shore. Be careful, especially with the Rum punch.

Arriving with the **ARC** was special. When I wake up, I see land. It's Martinique. Only that's not where we're going. Soon after, St. Lucia shows up. On the radio I hear another vessel, Rainbow, approaching the finish line. Civilisation is near. I see a fishing boat. St. Lucia gets closer. It is so green. The water is 30 degrees Celsius. The sun is shining on the water. I try to imagine what St. Lucia is like. Everyone is in the cockpit. We get welcomed by a photographer and pretend we're sailing like pros. "Congratulations *Eau Too,* you have passed the finish line!"—We hear on the radio. Time to get the sails in. We sail into Rodney Bay Marina. Dozens of boats have arrived before us. We're welcomed with an applause from fellow ARC participants. The yellow shirted ARC team, and local guys await us at the dock with Rum punch. That's a hospitable arrival! I can't wait to see my newly made sailing friends again! What's the time? No one has a clue. This crossing we were not really consistent with putting the clock back.

Waste disposal in Dominca

11.2 WASTE DISPOSAL

The boat will be trashed after the trip, so you will probably need at least a full day or two to clean it up. Hopefully, you can minimise your disposal impact by having provisioned consciously, and efficiently managed waste while at sea. What to do with the waste you have produced?

Waste disposal in the Caribbean

It's great to see signs around the place saying, 'Do not litter' and 'Keep our environment clean.' Yet, it's a common sight to see people throwing bottles in the bush. I can't blame them, to be

Common streetscene in the Caribbean

honest. Most of the locals don't have the education to know that this is harmful to the environment and that plastic will never ever disappear!

Popo (a lovely local man from Carriacou who sometimes brings me papayas and coconuts): "Do you have a black paper for me?" I brought Popo some **Callaloo** which I bought for him in 'town' (one street). Me: "I don't have paper." Popo: The one with the handles which they give you in town." I now realize he refers to a plastic bag so he could carry it easier: 'a black paper.' Since I brought my own reusable bag to town and said no to the plastic ones, I couldn't give him 'a black paper.' Many islanders simply may not know what is the difference is between paper and plastic and why the latter may be harmful.

Eyebrows are raised when you refuse a plastic bag. I must admit, I littered when I was a kid: ignorant and unaware. The awareness level of the impact of trash is still low amongst the general public in most tropical destinations. Disposable waste alternatives and waste disposal facilities in the Caribbean are limited. The islands do not have big landfills. Waste is often dumped near the road or burned. We can't blame them and point fingers. We must do what we can with the knowledge and resources we have.

It's therefore worth, or actually a responsibility, to make your first port of arrival on an island with a waste recycling system in place. I reached out to Greening the Caribbean (GTC), a local Caribbean organisation taking care of waste disposal in the Caribbean. The only marina they are aware of, that has a recycling and waste management policy and practice, is the IGY Rodney Bay Marina in St. Lucia. Antigua and Barbuda is one of the places most affected by yachters dumping waste because there are no facilities in place. This is "despite the fact that Antigua and Barbuda have more marinas than any of the other small Caribbean island states, which means that their sailing sector is generating a catastrophic amount of recyclable waste—especially electronic waste and plastic and glass bottles, which are all being dumped in their landfill and compromising their ecosystem."—stated Wayne of Greening the Caribbean.

From my own observations and explorations, Dominica, Martinique, Antigua, St. Vincent and the Grenadines, St. Maarten, the BVI, USVI, Dominican Republic, and Puerto Rico do *not* have a recycling system in place. The same for Trinidad and Tobago. Saba island does have an outstanding recycling facility, but the island itself is tiny, and not suitable for a regular influx of yachts with waste to discard. St. Lucia, then, is the only suitable island for disposing of your recycling waste in the least harmful way. If this isn't your first landing, keep your recyclables on board until you reach the island.

What and how to dispose of recycling waste at the recycling and waste facility in Rodney Bay (St. Lucia)?

- Plastic bottles. Remove the caps, crush the bottles, and keep it all in the same transparent bag.
- Glass bottles.
- Tin and aluminium cans. Crush them.
- Cardboard (must be flattened).
- Scrap materials (batteries, any e-waste items that used electricity, mechanical/or parts containing metal).
- Food waste and general waste (can be put in a non-transparent garbage bag).
- Rodney Bay Marina also has a storage facility for waste oil. Non-hazardous chemical waste can be set aside next to the waste oil storage container.

By following these suggestions, you help to make the on-island sorting and processing more effective. In St. Lucia they pre-process cardboard, aluminium and tin cans; and disassemble e-waste on the island. Once sufficient quantities are collected, it is shipped to recycling manufacturers abroad. Certain glass bottles are passed on to micro-businesses like bee farmers. Note that plastic bags and film foil is non-recyclable. This is a different type of plastic. Above all, try to arrive with as little recyclables and waste material as possible in the first place.

WASTE DISPOSAL IN EUROPE

The waste disposal situation in Europe is better with more recycling facilities in place. People understand the importance of recycling and responsible waste disposal. Every marina is different but generally, recyclables are collected. Horta, Faial (Azores), Lanzarote, Las Palmas, Fuerteventura and Palma the Mallorca all have waste recycling facilities in place. Carton, tins, plastic, glass, all is collected separately. You can apply the same procedures as described above.

If you're **heading** to mainland Europe, it saves logistics if you keep recyclables on board (instead of dispose it on an island) and dispose of them on the mainland. Recycled materials collected on the islands are often transported to mainland Europe.

11.3   THE NEXT ADVENTURE

You may have become a nice little family on the boat. Or perhaps you can't wait to leave.

The boat is cleaned. You have one last meal with the crew. Then what? Is it easy to find another boat to your next destination? Or a job? Or maybe you have had enough time at sea, and it's time to settle back on land. "It's about the journey, and not the destination", so they say. That certainly counts for an Atlantic Ocean crossing, although arriving to land after weeks at sea is a pretty exciting experiece. You don't want to have a return ticket booked just yet.

> *"Do not go where the path may lead, go instead*
> *where there is no path and leave a trail."*

> **– RALPH WALDO EMERSON**
> *(Lecturer, poet, and seen as champion of individualism)*

During my Atlantic crossings, I've met dozens of people with beautiful stories and dreams. Many of them are on a life journey, not knowing the destination. It's tempting to just go with the flow and keep on sailing and exploring with whatever opportunity comes up. There are so many options and adventures are around every corner. So what should be next? Most likely the adventure does have a budget or time limit. Perhaps you have a boss waiting for you to return, or you have to find a job, or you

On to the next adventure!

really have all your options open. But what is the next dream? And what next step will bring you closer to making that happen? Take that step! The Atlantic crossing surely has given insight about yourself, your dreams, your goals and your mission. The question is, what are you going to do with it?

What did I do after arriving?

Cheers to the adventure of a lifetime! The *Sea Ya* party crew with a Carib beer on the beach in the laid back fishing town of Charlotteville, Tobago! Today I'll leave Captain Rudy, Noor and boat *Sea Ya* behind! The *Sea Ya* moves on to Trinidad tonight, without me. I've decided to spend some more time exploring, kitesurfing and freediving in Tobago! I'm not done with this paradise island yet!

As much as I love the sea and sailing lifestyle, I also like to touch land and explore a new place inside out. Wherever I arrive I'd like to experience the full essence of it, and the best way to do that is by hanging out in a place for a while—living there, rather than just travelling through and ticking the 'been there, done that' box. I love to be on board a sailboat, but I also love to be off it, taking in the surroundings at my own pace, eating at my pace, and making fresh new connections with the people and places I visit. Sailing on someone else's boat requires a lot of adaptation.

After my first crossing on *Sea Ya*, I stayed on board for one more week to get a taste of Caribbean sailing. I fell in love with the island of Tobago.

I had the urge to explore the land and I wanted to be free to go where I wanted. Also, it was time to get work done on my websites. This is hard to do at sea with limited power and logistics. It was time to leave. I was not prepared for this and had to buy an onward flight ticket on the spot at the customs office so that *Sea Ya* could leave the country. Tobago allowed a one month stay. For the end of this period, I bought the cheapest flight I could find: destination Bonaire. I ended up taking the flight and spent a month in Bonaire doing some serious freedive training. From Bonaire, I found a consultancy gig in Saba. In Saba, I Skyped with the captain of *Cyclos II* to talk about the crossing back to Europe.

After the second crossing on *Cyclos II*, I spent a few more days working on the boat in Palma de Mallorca. It mostly involved cleaning the boat, and it paid me €120 per day. Great to raise the adventure fund a bit! I spent another week exploring Mallorca, which is a beautiful and peaceful island in the springtime. From Mallorca, I made my way to southern Spain and set up base camp in Tarifa, taking the first steps towards writing this book.

After the third crossing on *Eau Too*, all crew were asked to leave a few days after our arrival in Rodney Bay, **St. Lucia**. This was fine with me; It had been a great trip, but it was time to go my own way. My priority was to get this book finished! I started looking for a base camp on the beach somewhere, to live like a local, on a budget, with access to a power plug, WiFi, coconuts, and of course, the sea. Rodney Bay was not the right place. I found it expensive, busy and too commercial. I hopped over to join captain Mark on his boat *Fruit Salid 3* (not salad, sal-l-d), whom I met during the ARC+. He picked up a few more ocean nomads and together with three other ARC+ boats, we sailed to the south of St. Lucia (spectacular, a must-do!). After a few days of island exploration, we went north with *Fruit Salid*. I hopped off in Dominica. My curiosity for this island and determination to finish this book had me land-based in Dominica for a while. After a month, the ocean called and from Dominica, I hitch-sailed my way south to join the Grenada Sailing Week, followed by a dream week of exploring the Grenadines on a kitesurf catamaran. I spent a few months between the boat builders in Carriacou, and then helped to sail one of these traditional wooden beauties up to St. Bart's. I further hitchhiked my way to the BVI, USVI, and Dominican Republic, from where I could fly out on a budget.

What was next for the hitch-sailors?

"Back to the cold! I wish I hadn't already booked my flight!"

"I was planning to be back home for Christmas, so after I left the boat, I flew back to The Netherlands. I was working on projects for a website I run with a friend, but as a "digital nomad," I work on this most of the time anyway while travelling. Being on the ocean was very inspirational. I had many new ideas and managed to do a surprising amount of work, even though I was expecting not to have any time for this at all."

"I didn't have any plans set in stone for after the crossing but have now joined another boat and am sailing around the Caribbean!"

"I continued travelling, got to the Dominican Republic on another boat, fell in love, got married, spent 1.5 years there and then moved to Poland together."

"I flew straight back two days after clearing in. I shouldn't have done that!"

"For me it was just about the sailing. If I'll do it again, I'll combine it with scuba diving in the Caribbean."

"I stayed for a week in Saint Lucia enjoying the island life and exploring. I had to return to England for work commitments."

"I moved on to do Camino de Santiago from Porto to Santiago."

"I want to reach South America without using a plane."

"I have no idea!"

Finding another boat

You have to or want to leave the boat, but you want to keep on sailing. Or perhaps you want to reach a particular destination. You will have the best chance to find another boat by being proactively present in busy anchorages or marinas, on both sides of the pond. You may not sail across the Atlantic with a boat you meet, but perhaps you can share adventure time on the other side.

If you have the time and are keen to adventure more, explore the Caribbean. The Caribbean islands allow for endless discoveries, also possible on a budget. Learn more about the Caribbean paradise in the next chapter.

If you want to move on to Central or South America, it is more complex. Going from a random Caribbean Island to Central or South America can be as complicated and costly as going from Europe to the other side of the Atlantic. Flights from the Caribbean to South America are expensive. Only a few people sail to South America from the Caribbean because of unfavourable currents, winds and safety situations. Aim for finding a boat to cross the Atlantic with destination: Trinidad, Surinam, Guyana, Brazil in the first place. Once in the Caribbean, boats go from Grenada to Colombia or Panama during the season. Towards the end of the season (March–May), when the Atlantic **hurricane** season approaches, more boats, from any island but mainly the Caribbean harbour hubs, move towards the ABC Islands, Colombia or Panama. March and April is the ideal timing to go through the Panama Canal and move onto the Pacific.

How about moving on and sailing across the Pacific? This is the dream! Although, as cool as this ocean adventure sounds, and it surely will be, don't underestimate the Pacific passage. This is not a one-month time or money investment. The Pacific is severely off the grid and a journey through almost a third of the earth's surface. Catching a ride across the Pacific needs preparation and a thorough investigation for the right boat match.

If you want to find another boat in Europe, proactively chit-chat in the marinas and search online. The sailing scene in Europe is huge, so are the **charter** businesses. Discover more about Europe in the next chapter.

I have a zillion more tips and thoughts on hitch-sailing in the Caribbean, Latin America, Europe, and the Pacific. I am eager to share them with you, but I will have to leave that for the next book.

Working on boats

If you sail across the Atlantic and your next move is to find a job on a boat, I suggest making your way to the sailing hubs. Check with your nationality, if and where you are allowed to work and which visa or work permit is necessary. Sailing hubs in the Caribbean: St. Maarten, Antigua,

British Virgin Islands, US Virgin Islands, and the Grenadines. Sailing hubs in Europe: Palma de Mallorca and the French Riviera. Consider obtaining the **STCW10** and Med1.

Get stamped off

Keep immigration rules in mind if you decide to hop off a boat when you reach your destination. The crew list must be kept up-to-date when any crew member leaves or joins. In some locations, you need to provide proof of onward travel before you can be signed off the crew list. The boat itself cannot leave the country without you until this is done.
In Dominica and St. Lucia it was okay to be signed off the crew list without proof of onward travel. European Islands (like Martinique, Guadeloupe, St. Barts, St. Maarten, Saba, St. Eustatius) provide an easy entry with no onward travel proof needed for EU passport holders. In Grenada, Tobago and Antigua, and the BVI, you need proof of plans to exit the country before you can be signed off the crew list.

HOW TO PROOF ONWARD TRAVEL?

- Show a booking confirmation of a ferry or flight ticket out of the country.
- Show that you will join another crew list with a Captain's letter. You can get a letter from the new captain, stating that you will be crew on his boat, which must include the planned date of departure. You can download a template on *Oceannomad.co/resources*.
- Sometimes a hotel booking or proof of a place to stay will allow you to be taken off the crew list too.

Like many of us ocean nomads, you may go with the flow and can't prepare for this too far in advance. You could instantly buy the cheapest ticket to the next island, but be aware these are often not so cheap! You could book a flight and possibly cancel it in time if your plans change. There are also websites where you can 'rent' an onward travel ticket. Or you can look for another boat that can put you on their crew list.

Make sure you have your visa in place. Revisit the visa section in Chapter 7 for more info on this.

Navigational Hazard! Take your time for customs procedures. Whether you have arrived in Europe or the Caribbean, this often goes on 'island time.' Customs offices are usually closed on weekends, during lunchtime, and after 4.00 pm during the week. Sometimes the immigration officer door is next to customs office, sometimes not, and you have to walk to the other side of town.

Closing the Atlantic Ocean chapter

A few more actions to consider before you hop off:

- Ask for feedback from the captain and fellow crew. How have your fellow crew members experienced your company? How can you improve? On *Eau Too,* we discussed the best and worst parts of the trip. These are fun and valuable things to discuss and learn from.
- Ask for a reference from the captain, now, while your qualities and contributions are still fresh in his or her mind.
- Have your miles signed-off by the captain. If you ever want to pursue a yacht-master qualification (or equivalent), you then have those 2,100+ miles already in your **logbook!**

Submit your ocean research data collected to the organisations that are eager to receive your findings!

12

BACK ON LAND

"To move, to breathe, to fly, to float; To gain all while you give; To roam the roads of lands remote; To travel is to live."

– HANS CHRISTIAN ANDERSEN
(Writer)

WHAT'S IT LIKE IN THE CARIBBEAN? What's it like in Europe? How to go around on a budget? The following info on the Caribbean and Europe is intended as just a starting point. Use it as the first step for your own exploration! Where to find a coconut? First, some destination exploration bearings for the Caribbean. Second, information on navigating Europe.

12.1 THE CARIBBEAN

Before my first Atlantic Crossing, I had absolutely no idea about the Caribbean. I was super curious and eager to explore and learn more about this promising paradise. Now, I've spent around a total of ten months exploring this dream region of the earth. What's it like? Where to stay? How to get around?

A sense of place
With dozens of authentic and unique island nations, the Caribbean calls for exploration time. Every island deserves weeks, if not months around of exploration. From Tobago down south to the Dominican Republic up

north, the islands are blessed with tropical rainforests, happy coloured buildings, and it is just as scenic below the surface. Life happens outdoors and outdoors only. The Caribbean is full of character. But it is the people that create the ambience and make the place. Everyone is happy to stop and make a chat. I haven't seen two people with the same hairstyle; I was already wondering why there are more hairdressers than rum shops. And there are *a lot* of rum shops. The people are kind, funny and each one of them has a unique personality. The pace of life is slow and easy. Everyone is hustling, selling their fish, coconuts, bread and fruits on boats in the anchorages or on land near the streets. Reggae, soca and calypso music boosts from the speakers. You only know if it's a house, bar or supermarket after you walk in. Or sometimes it's all of it! Whatever image you have in mind of the Caribbean, will get beyond confirmed once you have arrived. You've got to go off the boat and explore!

On Island Time

These recommendations only scratch the surface of what the Caribbean has to offer. With so many islands to explore, you can be sure of adventure time wherever you go!

DO:
- Slow down. When heading from east to west, you will most likely arrive at an island. It's hot, and everyone is in laidback beach mode. Take the time to absorb the ambience. Drink a **coconut.** Take it easy.

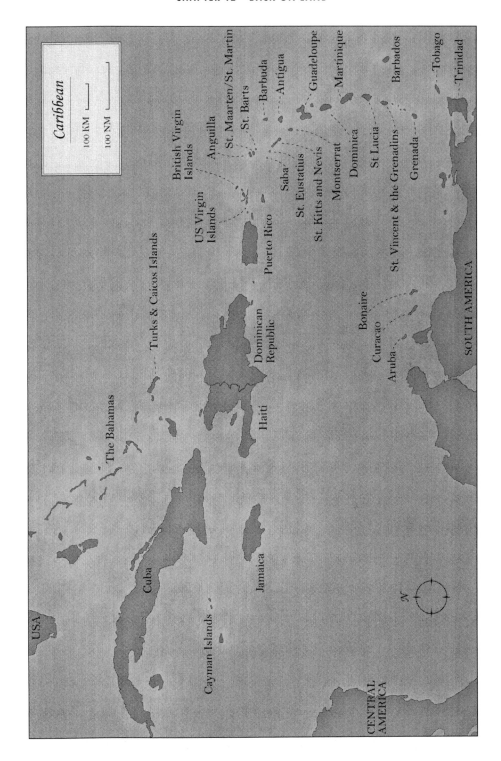

Caribbean

100 KM

100 NM

British Virgin
Islands

Anguilla

St. Maarten/St. Martin

St. Barts

Barbuda

Antigua

Guadeloupe

Martinique

Barbados

Tobago

Trinidad

US Virgin
Islands

Puerto Rico

Saba

St. Eustatius

St. Kitts and Nevis

Montserrat

Dominica

St Lucia

St. Vincent & the Grenadins

Grenada

Turks & Caicos Islands

The Bahamas

Dominican
Republic

Haiti

Cuba

Jamaica

Cayman Islands

USA

CENTRAL
AMERICA

SOUTH AMERICA

Bonaire

Curacao

Aruba

N

- Live the Caribbean instead of travelling through it.
- Wherever you go, connect with the locals. The experience of the island will be determined by the interaction of the people you meet. You'll meet them at your homestay, in the market, on the street, in the bus, bar or beach. If not, find them through groups on *Couchsurfing.org* or Facebook. Learn what drives them and how they see the world. You will get so much more out of your visit.
- Walk around the block from the fancy international restaurants the marinas to explore the cheap and tasty flavours of the food in the local shacks.
- Forget about the European foods like cheese and olives. Explore the local cuisine. It's pure, tasty, and a whole lot cheaper. Every island has an abundance of fresh fruits, vegetables, spices, produce and a special national dish. There's a reason why the Caribbean has one of the highest numbers of centenarians in the world. Go find out!
- Learn how to chop a coconut (and for the advanced: climb a coconut tree!). They are everywhere, delicious and superfoods. Try them on the grill too! Nothing like it.
- Be careful with the rum punch. Rum is part of the culture, but it's stronger than it tastes!

DON'T:
- Explore the island highlights during cruise ship rush hours. The Caribbean islands are a popular cruise ship destination. These floating cities arrive in the morning, invade the destination, and leave in the afternoon to check another country off the list the next day. It's 'bank day' for the locals. Prices for food, drinks and coconuts go up. Don't go to the local market or 'must see' waterfall at times the cruise ship is in. You will surely pay more for your banana. I've been charged US$10 for coconuts!
- Expect to find your favourite home foods. Instead, you'll find new exciting foods to try.
- Leave two days after arrival! That's when you just start to adapt to the local scene and become excited about a new place.

Windward Carriacou

The view from your bunk

Sailing in the Caribbean

Most likely you arrive in one of the **Windward Islands** in the Eastern Caribbean, which are the islands chain closest to the Atlantic.

Imagine jumping into warm turquoise waters just seconds after you wake up. Eating a freshly chopped papaya for breakfast, having consistent 15–20 **knot** breeze when sailing to the next island, hiking up a hill for the view, climbing a palm tree for a coconut, and enjoying a sunset chillax with a rum punch and green flash on the horizon. You can work on your swimming skills immersed in the evening bioluminescence, with the starry sky above you bringing back memories from all those nights out at sea. The Caribbean: lots of **'limin'.**

Many cruisers spend a few months exploring the Windward and Leeward Island chain in the Caribbean. With the trade winds from the east and the island chain going from north to south, turquoise waters and thousands of islands, bay and inlets, sailing conditions are just perfect.

The Caribbean hosts numerous sailing regattas. These multi-day events are a great place to meet fellow sailors, improve your sailing skills, fall in love with beautiful boats, and possibly find the next ride or job.

Read more on St. Lucia, St. Maarten, Antigua, and the Virgin Islands.

Accommodation

The challenge of being land-based in the Caribbean is the cost of accommodation. It's not a cheap place to stay or travel unless you are already on a boat. As crew, you're already in a good position to make this happen! Otherwise, if you don't plan ahead or aren't great at mingling with locals (who know the cheap and local way of getting by), a visit to the Caribbean can seriously drain your budget. There are very few hostel-type accommodations in the Caribbean. If you find an accommodation deal for US$40/night, it's cheap!

Getting around

How to get around on, between and off the islands?

ON THE ISLANDS

Take the local bus or hitchhike. It's a great way to meet the locals. There are no timetables; the bus simply stops when you raise your hand. Don't be surprised if the driver takes a detour via the bakery, his cousin, or the market to source or drop of some groceries. Buses get loaded—if you think there's room for ten people, double that! Buses have a great character, with colours, local music, awesome hairstyles and names like 'The determined,' 'Expect the unexpected,' 'Rastafariman.' Bus prices range from EC$1–10, varying across buses and bus lines. They stop driving around 10 pm. It's also easy to hire a car, with or without a driver. Prices are around US$50US per day. This is often cheaper than taking a taxi!

Taxis from one side of the island to the other can costs up to US$100 (in Martinique or St. Lucia at least).

BETWEEN ISLANDS

Whether you take a flight or ferry, travel between the islands is expensive. The **windward** and **Leeward** island chain is well connected with ferries (though not all islands are connected). A ride between countries, often between just 20–40 miles, can easily cost up to US$100. Keep hitch-sailing instead! I've hitch-sailed all across the Caribbean (that will be another book). It can be done! Especially in the high season (between December and April), there are many sailboats island-hopping the Caribbean. Distances between the islands are short. You can usually see the next one already lying ahead of you. There are also fisherman willing to take you to other islands. This is cheaper, but not always safer. Definitely adventurous! The best option to go to another island is to find another sailing boat! Whatever method you choose, clear out and in through customs properly. Flights within the Caribbean can be incredibly expensive, with one-way flights ranging from US$100–500 just within the region.

OUT OF THE ISLANDS

Flying out of the Caribbean doesn't come cheap. It's worth looking at flights from different islands and either hitch-sail or take a ferry to another island.

A few more take-aways

- What is the currency?
  - 'Eastern Caribbean Dollar' (EC$2.70 = US$1.00) in: Antigua and Barbuda, Dominica, Grenada, Saint Kitts and Nevis, Saint Lucia, and Saint Vincent and the Grenadines. Anguilla and Montserrat.
  - Euro (€) in: Martinique, Guadeloupe, St. Barts and St. Martin (the French part).
  - United States Dollar (US$) in: British Virgin Islands, United Virgin Islands, Puerto Rico, and the Caribbean Netherlands. Generally, US dollars are widely accepted everywhere.

- Countries not mentioned have their own currency which you can withdraw from the local cash machines.
- The Caribbean Islands are the tropics. It can rain a lot! Usually, it's just a **squall**—you should know what that is by now . . .
- The further away the island is you go to, the more expensive it usually becomes since foods have to be brought over. Plan ahead.
- Coconut Index: Ranges from free (when you climb a tree) to EC$2–7.
- Beer Index: EC$5–8. Three for EC$10 + cool reggae music in the local bar outside of 'yachtie' places.
- The avocado season ends in December. Mango seasons starts in May. It's worth being around in these months!
- I haven't felt unsafe one single second. Be open and friendly and you will get the warmest welcome, wherever you go. That said, pick pocketing happens. Don't show off your expensive phones and jewellery.
- The Caribbean region is obviously no secret when it comes to tourism. Don't let this hold you back. There's so much to explore! Cruise ships, sailboats, (lack of) local awareness on environmental problems, (lack of) regulation and enforcement, and lack of facilities and resources take its toll on the environment. Learn what you can do in Chapter 16.

Check *Oceannomad.co/resources* for recommendations on local style Caribbean budget travel, accommodations and logistics.

12.2 EUROPE

Since most boats cross the Atlantic to Europe in spring time, the timing to arrive in Europe is perfect! Everyone starts to go out of their houses again, to soak up the sun and live the outdoor life. What's it like in Europe? Where to stay? How to get around.

A sense of place
For me, Europe is familiar home ground. I was born in The Netherlands, spent most of the summer holidays camping in France, I have family in Portugal, and lived for a few years in Spain. Still, each of these countries is very different. From the middle of Norway in the north of Europe, to the middle of Spain in the south, it's about 2,400 kilometres in a direct

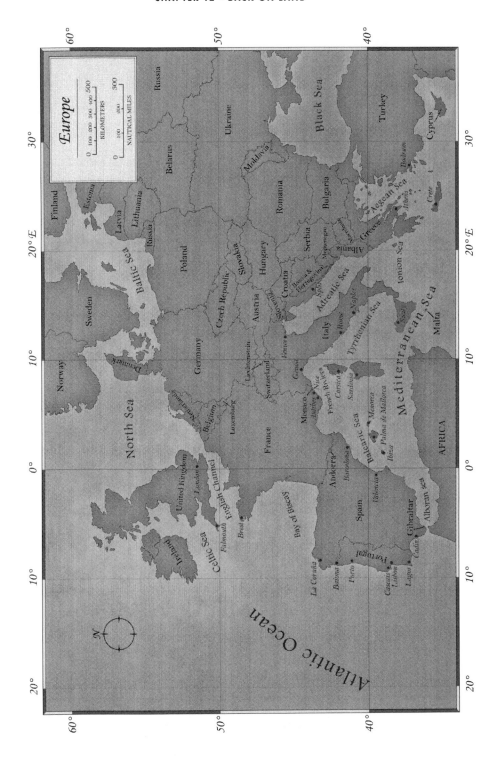

Greece

line. This may not seem so much, but in between, there are many different countries. Europe consists of 44 countries, each having their own cultures, languages, heritages, customs and foods. It's extremely diverse in beaches, mountains, historical architecture and foods.

Fascinating, isn't it? 28 countries have teamed up as the European Union. You only need to show your passport and visa once, and you are free to go to any country within the zone. With a different language and culture in almost every country, it's extremely diverse. From characteristic cities to the Alps to the islands in Greece. There are tourists trying to 'do' Europe in one week. Impossible! Just like you could spend weeks on one small Caribbean Island before you get the hang of life there, spend some time in each country if you want to get to know the place and its inhabitants. There is no "Europe in one week". Just enjoy every city or country that you visit and mingle with the people that live there. After some time in the Caribbean it's fantastic to have some wine (for just €1 in the Azores or southern Spain!), and springtime scents and flowers. The most special thing of all is when you smell land. Sailing into Europe, the ocean scent, which you've been smelling for weeks, gives way to the smell of pine trees. As a Northern European native, I'm particularly a fan of the south, where it's sunny and warm, and people are on the 'Mediterranean diet.' The Mediterranean diet is much more than fresh fruits and veggies, garlic, olive oil, tomatoes, and a glass of wine. It's a lifestyle. It's a way of life where socialising and sharing plays a vital part in life.

Faial and Pico in the Azores.

Sailing in Europe

With a seafarer history, the sailing scene in Europe has remained important and big. The Baltic, North Sea, Atlantic Coast, Canary Islands and Mediterranean are all spectacular cruising grounds. Especially in spring, the water can still be freezing. In the Mediterranean, the winds can be inconsistent and unpredictable. The sailing season in Europe starts around April and lasts until more or less October. The Mediterranean is particularly popular in summer, and that's no surprise. This sea is surrounded by dozens of countries, each having their own languages, cultures, islands and traditions. There's so much to explore! My personal favourite sailing ground so far: The Greek Islands and Turkish Riviera.

DO:

Make a local friend. Especially if it's your first time in Europe, it can be a big cultural difference from your home country. A local friend can help you understand and experience the place. You can meet them at the harbour, in the market, on the street, in the bus, bar or beach. On the internet, you can find them through *Couchsurfing.org* and local Facebook groups. Learn what drives them and how they see the world.

- Go to local little markets, bakeries and marketplaces to absorb the essence.
- Visit the local entrepreneurs who put their heart and soul in their businesses and need you! They are what makes the place.

- Adapt yourself to the local clock to get the most out of your time here! In the Mediterranean everything happens a bit later. Lunch is around 2 pm, and you don't even try to enter a restaurant before 8 pm—make it 9 pm in Spain!
- Learn a few words of the local language so you can exchange a word or two with the local waiter or vendor. The younger generation is usually more proficient in English, and in most countries you'll get by fine. But you get so much more out of your experience if you speak the language. Even if it's just 'Hello, how are you?'

At the market in Palma

DON'T:

- Try to explore a whole continent in one week. You can't see one country in a week, not even in a month. If you have limited time, pick one country, or two, and visit the others next time.
- Assume that everyone speaks your language. There are over 20 official languages in Europe and another 20 regional accepted ones. However, most Europeans speak English.

Accommodation

Hostels are easy to find and costs between €15–30 per night. July–August is high season. Prices go up and it will be more difficult to find a place to stay. It's fairly easy to find a free place to stay via *couchsurfing.org* or housesitting websites. Europeans generally love to meet travellers.

Getting around

WITHIN COUNTRIES

Trams, metros, busses, ferries, trains, bicycles, scooter, by foot, it's all possible! In most countries public transport is well set up and it doesn't break the budget to take a local bus. The bigger cities often have free bicycles to take. Car rental in mainland Spain is cheap. In other countries not so cheap. Ridesharing is common.

BETWEEN COUNTRIES

Once in the EU, you can cross borders without having to show your passport. You are, however, supposed to keep it with you. If you travel between countries, you can go by car, bus, train, or boat. Europe has a good train network and it's a cool way to travel! Flights within Europe are also relatively cheap. Much cheaper than in the Caribbean.

OUT OF EUROPE

The bigger cities have intercontinental flights. Or why not catch a ride back to the Americas? Go back to start.

A few more take-aways

- What is the currency?
  - Of the countries bordering the Atlantic or Mediterranean Sea, almost all of the countries use the Euro currency (€). The United Kingdom has the British pound (£).
- In most places you can safely drink water from the tap. Note that in some regions they put a lot of chloride in the water supply.
- Learn about the different customs in the country you're in. For example, every country has different customs when it comes to greeting someone. In Spain, for example, when you meet someone (even if you don't know them (yet)) you give two kisses on the cheeks!

- Europe is generally safe. Pickpocketing does happen, especially in big cities and tourist zones.
- Beer index: From €1 in Spain to €4 in expensive marinas.
- Coconut index: Forget about it. Coconuts are imported and expensive. For this you need to find a ride to the other side.
- Europe has other yumminess: olives for example! Also, as summer approaches the berry season starts. The strawberries, raspberries, and redcurrants are delicious little superpowers.

Check *Oceannomad.co/resources* for recommendations on local style Europe budget travel, accommodations and logistics.

Ocean Love & Conservation

13

WHY IS THE OCEAN SO IMPORTANT?

"The sea, the great unifier, is man's only hope.
Now, as never before, the old phrase has a literal
meaning: we are all in the same boat."

— JACQUES YVES COUSTEAU

THE OCEAN IS THE HEART OF THE PLANET. Water covers more than two-thirds of the Earth's surface. Ocean plants produce most of the oxygen we breathe, and the deep waters are home to wildlife and some of the biggest creatures on earth. It provides us with food, jobs, life, play, and sailing! It gives us everything; without it, we cannot survive. By experiencing the ocean first hand on a boat, you will be amazed by its beauty, gain a deep respect for its power, and also see its decline. Why should we care so much about the creatures that live in the ocean? Does it really matter if a species gets lost? What does that mean for us? Let's zoom in on seven reasons why the ocean is important.

Source of oxygen

We can go weeks without food, days without water but not even an hour without oxygen. It's is often thought that rainforests are the primary source of our oxygen on our planet, but it is the ocean that provides us with the most oxygen we breathe. It doesn't matter how far you live from the sea, for at least 50% of your breaths you are dependent on the ocean.

Don't worry; you won't need trees in the middle of the Atlantic—the **phytoplankton** has got you covered. These tiny little sea weeds act in the same way in the sea as tree leaves do on land. Plankton absorbs carbon dioxide and releases oxygen. You don't see them, so we tend to forget about them, if we even know about them in the first place. They are one of the tiniest beings on the planet, but one of the most important to have around, keeping us alive.

Climate regulator

In many ways, the ocean regulates our climate. It soaks up heat and transports warm water from the equator to the poles, and cold water from the poles to the tropics. Without these currents, the weather would be extreme in some regions, and fewer places would be habitable. The ocean regulates rain and droughts. With holding 97% of the water of our planet, almost all rain that drops on land comes from the ocean. The ocean absorbs **CO_2,** to keep the carbon cycle, and accordingly temperatures on earth, in balance. It makes the ocean our global climate control system. Learn more about how this works in the Climate Change chapter.

Food

The ocean is the number one source of protein for more than a billion people (8). With the world population growing by 1.5 million people every week, we are relying on the ocean more and more for survival.

Home

The ocean is not just home to us ocean lovers. The ocean is home to the greatest abundance of life on our planet. When you cross an ocean, you will see dolphins, whales, an occasional leaping fish, or a turtle popping up to take a breath. That's just what you see on the surface; there is more life below the ocean's surface than on land. With more than 60% of the world's population living on the coastline, we all depend on a healthy sea just as much as these beautiful creatures.

Play

The ocean is a happy-zone! The ocean is our temple, our life, our second home, our exhilaration place. It's where we swim, surf, sail, dive, chillax, and '**lime**'. Family holidays and Sundays often happen on the beach. For sailors, fisherman and islanders, it also is a transport zone. The ocean carries us to new lands. As sailors, we also serve as educators, ambassadors and advocates of a lifestyle on the water. Together we share a passion for the ocean, and an avid desire to keep our playground clean and safe forever. Waterways are key to our health, for us and future generations.

Jobs

The ocean gives jobs to fishermen, lifeguards, surf instructors, harbours, (free)diving schools, marine-based tour operators, water sports businesses, holiday accommodations, and, of course, sailors!

Health

Water means life. We are born out of water, our body is mostly made of water, our planet is two-thirds water, and we cannot live without it. Without it there would not be life on this planet. We live in a watery world. Don't you just feel great when you're near, in, or on the sea? Why is this? Breathing the fresh ocean air gives us oxygen and energy. The ocean is a powerful healing force. When we dip in the water, our inner dolphin gets released. It's called the "mammalian diving reflex." I learned this when I started freediving. When our face touches water, our heart rate immediately slows down, and blood moves from the extremities to the brain, heart and vital organs of our body. Seals and dolphins have this reflex, and so do we! It wakes us up and makes us feel vibrant and alive. This is pure science. The ocean is therapeutic. When we see, feel, hear, smell or taste water we're happy and at peace. Yet, we still know more about Mars than we know about the ocean.

A healthy ocean keeps us healthy on earth. We are alive right now because of the oceans. Now the ocean needs to be kept alive by us. The choices we make now determine our future, and our children's future. We have the responsibility to care for the ocean as it cares for us.

14

WHAT'S HAPPENING
TO THE OCEANS?

*"Knowing is the key to caring, and with caring
there is hope that people will be motivated
to take positive actions."*

— SYLVIA EARLE
(Ocean Explorer)

WE HEAR ABOUT CLIMATE CHANGE, plastic pollution, overfishing and many other challenges! Many things are happening, and they are all interconnected. But what is actually
happening? Why does it matter for the ocean? And for us? First, I share
with you what I've seen during my ocean adventures. Then I'll zoom in
into a few major ocean challenges.

14.1 RECENT OCEAN EXPLORATIONS

Local fishermen have trouble catching, corals don't look as colourful
as they used to, and waters aren't as clear. For the last ten years, I
have travelled the world, visiting every continent and sailing on every
ocean (except Antarctica). I have walked on remote beaches on islands
hundreds of miles from any mainland. I explore the bottom of the sea
whenever I can. I've explored below the surface in Tonga in the middle
of the South Pacific, in the Galapagos, the Mediterranean, East Africa,

Australia and the Caribbean. Everywhere I get confronted with the same: man-made situations to the detriment of the ocean. Plastic is everywhere, coral **reefs** are bleaching, fishing lines discarded, and endangered fish are on the menu and in the supermarket. We are destroying our planet, and we don't realise it. Most of us only see coastlines and water surface, but when you are out, on, or underneath the ocean, you are constantly confronted with the damage we collectively are making.

I am not a scientist, but I explore, observe and learn every day. My ocean explorations have shown me the tsunami of challenges our oceans are facing. I've been dancing with manta rays in a plastic soup, watching them funnel in plastic instead of plankton. On more than one occasion I did not know where to resurface after a freedive because above me I saw nothing but trash. I've seen fish eating plastic bags. I've had plastic stuck to my fins. On a recent dive trip in Bali, we had to stop the boat every five minutes because a plastic bag got tangled

The beach is a colourful plastic disco. The whole shoreline is like this.

in the propeller. In the middle of the Atlantic, I fished water samples that appeared to be clear but actually had 47 parcels of plastic. Sailing on the Andaman Sea, I've had to zigzag to avoid the hundreds of trawling fishing boats. I've cleaned up beaches on uninhabited islands. I've stared at floating parades of plastic in the Mediterranean, Caribbean, South Pacific and in the middle of the Atlantic. In the open high seas, we thought we caught a fish but caught a plastic bag. In the Azores and Greece, I built castles of plastic sand. I've been looking for fish on freediving sessions and couldn't find any, even in places where they're supposed to be abundant. Then I go out for dinner, and the menu has shark, snapper, swordfish, tuna, salmon, and shrimps. The people catching, serving, ordering and eating, do not know that these species are exploited, endangered and loaded with toxins. I didn't know that before either.

I want to drink water, but they only serve in small plastic bottles because it's convenient, available and the social norm. I've explored bays in Turkey and Greece, and at every anchorage, I had to do a beach clean-up. I couldn't just look at it. When I check out the bottom, there are hundreds of cans just sitting at the bottom of the sea, and sadly not a single fish in sight. In the Caribbean mangrove forest, the oyster man who has been harvesting oysters for 50 years has a hard time finding them today. Last summer in Turkey, as always, every day I jumped into the sea to explore. In two out of three days, I did not see *any* fish.

These are just a few fragments of the many man-made consequences of climate change, plastic pollution, overfishing, and biodiversity change that I cannot get out of my mind. My nephew is almost two now. I'm curious about what the ocean will be like when he starts snorkelling, and once he has kids. In the next section, I'll address these challenges one by one.

14.2 CLIMATE CHANGE

2016 has been recorded as the hottest year in human history. Since 2001 we have had 16 of the 17 warmest years recorded (9). A few **degrees'** change may not seem like much, but when we take the average on earth, things change. We can already see the changes happening: wildfires, droughts, extreme rainfall, super-hot days, super cold days, and tropical storm development outside 'the season.' Weather patterns have never changed at such a rapid pace as we see today. It's called Climate Change. And it's not a distant reality anymore.

It's hard to get a grasp on climate change since for most of us, it doesn't directly affect us much (yet!). Yet, islanders, farmers, and fisherman have already experienced the consequences first-hand. When I was a kid, building snowmen and ice skating were guaranteed in winter in The Netherlands. Now we walk around in a T-shirt at Christmas time. While I'm typing this in Grenada, in the Caribbean the biggest storm surge is taking the coastline away. Locals have never seen the water reach this level before! In Tonga, the locals told me they already have had islands disappearing. The North-West passage, which used to be the most challenging passage where ships got stuck with the ice around them, is even opening up as a cruising ground.

How does climate change happen?

The atmosphere plays a fundamental role in the regulation of the climate. During the day, our planet warms up in the sunlight. At night, it cools, and the heat absorbed during the day goes back into the atmosphere. Some of the heat goes into space, but some of the heat is trapped by so called 'greenhouse gases', which includes Carbon Dioxide (**CO2**) and Methane, in the atmosphere. This has provided our planet with a consistent temperature and has made life on earth possible.

By nature, our planet produces and processes CO2. Plants, above and below the surface, take in CO2, and convert it into Oxygen. Animals, including us humans, breathe in the oxygen and breathe out carbon dioxide to live and thrive. What is now happening is that too much greenhouse gases (like CO2) are released into the air. More gases are trapped, and earth becomes warmer and warmer. We're messing with the balance by adding more CO2 (by burning fossils fuels like oil, coal and gas) and removing what the planet needs to absorb CO2 (trees, seagrass, **phytoplankton).** It's a double-edged sword! It makes it difficult for marine life, but also for us humans to adapt.

The changes in nature are not happening as a cycle of nature. They are man-made. We drive cars, browse the internet, eat meat, take airplanes, make babies, and use all sorts of products coming from the factories burning fossil fuels like there's no tomorrow. We burn fossil fuels to create energy to make things, eat things, and move ourselves around. The biggest CO2 emissions come from agriculture and deforestation (10). Waste products from the creation process include carbon dioxide (CO2) and methane (another gas). Some of it is seen, like that exhaust you see when driving by a factory, but some of it is unseen.

Why is this a problem for the ocean and for us?

As long as CO2 levels continue to increase, so will the temperature. Sea ice and glaciers are melting around the world, causing sea levels to rise. As the oceans become warmer, the water expands, making the sea levels rise even faster. Less ice also means warmer oceans since less sunlight is reflected back into the atmosphere. With warming oceans, there is less circulation of warm and cold water, bringing fewer nutrients to the surface for plankton to eat. With **Phytoplankton** being of huge importance for absorbing carbon and producing oxygen, sea temperature rise disrupts this process. Some fish species are already going deeper. Fish and plankton move toward the poles for colder water with more nutrition near the sunny surface where they thrive the best.

Not only the temperature upsets the balance. When the ocean absorbs CO_2 from the atmosphere, a chemical reaction occurs that makes the water more acidic. This process is called **Ocean Acidification.** For millions of years, the acidity level in the oceans has been stable. This steady pH balance (a numeric indicator of alkalinity or acidity) created a rich and flourishing marine life. Now, with our demand for fossil fuels and accordingly more CO_2 out there, we have managed to change the pH in the ocean.

Warming and acidity of the ocean affect **reefs,** marine life, shellfish and **Phytoplankton.** If it gets out of balance to the point where **Phytoplankton** can't survive, then other fish further up in the food chain can't either. Plankton has already decreased by 40% over the last 50 years (11; 8).

How much CO2 can our earth deal with?

At present rates, carbon dioxide is expected to reach 500ppm (parts per million) by 2050. The last time CO_2 levels were this high, humans did not exist. Scientists say that CO_2 levels this high would cause extreme weather changes that would endanger food supply, cause major mass migrations, species of plankton will be wiped out, and forests will be destroyed through droughts and fires (12).

To better understand the problem of CO_2 in our oceans, let's compare it with the carbon cycle in our bodies. It kind of works the same. We breathe in oxygen to convert nutrients into energy. A waste by-product of this process is CO_2, which our lungs normally breath out. The more CO_2 in the blood, the more acidic the blood is. As humans, we can also only tolerate so much CO_2. If our blood pH levels become too acidic, because of consuming too many acidic foods and drinks like coffee, alcohol, tea or meat, this can lead to disease. We can balance it by eating alkaline fruits and veggies to stay healthy.

With freediving (breath hold diving), I don't want to reach the surface because I need more oxygen. Rather, I need to go to the surface because my body gets sensitive to the acidic pH of my blood and needs to release CO_2! What if it cannot go anywhere? It will disturb the functions in every cell of my body.

Minimising the stress on our bodies with pure foods and proper breathing keeps us healthy. The same must be done to keep our oceans healthy. We must minimise the acidic load on the lungs of our planet, the oceans, and keep the oceans in balance to neutralise the acids. In the oceans however, we're not balancing it, this results in diminishing the health of the ocean. What if the CO_2 in the atmosphere cannot go anywhere? It will disturb functions of life in every layer of the ecosystem.

We need to proactively tackle climate change, now! Shifting away from fossil fuels, adopting to simpler and less polluting lifestyles, and renewable energy sources like wind, sun, tides and certain **biofuels** (not all!) are critical in order to avoid climate change getting worse. It's really urgent! Learn more about what you can do in the solutions chapter.

14.3 PLASTIC POLLUTION

"Pollution is nothing but the resources we are not harvesting. We allow them to disperse because we've been ignorant of their value."

— R. BUCKMINSTER FULLER
(Inventor and Poet)

Plastic pollution is choking us and the ocean. Via rivers, rain and wind, this never-disappearing material ends up in the sea. It is estimated that more than 8 million extra tons of plastic join the plastic soup each year (13). That is one garbage truck every minute! At this rate, there will be more plastic than fish in the ocean (by weight) by 2050 (14). Why is plastic such a problem? Do you know the full scale of the issue? What is plastic in the first place?

hear Valére in the cockpit. "Bart, wake up wake up! I need your help to get the fish in." I'm down in the **galley** attempting to work on my book. I think: Oh boy, not again." Line fishing is one of the least harmful fishing methods. It's a much better choice than opening a can of tuna. But we have lost four fishing lines by now, which will just end up floating around until a fish or turtle somewhere gets caught. Bart: "It's white. What kind of fish would this be?" Valére: "I don't know. Let's get it in." I try not to listen. The boys have been trying to fish for days. Bart enthusiastically announces "Suz, we caught the biggest thing ever." But it was not a fish. It's a plastic bag! They caught a plastic bag in the middle of the Atlantic. "There are some dolphins on the **bow** if you want to see them"–Valére says. Kerstin: "You know why there are coming? To thank us for fishing out the plastic."

I've seen bottles, bags, pieces of this, pieces of that, floating by in the middle of the ocean. Thousands of kilometres from civilisation. Most likely you already know plastic is an issue. Shops have started charging for plastic bags now, or even banning them altogether (hoorah Hawaii and Delhi!) so you might already be bringing your own. Your municipality might ask you to separate your plastic waste. Perhaps you've seen a picture of a sea creature tangled in plastic. And realise that in the western world we're way ahead of it. In the Caribbean, they raise an eyebrow if you say no to the convenience of a plastic bag.

A few plastic facts

- 5.25 trillion plastic particles weighing a total of 268,940 tons are currently floating in the world's oceans (15). That is almost the equivalent of the European population in weight! Look up 'Sailing seas of plastic' to zoom in and out on the ocean and see the data of this global plastic study swimming in the ocean. If current trends continue, this will be two trucks per minute by 2030 and four per minute by 2050 (13)!
- An estimated 80 percent of the plastic in the ocean comes from land, the other 20 percent from practices at sea (16) (remember those fishing lines we lost)!
- 94% of plastic ends up at the bottom of the sea (16).

Paradise, until you have a closer look. I'm in the Tobago Cays: a protected marine reserve. And let's assume, no one would litter here. So where does this trash come from? It's washed up ashore, thrown 'away' elsewhere in the world. Today I found fishing lines, flip flops and bottles.

What is plastic?

The word "plastic" comes from the word *plastikos*. This means to mould or form. It is made from processed oil and exists as a chain of molecules called **polymers.** The special property of the polymers is the large size of their molecules. These "super molecules" allow for bending, and for adding different types of chemicals to produce plastic in any shape or colour. And indeed, we can make any shape, colour or substance from plastic.

Try going for just ten minutes without touching plastic . . . I've already failed! The buttons of my computer are made from plastic. It's everywhere—shoes, plates, forks, spoons, toothbrushes, toys, straws, cups, shavers, chairs, bottles, bags, shampoo wrappers, pens, diapers, cookie-wrappers, even the ink on your grocery receipt is plastic. There's even plastic in our shampoo, toothpaste and scrub. Our clothes are plastic: acrylic, nylon and polyester are all types of plastic. Go beyond the veggie department in the supermarket, and almost everything has plastic. Even the veggie departments are great at wrapping things in plastic these days. Regulations. My freedive mask and fins are made from plastic, my backpack is plastic, my nylon sweater is plastic. Most boats are made of plastic these days. Sails are plastic. The boat toys are plastic.

It's great, right? We can make everything from plastic! It doesn't corrode. It's cheap, lightweight, help us to store food, drinks and other stuff. It's convenient. Plastic makes our food last. We don't have to do the dishes at the BBQ party. We can take away our food. We sip cocktails and coconuts through plastic. We have made ourselves very dependent on it. We are living in a plastic age.

Why is plastic a problem?

Plastic is designed to last forever. Plastic may be derived from natural materials, but in the process, molecular structures are changed, chemicals are added, and become too strong and durable for the planet to digest. There is no bacteria or enzyme that effectively eats plastic and closes the natural cycle, which means it just keeps piling up. Every piece of plastic ever manufactured is still on this planet. We may throw it 'away.' Only there is no such thing as 'away.' Where's away? Plastics accumulate in garbage dumps, landfills, and eventually the ocean. Our creation has become our enemy.

You may have heard that are islands of plastic floating in the ocean. While it's not really an island, it's almost like one. These 'islands' are gyres. A gyre is where ocean **currents** come together in a circular pattern and where plastic accumulates. Five main ocean gyres exist. Here the plastic soup is densest. Where outside the gyres plastic density has been estimated 1,000–100,000 pieces km2 and even up to 890,000 pieces km2 in the Mediterranean (15), the density in the gyres are multifold. Here marine life rampantly ingests plastic and gets entangled.

Scientists have also found that plastics carried in the **current** are contributing to the spread of invasive species. Plastic functions like a transport mechanism, and algae and crabs for instance hitch a ride on the plastics (17). As foreign species in a new environment can be invasive and destructive by altering the balance of an ecosystem.

The most worrisome types of plastic are the 'disposables' that we only use for ten seconds, ten minutes or maybe an hour and then throw 'away.' Packaging, bottles, bags, straws, take away boxes. Take a water bottle: It's manufactured using energy and petrochemicals, packed, shipped, flown, trucked, driven, cooled, drank and then tossed away. So much energy for such short use, and an endless lifespan in nature. It doesn't make sense, does it? Tossed 'away' means it either ends up in landfill for hundreds of years, is burned releasing toxins into the atmosphere, ends up in nature, or is recycled.

Disposable plastic

The four biggest polluters of the oceans

Only a tiny fraction (Scientific data ranges from two -15%) of the plastic produced is recycled, which again takes oil and energy to turn used bottles into other plastic items. Plastic comes in many forms, and each type has to be recycled through a different process. This takes a lot of resources. Only certain plastics can be recycled, and only into a different type of plastic. A bottle can never be a bottle again, only a bench or a car. It's called 'down-cycling.'

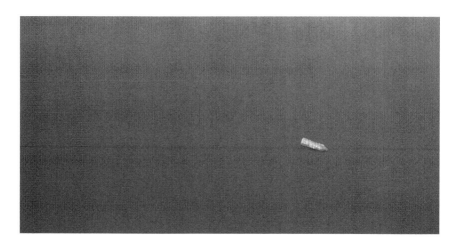

A lot of plastic is seen. Even more of it is unseen. Through exposure to the sun, salt, wind and waves, plastic break down into **microplastics.** It does not biodegrade, but fragmentizes. 3.2 million tons out of 9.5 million tons of plastic that enters the ocean yearly is in the form of microplastics (small particles of plastic, less than 1mm in size). These are a big threat to  marine life. The latest research says that most of it comes from clothing fibres or tires (18). Every time we do the laundry more than 20 million microfibers are released into the wastewater (19). These fibres eventually find their way into the stomach of a fish. Into your stomach?

Me taking water samples during my hitch-sailing trip around the Atlantic. The samples I took seemed like bright, clean ocean water. No plastic to be seen! Adventurers and conservation scientists then tested them for **microplastic** pieces. They all contained plastic, except for one! The rest of the samples, I took in different locations in the Atlantic Ocean, had more than 11 micro pieces per litre. One of the samples taken between the Canary Islands and Cape Verde had 47 micro pieces! Of all the samples collected during the **ARC** across the Atlantic, 97.5% of the samples contained microplastic!

A piece of plastic in the ocean is a million times more polluted than the water around it (20). Water repels chemicals and metals like mercury, arsenic. Plastic, on the other hand, attracts these toxins like a sponge. Led, chromium, and tin are found in plastic litter (21). Fish and sea mammals mistake microplastic particles for food and ingest them, making them sick. The higher the plastic moves up in the food chain, the more toxins accumulate.

Fish eating Plastic

Besides impact plastic has on our ocean, wildlife and environment, plastic is a concern to human health. Plastic isn't just around us, it's in us! Through food we eat, water we drink, products we use, things we touch, and the air we breathe. Plastic is found in a third of UK-caught fish, including cod, haddock, mackerel and shellfish (22). Shellfish lovers could be eating up to 11,000 plastic fragments in their seafood each year (23).

It's not a question anymore if we are eating plastic from seafood, the question is what is does to the health of animals, the ocean, and us. Plastic in the ocean contains high levels of pollutants such as **PCB, Phthalates,** organic pesticides like **BPA,** and heavy metals like mercury, arsenic, and lead. These are proven poisons linked to all sorts of diseases, including cancer, hormone disruption, and infertility issues (24).

Another plastic problem is known as **ghost fishing.** Hundreds of kilometres of fish lines and nets, made from plastic, get lost every year at sea. This kind of trash doesn't only pollute; it is one of the biggest killers of wildlife living in or near the ocean. Fish get tangled or trapped. These lines, an estimated 10% of all marine debris, will never ever disappear unless we take them out. An estimated 640,000 tons of fishing gear is lost or abandoned in the ocean each year, killing more than 100,000 seals, sea lions, and

Ghost fishing in the afternoon office. . . . Picked up this line from the shore. It's dozens of metres long. That's a few metres less of ghost line in the sea, along with a few items of plastic caught up in it. The positive side of a ghost line: it can clean up too.

whales (25). These ghosts continue to accumulate in the ocean, catching and killing birds and marine life. Whales wash up ashore with not just one or two, but dozens of plastic items in their stomachs.

Bioplastic

What about bioplastics like biodegradable plastic and bio-based plastic? The names sound great and natural, but these types of 'plastic' come with other problems. They can do more harm than good.

Biodegradable 'plastic', which breaks down completely in nature with the help of bacteria, fungi or algae, comes with other problems. In landfill, there often is no sun or oxygen which the 'plastic' needs to biodegrade. Producing biodegradable plastic still takes a huge amount of resources. They're often still made from similar petroleum based materials to plastic, only with some ingredients added that make it decompose, still leaving toxic leftovers. Also, when a product is 'biodegradable,' one may be less likely to reuse it.

Bio-based plastic, which is 'plastics' based on natural material (for example made from corn, potatoes, soy, wheat, seaweed, coconut, sugar cane), can result in problems with food security. We need our land more for food production than 'plastic.' The breakdown of these products results in co2 and methane release which contributes to global warming. Bio-based plastics are also hard to recycle since they need to be separated from other plastic to be able to be recycled.

One day, we may find a way to make the perfect material which is available in abundance and can be completely eaten by nature. But until then, we need to produce, re-use and refuse more smartly. We must stop the creation at the source. Cleaning up is great, but it's like trying to empty the ocean with a thimble. We must reduce, redesign and push out plastic packaging in favour of more environmentally-friendly alternatives, and altogether just simplify our lives in general. Find out what actions you can take as an individual.

14.4 BIODIVERSITY CHANGE

"Great attention gets paid to rainforests
because of the diversity of life there. Diversity
in the oceans is even greater."

– SYLVIA EARLE

Two words: Bio and Diversity. Bios comes from the Greek and means 'life'. Biodiversity is a variety of life. Biosiversity sustains life in the sea. To have a healthy fish population there needs to be a healthy predator population. Predators prey on the weak and sick, keeping it all in balance. But the diversity is changing. Rapidly! As humans, we are not a healthy predator anymore. We have become more like monsters, interfering with the system like we're the last generation on earth.

Climate change, **ocean acidification** and plastic pollution all make it harder and harder for marine life to thrive. We speed up the degradation process with fertilisers, chemicals, pesticides, herbicides, sewage, oil, plastics running down from land, and nuclear disasters. This results into '**dead zones.**' which are zones in the ocean where no life exists at all anymore due to a lack of oxygen.

A 2017 published study by the Tropical Research Institute found that coral **reefs** are associated with more than half of the known tropical dead zones worldwide, concluding that the risk of dead-zone to reefs has been severely underestimated. The same study estimates the number of dead zones far greater (441 in the tropics, and 447 outside the tropics), than previous estimates (26).

Coral reefs are complex underwater ecosystems. Reefs are the "rainforests of the sea," and home to many living beings. Half of the shallow coral reefs globally are gone or in a serious state of decline. In the Caribbean, 80% of the reefs are already believed to be dead. One in every eight birds is in danger, one in every four mammals, and one in every three amphibians. Seal populations are now less than 10% of what they once were in the North Atlantic 500 years ago (27).

With fewer species, the greater the challenge becomes to maintain a healthy ocean, food security and the health of everyone on earth. It's a bit like the game *Jenga,* where the aim of the game is to make a tower as high as you can (more money and appetite satisfaction). You take a block (a fish species) out of the bottom foundation (the ecosystem) and put in on the top of the tower (our appetite). We can only do this so many times until the tower (the ecosystem) collapses. Fish species collapse when only a few fish are left and are not able to reproduce fast enough to replenish the population.

The primary cause of the changes in biodiversity is: overfishing. The next challenge to tackle!

14.5 OVERFISHING

"The cause is simply to save humanity from humanity. The solution is to learn to live within the biosphere instead of dominating it."

— PAUL WATSON
(Captain, Ocean Activist—founder of Sea Shepherd)

The saying goes: "there's plenty more fish in the sea." Well, this saying is outdated! There's actually not much left. Not so long ago, we thought that the ocean could replenish whatever we take from it. After all, the oceans are huge! Now we know that that is not the case. For fishing to be sustainable, we need to allow enough time for new ones to be born so the population can be maintained. The reverse is happening. We have taken more than the ocean 'produces', and we're taking fish faster than they can reproduce. It's called overfishing.

Overfishing has wiped out 90% of the ocean's large top-predators, like sharks, tunas, cod, and groupers. And we need the big fish in the ocean because they eat the weaker ones. They prevent the *'jenga'* from collapsing. The big fish that are still out there weigh 50% or less than they did 50 years ago. The average weight of a swordfish caught today is 45 Kilos. In the 60's this was 130 kilos (8). Of all fish species, 52% is fully exploited, 17% is overexploited, and 7% is depleted. Common seafood choices such as tuna, shrimp, and salmon are among the worst affected. (28) I don't want to withhold the good news from you: a whopping 1% of species are recovering from depletion.

The problem is not just the fish we're taking; the problem is also *how* we're taking it. We have advanced and crazy destructive technologies these days to find and catch any size of fish. Modern fishing techniques destroy habitats, damage ocean floors, and wipe out species. Most devastating are the fishing trawlers, which literally scrape the sea floor taking everything along with it. It's like wanting to pick a flower by bulldozing the whole garden! How can the next flower flourish? Another fishing method that does more harm than good is 'longlining.' This method involves throwing out a long line with dozens of hooks. The fisherman aims for tuna, but in the process dolphins, sharks and even seabirds are also caught. This is called 'bycatch.

At some fisheries, for every kilo of fish that can be sold at the market, ten more kilos are thrown back, dead or half alive, as bycatch! This is sorted out offshore so the fleet can be out at sea longer, go further, and catch more of what the market demands. It is estimated that global bycatch is 40% of the world's total fish catch, with fisheries throwing back more than 28 million tons of non-targeted fish every year. 28 million tons (29). That's comparable to the content of 28,000 Olympic swimming pools full of dead fish that don't qualify for our appetite. It makes bycatch on of the largest threats to maintaining healthy fish populations.

Despite the scooping, seafood consumption is rising because of diet shifts and population increase. Bluefin tuna, swordfish, and shark are still on restaurant menus. And since it's called 'fish of the day', we think it's fresh, local, healthy and acceptable. Food advice around the world recommends eating fish because of the omega health benefits. Fish are even squeezed to create fish oil pills. The Dutch 'Voedselcentrum' (Food Advisory institution) recommends people to consume one portion of fish per week (30). That means 17 million dead fish each week for a country that's not dependent on fish for survival. What only a few know is that the healthy omegas originate in sea algae and weeds, of which almost all are edible.

People currently most affected are the ones that need fish as a food source the most. In the developing world, especially on the islands, fish is vital as a food source. There is simply not enough available land to produce for agriculture. Yet only fewer and fewer fisherman can obtain a living from fishing. With fewer fish in the ocean, there is less to catch for the local fisherman, less to see for divers, and less business for dive tour operators. When the ocean ecosystem collapses, humans go too. It might sound like a distant reality, but it's not! If the current rate of exploitation is maintained, the ocean will be empty in 2048! (31)

Check *globalfishingwatch.com* for a live map of fishing vessels (only those trackable on the **AIS**!), to see for yourself the insane number of commercial fishing boats out there. Taking them is still possible because fishery management is practically non-existent at sea. It's hard to measure, but there are numbers out that between 30% and 70% of fish are caught illegally! Fisherman are getting desperate to sustain a living, catching more and younger fish than they are supposed to, or fishing in prohibited areas.

What about farmed fish? Aquaculture, or fish farming, is a fishing method that is overtaking wild-caught fish. A solution? It's like chicken farms. It might be more productive and quicker in volume but with it comes disease, antibiotics and pollution. Fish farms destroy surrounding habitats and mangrove forests in the process. Farmed fish are fed all sorts of fish and lots of it (but also meat!), which puts pressure on wild fish stocks. Fish like salmon, tuna, grouper are carnivores and need to be fed fish to be healthy. Farming fish in a closed space where waste is controlled, and there is little chance for fish to escape, seems better, but other challenges exist in managing the water quality for the health of the fish and the surrounding environment.

While governments debate fish quotas and 'sustainable' practices, and chefs debate which fish they can still "sustainably" cook, fish are continually taken without considering how much is left. Globally, we need to reduce our fishing efforts and fish consumption. Commercial fishing practices should all be banned. As long as we keep demanding, businessmen keep finding a way to supply. Action must be taken at global, national, local and individual levels. Learn what you can do in Chapter 16.

"The most important thing we take from the ocean is our existence."

– SYLVIA EARLE

14.6 MANAGEMENT AND PROTECTION OF THE OCEAN

"The greatest threat to our planet is the belief that someone else will save it."

– ROBERT SWAN OBE
(Polar explorer)

Every inch of land has been claimed by someone, managed through laws, policies, and regulations. On the ocean, the situation is different. No one owns the ocean. But everyone uses it. Little is protected, managed and regulated. Learn about the challenge of ocean management and protection.

In 1609, the Dutchman Hugo Grotius made the first attempt to create an international regulation on the ocean. His document 'Mare Liberum' (freedom of the seas) proposed that the ocean belongs to everyone. There is freedom to take what's swimming or floating around. If you find a ship, it's yours. Only 35 years ago, in 1982, the United Nations established a global framework governing human activities on the world's oceans, the Convention on the Law of the Sea. Only 167 countries in the world have signed it though—with the United States, one of the biggest importers of seafood, notably absent on the list! The ocean belongs to everyone, but especially to those living in it.

Too little of the oceans are protected areas. The oceans account for 71% of the planet's surface, but less than 3% of the oceans are protected. Protections are in place for nearly 12% of all land (through areas like national parks) (8).

Although there are Marine Protected Areas, the challenge lies in upholding laws and regulations. Within 200 nautical miles from the coast, waters are an Exclusive Economic Zone. Beyond that, the oceans remain ungoverned. There are international laws and agreements, like for instance the ban on whaling, but on the high seas, there is no enforcement of these regulations.

Marine Protected Areas (MPAs)

They are the "National Parks" in our oceans (and big lakes). These are protected areas with a specific conservation purpose, and they limit human intervention by fishing, building, or mooring/anchoring with your boat. For example, in Carriacou (Grenada), there is an MPA for a mangrove forest, an important nurturing ground for small fish and oysters. These MPAs are overseen by the government of the country. It's a way to restore the rich biodiversity of our oceans. The world has

Protecting 2.8% of the Global Ocean

Source: IUCN and UNEP-WCMC (2013). The World Database on Protected Areas (WDPA) Official Map Series: Marine Protected Areas. Series M01. WDPA October 2013 Release. Map available at: www.protectedplanetocean.org; WDPA available at www.protectedplanet.net.

(34)

around 5,000 MPAs. All together they cover an area of not even 3% of the world's ocean! That's about the size of Europe. A huge win in 2016 was the decision to make the Ross Sea in Antarctica an MPA, one of the earth's most pristine marine ecosystems. A special type of MPA is a marine reserve, a 'no-take MPA.' In a marine reserve, nothing may be taken. Only 10% of the MPAs are a marine reserve. So much remains unprotected (32) (33).

If everyone just keeps taking what they want from the ocean, eventually no one will have anything. It's called the 'tragedy of the commons.' It means that individuals try to reap the greatest benefits for themselves from a shared resource. Until the resource is gone . . . If we want to keep enjoying the ocean and give our children a healthy environment, we need to shift our thinking and behaviour. We only have one planet, and it's not expanding. But we're breeding and using the planet like we have a spare.

There is only so much space and resources. Each day the number of births double the number of deaths (35). When my parents were born (in 1960), there were only three billion people on the planet. Today we approach 7.5 billion, and by 2100, 11 billion people are expected to be on this planet (36). The planet has room for more, but there's no room for all these people to keep consuming the way that we do. We as humans are pretty destructive to the planet that gives us life, often without even realising it ourselves. We have become disconnected from nature, and connected with work, money, and convenience. Too many people consume too many resources and return toxic poisons, plastic, radiation and chemicals to the sea, often without even knowing.

*"We can learn from exceptional people of our own culture, and from other cultures less destructive than ours. I am speaking of the life of **a man who knows that the world is not given by his fathers, but borrowed from his children;** who has undertaken to cherish it and do it no damage, not because he is duty-bound, but because he loves the world and loves his children . . . .*

– WENDELL BERRY
(Writer and Environmental Activist)

The responsibility of ocean protection lies within each one of us. We all need to team up to keep our ocean playground and the lifeblood of our planet alive! As individuals we make an impact, for better or worse, with the choices we make in all aspects of our lives: work, food, time spent, and things bought.

14.7 WHAT HAPPENS IF WE DON'T CHANGE ANYTHING?

"If the oceans die, we die."

– PAUL WATSON

Reefs will die, fish species will be gone, colourful plastic beaches will be the norm, and our children will have to deal with it. If we don't change our rate and ways of consumption now, within 100 years jellyfish might be the only wild seafood option left (8). Oxygen will be the new gold. For as long as it lasts. . . .

I hear it often: "The world has been able to recover for over millions of years. Why not now?" The biggest difference is that we as humans are the dominating race now. As a result of our actions, the ocean is getting emptier, warmer, and more acidic, putting life under pressure. We cannot just take what we want and throw back what we don't want. Without life in the ocean, we would lose 50%, if not more, of our oxygen supply as well as absorption of carbon dioxide.

But there is good news: the ocean can regenerate! We know much more now than we did in the last century. It's not too late to rebalance the oceans! There are many causes, but also many solutions. Only we cannot sit back, relax and just point our fingers towards others to take action. For real environmental change, we must ALL take action, now, to protect and restore the health of the ocean. We must work together to get the abundance of wildlife back and help everyone on this planet thrive! We owe it to our children and all living beings on this beautiful planet.

15

WHAT IS BEING DONE
TO SAVE IT?

*"Like drops in the ocean, sailors and boaters are
individuals. But together we're creating a powerful
wave of change that is sweeping the globe."*

— SAILORS FOR THE SEA

GREAT ACTION IS TAKEN TOWARDS A HEALTHIER OCEAN.
Thankfully, there are many more ocean conservation groups and
influencers out there than I'll be able to cover in this book. Here
are a few of my favourites, that have inspired me, provide useful data,
and can help you learn more about the ocean. They are all eager for you
to get involved!

15.1 OCEAN CONSERVATION & RESEARCH

Marjo and Edwin, the adventure couple behind Ocean Conservation, sail
around the Canary Islands aiming to provide a worldwide platform for
research, education and connection, contributing to the sustainability of
the oceans. Their slogan is 'to bring awareness into action.' And they do
act! They are steadily moving onto the global stage. They recently became
owners of Grace, a 85 ft. Danish Cutter from 1925. "A solid wooden ship
with history, and ready and able to make more history. . . ." as they state on
their website. I'm sure they will because they already made history them-

selves. With the Atlantic Rally for Cruisers (ARC) of 2014, they managed to get 100 boats to take water samples from different parts of the Atlantic during their crossing. This project thus covers a whopping 602,000 square nautical miles to measure the amount of **microplastic** in our ocean—the widest scale of research ever conducted in this field! Microplastic is just one of their areas of focus. Their new focus area is the creation of a platform for Personal Development, through which which they aim to involve more people; helping them become aware of their own talents and skills, and to apply these with respect for our planet. They facilitate and work together with scientists aiming to involve more sailors and other citizens in science projects. They have found that helping collect data is an excellent way to make people more aware and willing to take action in their own lives. And it's just the beginning. With sustainable sailing and many conservation projects ahead, there is a lot more in the pipeline for Ocean Conservation! Marjo and Edwin have broadened my horizons and radiated their passion for the

Microplastic Research ARC Fleet

ocean to me. They are the best example of 'whatever the situation, it can be done' They don't only chase their dreams; it's their mission to make a difference in the world. It's a powerful concept and enhances real change.

Learn more at *OceanConservation.org.uk*.

15.2 SAILORS FOR THE SEA

Sailors for the Sea helps water-based events reduce their environmental impact. Over 1,000 regattas, events, rallies and cruises are taking part in their Clean Regattas program, which educates and activates event organisers to reduce their impact on the environment.

They have also developed a program for school children: Kids Environmental Lesson Plans (KELP). They have developed a fun, easy to use tool to help kids understand the ocean's influence on them and their impact on the ocean.

Learn more at *SailorsfortheSea.org*.

15.3 OCEANSWATCH

Their slogan is Cruising with a cause. With their own yachts and members' boats, OceansWatch supports coastal communities in developing conservation action plans, sustainable livelihood projects, and help in mitigating and adapting to the effects of climate change. OceansWatch is active in the Pacific and Atlantic.

Learn more at *OceansWatch.org*.

Team *Sea Ya*, OceanConservation.org.uk, and Oceanswatch.org

15.4 THE 5 GYRES INSTITUTE

5 Gyres Institute undertakes some of the most cutting-edge research on plastic pollution in our oceans. They take action against the plastic pollution challenge through science, art, education, and adventure. You can become a 5 Gyres Ambassador and use their resources to create awareness in your school and community.

Learn more at *5gyres.org*.

15.5 PLASTIC POLLUTION COALITION

Plastic Pollution Coalition is a group of over 500 organisations, businesses, and individuals working towards a world free of plastic pollution. They create impactful videos and actionable guides to tackle the challenges of plastic.

Learn more at *PlasticPollutionCoalition.org*.

15.6 PANGEASEED FOUNDATION

I went for a stroll in Grenada and came across this powerful ocean-inspired wall painting by artist Aaron Glasson. Locally in the Caribbean is how I learned about the PangeaSeed Foundation. PangeaSeed raises awareness through 'ARTivism.' Through art, science, and creativity, they connect individuals and communities to the ocean. Art can be an effective trigger for the local community and travellers to rise against plastic.

Learn more at *www.pangeaseed.foundation*.

15.7 ONE WORLD ONE OCEAN

One World One Ocean is 'the ocean's storyteller.' They create high-quality educational films and videos to educate on the challenges of the ocean. Powerful visuals.

Learn more at *OneWorldOneOcean.com*.

15.8 MISSION BLUE

Founded by 'her Deepness', Dr. Sylvia Earle, Mission Blue aims to provoke public support for a global network of marine protected areas. Earle's organisation identifies 'Hope Spots', which Mission Blue describes as "any special place that is critical to the health of the ocean, Earth's blue heart. Hope Spots are about recognising, empowering and supporting individuals and communities around the world in their efforts to protect the ocean." Anyone can nominate a site unique to him or her—a site that gives them hope!

Learn more at *Mission-Blue.org*.

15.9 SEA SHEPHERD CONSERVATION SOCIETY

Sea Shepherd is one organisation that takes Action with a capital A. Since the 1970s, they have been taking direct action on illegal activities on the high seas, and to end poaching on the high seas. Their mission: Defend, Protect, Conserve. Sea Shepherd has helped to decrease the number of whales killed each year hugely. Captain Paul Watson, Sea Shepherd founder, also conveys powerful messages through social media. Sea Shepherd has some great volunteer opportunities both on shore and at sea.

Learn more at *SeaShepherd.org*.

15.10 OCEAN UNITE

Ocean Unite brings together powerful voices for the health of the ocean. With scientists, business, organisations, world leaders and everyday citizen taking action, knowledge is fragmented. Ocean Unite coordinates high-impact efforts to get key messages to the right people at the moments that matter. Their website is packed with ocean information and resources.

Learn more and unite at *OceanUnite.org*.

15.11 OCEAN CONSERVANCY

The Ocean Conservancy is an American non-profit organisation, advocating for policy changes and organising cleanups, including an annual international ocean clean-up. They have a cool app called 'Clean Swell' where you can report your trash collections and add to the research database.

Learn more at *OceanConservancy.org*.

15.12 PARLEY TV

Parley TV is a collaboration network and accelerator of important ocean messages and innovative solutions. They are aware that we have no time to lose and therefore reach beyond the ocean conservation 'community.' They bring creators, thinkers and leaders together to raise awareness and amplify voices on ocean problems and solutions, to accelerate a process of change that is already in progress.

Learn more at *Parley.TV*.

15.13   PLASTIC SOUP FOUNDATION

The Plastic Soup Foundation is a Dutch organisation fighting the plastic challenge in our ocean. They make the ocean challenges understandable for everyone and have actionable campaigns and initiatives to involve citizens fixing the plastic soup.

Learn more at *PlasticSoupFoundation.org*.

15.14   PLASTIC OCEANS FOUNDATION

Plastic Oceans is a global network of charitable organisations united by a common goal to change the world's attitude towards plastic. They make the plastic problem understandable for everyone, and have recently released a documentary exploring the issue, entitled "A Plastic Ocean". Through education, business and sustainability, and science, they promote solutions for the plastic in our ocean.

Learn more at *PlasticOceans.org*

15.15   THE INSPIRATES!

Together with my adventure sister Roline Prummel, I've set up The insPirates. With the insPirates we unite people with a spirit of adventure and a drive for entrepreneurship in sustainable innovations. We see the combination of nature, inspiring experiences and adventurous game-changers as the accelerator for creativity, social entrepreneurship and positive change. We do this in cool outdoor settings to maximise play, inspiration and adventure time. We have kicked-off with an insPirate-tional Sail flotilla in Greece and are currently insPirating the next adventure.

Learn more on *theInspirates.co*

15.16   SAILING CONSERVATIONISTS

There are awesome ocean-based sailing conservationists out there too! These are a few of my favourite sailing ocean savers that operate in the North Atlantic region. Hop on board, participate in research, and become excited about saving the ocean!

- Science Under Sail Expeditions (SUSIE—*Scienceundersail.org)*
- Grace—*(OceanConservation.org.uk*—Canary Islands (for now))
- Pangaea Exploration *(PanExplore.org*—Around the Atlantic)
- eXXpedition *(eXXpedition.com*—Around the Atlantic)
- Making Waves Sailing *(MakingWavesSailing.com*—Caribbean)
- By The Ocean We Unite *(ByTheOceanWeUnite.org*—North Sea)
- The Watermen Project *(TheWatermen.org*—Global)

16

WHAT CAN YOU DO AS CREW?

"Our actions over the next ten years will determine the state of the ocean for the next 10,000 years."

—SYLVIA EARLE

A T SEA, THE LIFESTYLE IS SIMPLE. You will experience the preciousness of drinking water and electricity and will learn to use every drop and amp consciously. But what else can do you to minimise impact? How can you make a difference during an ocean adventure? What can we do at the frontline, as sailors, with our special connection to the sea.

The time for raising awareness is over; it's time to act!

We have some situations to tackle. The good news is that oceans are resilient and can get back into balance—but they need our help! Lots of solutions are in the hands of governments, policymakers and corporations, but we don't have time to wait for politicians to prioritise the ocean in their agenda. We can travel oceans, do good, save money, *and* have fun. When we plan, prepare and make conscious decisions, we can minimise our negative footprint and maximise the benefits for the place we visit and for the planet as a whole. All together we are responsible for the life that is depleting in the ocean. All together we can also bring it back! Collectively, our impact can be major. It's our responsibility to become part of the solution, not the problem. Governments and businesses respond to the choices of the public. By making conscious decisions as a consumer, you can influence what will be on the market tomorrow.

16.1 BE AWARE

"It ain't what you don't know that gets you into trouble; it's what you know for sure that just ain't so."

– MARK TWAIN
(Writer)

I hope the previous chapter has made you a little more aware of the urgency of our actions. It all starts with that: awareness. We can only do good if we know what the problem is in the first place. We are so used to doing things the way we do, that often we're not even aware of the impact. Take notice of what's happening around you in your daily lives and how it may affect the environment. It's easy to look away, but that's not a solution. What is the impact that you are making, right now? It's fun to calculate your carbon footprint. Here's a cool carbon calculator: *oceanfdn.org/calculator*. You can also calculate roughly how many toothbrushes, and shampoo bottles you have used in your life! Whoopsy! Time to rethink, refuse, reduce, reuse, recycle, and research (more about that later).

16.2 DISTRIBUTE GOODS

Use a small amount of space in your luggage (ask the captain to free up some storage) and use the extra space to support community projects around the world.

Correos del Mar
Going via Cape Verde? Marta from Las Palmas set up 'Correos de la Mar' (Mail of the Sea). She's always looking for boats that can transport clothes, toys, and other helpful things to Cape Verde or the Caribbean for children and older adults in need. Goods that are especially needed

Taking goods on board from Correos del Mar

in Cape Verde include school supplies (pencils, pens, papers), sleeping clothes, and cold-weather clothes for the elderly which are not for sale at all in Cape Verde. A good moment to give your thick sweater away which you don't need in the Caribbean.

Get in touch with Marta via *facebook.com/correos.de.la.mar*.

Pack for a Purpose

Check this website to see what goods are in need in the destination that you're heading to. Communities in Cape Verde, the Caribbean and South America are eager to receive your help.

Learn more at *PackforaPurpose.org*.

Hands Across The Sea

An organisation dedicated to raising the literacy levels of eastern Caribbean children.

Learn more at *HandsAcrosstheSea.net*.

16.3 PACK & STORE SMART

As my dad always said, '*Een slimme meid is op haar toekomst voorbereid*' (literally translated as 'as a smart girl, has her future prepared'). While he is usually talking more about my pension, he has taught me to prepare for the unexpected. He still shows up with a piece of rope ('always handy'!) whenever I head out for another adventure! My years of travel have taught me what to expect and what is of use in this crazy adventure lifestyle. Preparation is key to be able to make a difference! That's why I'm thrilled you got your hands on this book! As discussed earlier in the dedicated packing section, you can make a huge difference by packing smart. In addition to the ocean-friendly packing tips, *store* smart once on board. I've seen it all falling overboard: hats, coffee machine parts, **winch handles,** fuel tanks, keys, spanners, screws, shackles, towels, pegs, bottles, and thousands of polystyrene balls when the bean bag got a hole. Be smart about leaving water bottles, sunglasses or caps lying around. Boats move, and the wind blows. It's easy for things to fall over board accidentally. Although if it does happen, it can be an excellent opportunity to practise the 'man' overboard drill.

16.4 MINIMISE WASTE IMPACT

"If you think you are too small to make a difference,
try sleeping with a mosquito.

– TENZIN GYATSO
(14th Dalai Lama — Monk)

We've already seen how you can manage your waste responsibly when you're out at sea and when you arrive at your destination. Go back to the relevant chapters to refresh your memory:

1. Pack smart (Chapter 7)
2. Provision smart (Chapter 8)
3. Dealing with waste on the ocean (Chapter 10)
4. Dispose smart (Chapter 11)

The amount of energy and chemicals used for constructing and maintaining a boat can be horrendous. Having been on many different boats and having seen procedures taken with provisioning, waste disposal and (lack of) awareness level on the impact of it, there are huge differences to be made in behavioural changes. Rethinking the way of doing things and contributing with the skills one has. Above all, before you even hop on board—minimise, minimise, minimise.

16.5   DO YOUR RESEARCH

Will you be sailing through any Marine Protected Areas? They are often indicated in charts, but also on *mpatlas.org* and *protectedplanet.net*. Know where they are in advance so you can be prepared to spot magnificent wildlife and share it with the world. Or to detect an illegal fishing vessel and help enforce governance at sea!

Do your research on the destination you're going to. How are the waste recycling facilities? Download blogs and travel guides so you have the information at hand offline when you don't have internet access—then you can say no to the maps and brochures locally.

16.6   CONTRIBUTE TO RESEARCH

There is so much we don't know yet about the ocean. Especially outside coastal zones, it's logistically and economically challenging to collect data for research. As sailors, we are already out there, and we can reach places far away from civilisation. Why not make your wildlife sightings part of something bigger? Our observations on location can be extremely valuable to gain better insights on what's going on with the ocean and its wildlife. The more we know, the better solutions we can create. Here are a few initiatives that would welcome your contributions and sightings from the ocean. Be sure to check these out beforehand, so you know what data is welcome.

Spot wildlife and plants

WHALES

If you see a whale on your travels, remember that whale tails serve as unique identifiers for each whale, like fingerprints. Snap a photo and submit them, along with sighting coordinates to:

- Sail & Whale *(sailandwhale.com)*
- Carib Tails *(caribtails.org)*
- Flukebook *(flukebook.org)*

Be careful! If a whale is close to your boat, slow down to avoid a collision.

BIRDING ABOARD

A citizen-science project organised by a group of long-distance birding sailors from around the world. Join the bird count and contribute information about bird migrations. Simply take a photo of a bird and write down the location coordinates. The data goes to *eBird,* a worldwide resource for scientists and conservation groups.

Learn more at *BirdingAboard.org.*

PHYTOPLANKTON

Contribute to the seafarer study of **phytoplankton.** Plankton is particularly sensitive to changes in sea surface temperature. You can help to get more insight into the plankton changes by making a simple piece of scientific equipment called a 'Secchi Disk' and getting the Secchi app.

Learn more at *SecchiDisk.org.*

SEAWEED

There has been a massive increase of **sargassum** (a type of large brown seaweed) in 2015 and 2016, especially in the Caribbean. During my first crossing in 2015, we had massive parades of seaweed next to our boat, for almost the full route. It impacts shorelines, marine life, waterways and tourism. Trinidad and Tobago even declared this abundance of sargassum a natural disaster! You can help to add to the data set. Report your observations at sea, in harbours or on the beach through photos, dates and location data to the University of Southern Mississippi Gulf Coast Research Laboratory. Try some for dinner! Sargassum is edible (in soup or stews, or raw when dried), and a high nutrition dense source of omegas.

Learn more at *gcrl.usm.edu/sargassum*

Note: Check these organisations out beforehand to find out more about the data collection methods. Even if you forget those details at the time, collect as much data as you can on the spot. Think of: **latitude/longitude,** *date/time, wind speed, wind direction, sea and air temperature. Take a photo or video if possible, and add any descriptive observations you can make during a sighting.*

Report plastic

What plastics do you see in the middle of the ocean? Report marine debris on the *Marine Debris Tracker* app or *Clean Swell* app.

Learn more at *marinedebris.engr.uga.edu.* and *OceanConservancy.org.*

Take water samples

You can help Adventure Scientists to study the sources, composition and distribution of **microplastics** pollution by taking samples of Atlantic ocean water.

Learn more at *AdventureScience.org.*

	DATE mm-dd-yyyy	TIME (UTC)	SAMPLE ID Micro-ww-mmddyyyy-sample#-boat name	LOCATION Latitude	(decimal) Longitude	WIND SPEED knots	WIND DIR.	WATER TEMP (c)
1	15/2/15	1:55		18 07 70	05 19 21.44	NNW		22.5
2	20/1/15	12.45	#Sea-ya	24°07 651	17°35 001	15	NNE	24,2
3	28/1/15	16.15	#Sea-ya	25°13 306	16°40 487	20	NE	26.5
4	3/2/15	13.10	#Sea-ya	38 23 500	11 23 762	18	NE	29,5
5	10/2/15	13.10	#Sea-ya	52 54 712	12°10 310	12	NE	30,5
6	14/2/15	16.40	#Sea-ya	59 30, 300	11°04 6.9	17	NE	31,5

Data collection sheet for the samples

Set up a measurement station

Team up with the SeaKeepers Society by becoming a Discovery Yacht and launching their Drifter or Argo Float instruments in the ocean! These devices collect temperature and salinity profiles up to 2,000 metres deep.

Learn more at *SeaKeepers.org.*

Report illegal fishing

Despite regulations, quotas, restricted and prohibited areas for fishing vessels, no enforcement eyes are out there. There is lots of illegal fishing going on, with ships simply turning off the (required to be on) **AIS** system. If you see a fishing vessel and you think it's suspicious act! If for example, it meets up with another boat, or if it's in a Marine Protected Area, you can track the navigational history of the vessel through Global Fishing Watch. Global Fishing Watch tracks and traces fishing boats based on their AIS. If it doesn't seem right, report it.

Sign up and learn more at *GlobalFishingWatch.org*.

16.7 FISH RESPONSIBLY

Fishing can be an exciting part of the Atlantic crossing—but catching is a different story! Many sailors like to fish. It's a better way to source your fish than buying them in cans, where we often don't know how and when it's been caught and mixed. You can enjoy the fishing experience while minimising your impact. Here are a few suggestions to bear in mind to help protect the marine life.

If you fish

- Fish with the right gear or not at all! Choose the right hook and line thickness. Ocean fish are big guys. A thin line will not hold and will end up at sea as a **ghost fishing** line.
- Do your research to find out if your catch is a threatened species or not—then either release or eat.
- Only catch and kill what you can eat.
  - Catch something you can't eat? Throw it back within seconds, not minutes.
  - Is it too big to eat? Throw it back!
- Kill the fish right away once you caught it. A handy trick is to spray alcohol in the gills. If you don't, the fish will suffer tremendously, and all that stress will affect the quality of the flesh. It's not healthy for the fish, or for you!
- If you fish near the islands:
  - Check the local situation and rules for species, size, and sustainability.
  - Spearfishing is prohibited almost everywhere in the Caribbean (except for often lionfish, which are an invasive species and need to be reduced for the ecosystem to be in balance).
  - Be aware that many fish in the Caribbean are poisonous.
- Wherever you are, take it easy on the bigger guys. We need them in the ocean! They eat the weak and sick ones to keep the system in balance.

Few are left because it takes so long for them to mature. The higher up in the food chain, the older the animal, the more contaminants have been built up. Tuna, swordfish, shark, cod or sea bass all have danger-ous levels of **mercury** and **PCB** accumulated in their bodies.

- By eating some species, you can even help the ecosystem, such as lionfish in the Caribbean. While they were a rare sight just ten years ago, the population is now out of control.

Don't get your hopes up too high. On my three crossings (combined), we caught a total of three fish that made it up to the dinner plate. In the pro-cess, we lost about ten lures and eight fishing lines that are all still floating around, '**ghost fishing**' somewhere in the ocean. Only **Neptune** knows if a dolphin or sea turtle may have gotten injured, entangled or killed by it. Or maybe the lines got stuck in a boat propeller. Every bit of fishing gear lost will continue to damage in the ocean. It will never disappear.

'Fish' for seaweed

We have a lot of food to choose from these days with healthier alterna-tives that still provide the same benefit without killing life. An exciting option I have found is consuming sea algae like kelp, nori, spirulina, dulse, and **Sargassum.** Hundreds of edible sorts of sea vegetables are known. Seaweeds are real super foods that mostly need sun and **current** to thrive. These vegetables of the sea are where fish get their omegas from in the first place. It's a healthier food choice for you and the ocean. And they just float by your boat!

16.8   RETHINK—REFUSE—REDUCE—RE-CHOOSE— REUSE- RECYCLE

Rethink

"We are living in an interminable succession of absurdities imposed by the myopic logic of short-term thinking."

— JACQUES YVES COUSTEAU

SECTION 4 – OCEAN LOVE & CONSERVATION

People often say 'you are what you eat.' I can certainly resonate with that. But it's not just that. You are also what you buy, use, put, wrap, and present yourself with. Making a difference and living sustainably is not just about having solar panels on the boat or roof (although that is a great investment to reduce reliance on fossil fuel!). Responsible living is about how you think, buy, plan and prepare, and where. Whether you go around the world or to the market around the corner, thinking ahead helps. Start questioning where things come from, how it has been made, and by who? Where do things go after we throw it 'away'? By making a shift in our thinking, and putting our inspector hat on, we can better engineer our lives to reduce our environmental impact. I can tell you many things. But the most fun and effective way to make a change is by finding out yourself! Sailing the Atlantic will give you that pause, to think, reflect, and plan for the way forward. Here is some food for thought:

RETHINK SHOPPING

Who do you give your money to? Do you help Mr. Supermarket CEO finance his second boat or are you bringing benefits directly to a family by shopping locally? Help to shorten the supply chain, which reduces transportation energy cost, use of packaging, and increases nutritional value, and benefits for those down at the bottom. Support the small entrepreneurs and go against mass consumerism. We live in a demand-driven society. Help the good brands, those without lobbying power and big advertisement budgets, to climb the ladder. Support the local coconut art and straw hats in the Caribbean. This is art that doesn't harm the environment. As opposed to jewelry made from turtles, corals or sharks. Besides, do you *need* to go shopping at all? If so, do you need to buy new clothes, gadgets and gear? Take over second-hand, borrow from the neighbour, save resources and things from the trash pile.
Rethink food

"We live on a planet where pigs eat more
fish than sharks and where the domestic house cat
eats more fish than all of the seal in
the North Atlantic Ocean."

– CAPTAIN PAUL WATSON

Where does your food come from? Do you know its source? The source is not the supermarket. It's the soil and the water that determines the quality (or harm) of the food. Rethink food recommendations. Who sponsors the food advice you're reading? Is there maybe a financial gain involved? Do you know what's in your processed food? Go find out! Consider and explore alternatives for the sake of your own and the planet's health.

RETHINK WASTE

How much waste do you generate each week? What is it? Food, packaging, paper? How much of that could you refuse, reduce, reuse or recycle? We all still use plastic bags, but not because we want them. We know it's not the way to go by now. We simply forget to bring reusable bags in the first place. Before you purchase something packaged in plastic, consider if you need it. If there's a different option, choose the one where you can reuse the packaging and don't have to toss it away. For example, take a toothbrush. With let's say eight tooth brushes per year, in a life of 30 years brushing my teeth I have thrown 'away' 240 toothbrushes (as well as the plastic wrappers they are packed in)! And that's just me! I can circle an ocean-worthy boat with that! Be creative and inventive. See what you can reuse, borrow, swap, buy second-hand or make yourself. Every piece of plastic ever made is still out there in some form. If you throw plastic away, there is no 'away.' We all have a desire for convenience. We organise a BBQ and can just throw the dishes away. It may save a few minutes of your time. But the effects of it cost us greatly. We do take-away but what do we do with the (often **styrofoam**) box it's delivered in? We order online and have another plastic taped box. We opt for one-time usage products like tampons, diapers, straws, bags and bottles because it's convenient, or the advertisement has made us believe it's convenient. We don't even know what's the alternative because we accept things as they come. Our system makes it difficult to make sustainable choices because money drives our society. Think about the journey things make before it arrives into your hands. What choices can you make to reduce the number and impact of those journeys? Not only plastic items make their impact. Glass, metals, wood, coal are also resources used to produce *things*. What can you do to reduce energy demands?

Another big waste is food. In the western world, an estimated one-third of the food we buy, we throw away. What a waste. How can we plan smarter than that? Here's something fun to try: Aim to continue seeing the bottom of the garbage bin (put the organics separately if you don't do so yet). How long can you manage?

RETHINK THE PAST

Before the 1960s the world was doing fine without plastics. There simply was no such thing as a plastic bag, diaper or shoe. Since then, it has found its way into every corner of our society. We have to think about alternatives that work. And support those accordingly. Think, what would your grandmother do?

Just wash the spoon—by Max Temkin

RETHINK ADVERTISING

'Eco,' 'sustainable', 'organic' or 'green' have become fashion words. In most countries, anyone can put that on there, and it can legitimately be sold. Question advertising messages. These messages are created for the purpose of selling, not saving the planet. Certifications are a step in the right direction but don't just take certified products for granted either. When a brand is a certified B-Corporation, it's using business as a force for social, environmental, and economic good, which is a positive step forward. Nevertheless, read labels, read stories, and ask questions. Advertisers are smart, and they know how to find you at the right spot.

RETHINK THE INVESTMENT

Sometimes organic is more expensive. Realise that it's only expensive in the short term. In the long run, it will be healthier for you, our children, and the planet because the soil is preserved and not damaged with harmful pesticides, herbicides and insecticides for the sake of volume and price. As much as you and I may live on a budget, cheaper is not always better. By supporting organic producers, we keep them in business, enabling them to bring more purity to the consumer and keep our soils healthy for the future. Also fun, invest in some seeds and basic materials and start growing food and making cosmetics yourself!

RETHINK ON WHAT MATTERS

For whom are you doing what you're doing? And why? What are the consequences of what you eat/drink/buy/do/plan for/work for, for the next ten minutes, ten months, ten years and 100 years? What impact do those actions make on yourself, our children, and the world as a whole? Instead of spending money, time and effort in keeping consumerism going, what can you do at the core? Work harder to earn more money so that you can buy organic (which unfortunately is often more expensive)? Or instead, use your time creating solutions and advocate to ban harmful practices, subsidize organic farmers to make it less expensive? Money, fun and 'owning' stuff are all temporary. Our impact will last beyond our lifetimes, so we better make it a good one!

> "The significant problems we have cannot
> be solved at the same level of thinking with
> which we created them.
>
> — ALBERT EINSTEIN

Thoughts become actions. What can you *do?*

Refuse

- An easy action we can take is to refuse single-use plastic. This is plastic that is used one time only. The most troublesome part of the plastic challenge is the magnitude of plastics we only use for a few minutes to eat, carry stuff, and take away. These single-use items have an average life span of 15 minutes and then are thrown 'away.' Only there is no such thing as 'away.' Where's away? Eventually the ocean. 50% of the plastic problem in the ocean is disposable plastic like plastic bags, water bottles, takeaway containers, cups and straws. This is a relatively easy problem to tackle. We don't *need* single-use plastic. Pro-actively say NO. With your drink order, ask for no straw. Refuse to accept a plastic or paper cup at the coffee machine or water cooler. With your shopping, say no to the plastic bag. Stay, don't take away; have your coffee or lunch on the spot. You can save a plastic item and have a nice chat! Refusal is easier in some countries than others—especially in developing countries you need to be equipped to be able to refuse. Be prepared and bring your reusable items.

- Refuse to buy cosmetics with plastic ingredients. Common ingredients are polyethene and polypropylene, polyethene terephthalate (PET), polymethyl methacrylate (PMMA), and nylon (PA)—and dozens more complicated plastic names are out there. These words are impossible to remember. Thankfully there is a great app to help. Use "Beat the Microbead", to check if your mascara, shower gel, toothpaste or sunscreen use plastic ingredients. Learn more at *BeattheMicrobead.com*.

- Refuse to accept that 'it's just the way it is'—it may used to be. Now we know more, have developed more, it doesn't have to be!

- Refuse to eat fish that are overexploited or endangered and explain why to the vendor or restaurant owner. Shark, whale, and bluefin tuna are still commonly found on the menu. More about seafood solutions further down.

Re-choose

Our greatest and most exciting individual power: the power of choice!
To a large degree, we can choose what to eat, drink, wear, believe, say, do,
create, and buy. We can choose with whom to play, talk, sail, date, marry.
Each choice comes with its consequences, good or bad. With an abundance of options in everything these days it's sometimes hard to choose,
isn't it? Do your best with whatever choice you make it's a good one for
you and the ocean! Not sure what the best option is? Explore, discover,
learn, and then choose.

Reduce

To be 100% is super tough (for now!), but we can drastically reduce our
usage. A few ideas to get you started:

REDUCE PLASTIC USE

Choose products made from natural fibres and materials. Immense
amounts of crude oil and chemicals are used to produce plastic, polyester, nylon and other synthetic materials for your backpack, clothes, and
technical gadgets. Not to mention the amount of waste generated. . . . All
sorts of plastics with complicated names exist: polyethylene terephthalate (PET) (bottles are made from this), polyvinyl chloride (PVC) (the garden hose, vinyl plates, pipes and fake 'leather' shoes are made from this),
polystyrene (Tupperware is made from this), polymethyl methacrylate
(windows are made from this), nylon (our clothes), polytetrafluoroeth-
ylene (PTFE/Teflon—the famous non-sticky pans)—they are all plastic!

- Place a filter in your washing machine. Did you know that with every
  wash of a synthetic cloth item, thousands of fibres end up in our
  waterways? I'm not even talking about the chemical colouring techniques (and labour efforts) used to produce our clothing. Synthetic
  (read: plastic) fibres act as a sponge for metals and chemicals. Fish
  see this as plankton, and the toxin-loaded fibre stays in the fish for
  months. Alternatives can include (organic!) cotton, hemp, bamboo, or
  eucalyptus. Learn more about this challenge on *Life-Mermaids.eu*.
- Particularly in the cosmetics department, we can reduce a lot on plastic waste. Almost all toiletries, like shampoo, toothpaste, or sunscreen,
  come in plastic packaging and are thrown 'away' once finished. Save

yourself and the ocean from toxins and plastic pollution. Buy natural shampoo in bulk bottles, get a block of soap instead of the liquid stuff. Or even better, make your own toothpaste, shampoo, moisturiser, facial cleaner or mosquito spray. Choose a hairbrush, hair ties, toothbrush and razor all made from other materials than plastic.

- Bring your own toothpicks. In many restaurants, toothpicks are individually wrapped in plastic. Be prepared and bring your own.
- Source food from places that use less packaging, like the local market or even better, grow your own.
- Filter water (with a filter on your tap or with a reusable water bottle)
- Bring your own bag, spoon, cup, and bottle, and keep saying *no*!
- If you order online, kindly request the sender to use as little packaging as possible, and without plastic tape. Demand minimal or better *no* packaging in general wherever you go. Buy from sellers located close to you to avoid a package going from a plane to a ship, to a ferry, to a truck, around the world.

REDUCE RESOURCES USE

- Cut down on power. Reduce your own carbon footprint by sourcing locally. Walk, bike, hike, share rides, take public transport, turn off the lights when not in use, switch to more efficient light bulbs, reduce airplane trips, reduce meat and fish intake, and waste less food. And hitch-sail the Atlantic Ocean where you must be very conservative with the resources you have on board. After this journey, you'll treat every drop of water like gold.
- Reduce the amount of paper you consume. Read online newspapers, brochures, blogs, e-books. Say no to the receipt at the ATM. Do you need a receipt for everything you buy? The paper is often bleached, and the ink is plastic. Paper often ends up with organics further polluting the soil. Save a tree so more carbon can be absorbed; keep it digital.
- A significant impact we can make is to reduce the number of babies we're making. Researchers calculated a reduction of 58 tons of **CO2** for each year of a parent's life, as compared to 2.4 tons by living car free, 0.21 through recycling, and 1.60 for a roundtrip Atlantic flight

(37). This study is based on people living in the Western world, consuming as an average westerner.

• Reduce buying new things. Our resources are finite.

REDUCE THE CHEMICALS

Cleaning products, cosmetic products and plastic products are often loaded with toxins, harmful for the ocean, and yourself. Why use them?

• **SUNSCREEN** The average sunscreen has lots of chemicals affecting corals, fish, and your own health. Some tourism destinations (for example Bonito in Brazil, and Palau in the Pacific) even prohibit sunscreen to protect nature since this product has already negatively affected the natural state of the destination. It's that destructive! Using biodegradable sunscreen is not only better for the environment, but it's also much better for you. Ingredients that are found to be biggest hormone disruptors are oxybenzone and octinoxate, and homosalate, octisalate, and octocrylene) (38). So, what to do? Do everything else right before applying sunscreen in the first place. Protect yourself from the sun with a cap, and clothing. Use sunscreen only when you have to. More and more biodegradable sunscreens are available on the market. Zinc oxide and titanium dioxide are working ingredients that are more ocean and human-friendly alternative. Finding one that does not *come* in plastic is the biggest challenge! Or just make your own.

• **SHAMPOO, SOAPS, AND LOTIONS** How many words do you see on the back of your shampoo that you can't even pronounce? Google them and educate yourself. All the fragrances, chemicals and other stuff the big corporations put into our shampoo, shower gel, make-up, and mosquito spray may smell great but are loaded with harmful toxins that end up in our waterways and bodies. We often assume that if it's on the shelves or if it says 'natural', it should be okay, right? It's not. The cosmetic industry is shockingly little regulated. Luckily there are many real natural cosmetics out there. They are only not penetrated into the big supply chains. You could get a block of soap instead of the liquid stuff. Or even better, make your own toothpaste, shampoo, moisturiser, facial cleaner or mosquito spray.

- **CLEANING PRODUCTS** What about aggressive cleaning products? They work so well! Aside from the residue that stays on the floor where you walk or on the **galley** counter where you put your food, we just wash it down. Where does it go then? The ocean! With a combination of vinegar, baking soda and cold pressed plant oils, we can clean almost anything!
- **OUTDOOR GEAR** Many outdoor brands produce clothing with **PFCs,** a highly toxic chemical which has now been found in the highest snow peaks, waterways and ocean. Check *detox-outdoor.org* to learn how green or pollutive your favourite outdoor brand is.

REDUCE THE TRASH PILE

Our world is filling up with trash at an exponential rate. I can't even be sure if that water bottle floating around the ocean wasn't formerly used by me! Either way, the planet is everyone's. Everyone should take care. Reduce plastic in the ocean by helping clean up. The ocean is downhill from everything. Wind and water ways bring it in. If you see it on the ground, take the opportunity to pick it up, preventing it from ending up in the oceans.

A few initiatives to make cleaning up more fun, easy and impactful:

- Take3forthesea. Collect three trash pieces every day you go out and play. Tim Silverwood sailed through the great Pacific garbage patch and realised something had to be done! He founded #Take3fortheSea with a simple message: take three pieces of rubbish with you when you leave the beach, waterway, or . . . anywhere. If you do this every day, you can save thousands of pieces of trash from ending up at sea. Simple but impactful. Imagine what we can accomplish if everyone does this. Learn more at *Take3.org*.
- Join a beach clean-up or organise one! Check #CleanSwell on social media for inspiration.
- Document what and where you find.
- Become a Trash Hero (*TrashHero.org)*
- Order your 'Trash Hunter Kit' and help to identify where it comes from in the first place. Who are the producers and who are the polluters? Learn more at *TrashHunters.org*.

Reuse

As we have already learned, the problem with plastic waste is that it doesn't go away. Before you toss something away at all, perhaps the item can serve another purpose?

Packaging is a big waster. Reuse packaging when you can. Reuse the peanut box, pill jar, spice pots, or zip-lock cereal bags to store other items. Old pill jars are especially useful when travelling. Reuse plastic bags as garbage bags.

To be able to refuse plastic, you should be equipped with something you can reuse. We can all make a huge difference by being prepared with **reusables.** Going to a friend's BBQ party where 'throw away' is usually the norm'? Bring your own cutlery, plate, cup and straw. You will surely make an entrance, and it's a great conversation starter. Make it a habit of

Reusable alternatives for single use plastic

bringing your **reusables** items wherever you go. By being well-prepared, you can avoid 'having' to accept hundreds of plastic items. Hit the road with a spoon, fork, knife (or spork), straw, bag, cup, a storage container for takeaway, refillable bottle and filtered bottle.

Reusable lifesavers

BOTTLES

Access to drinkable tap water might be normal at home, but in many countries buying plastic bottled water has become the norm. It already makes a great difference to have a reusable drinking bottle with you all the time. At home, at your office, and especially during your travels. If you don't like the taste of tap water, put a filter on it. This might be the best investment for your health too. In addition to a refillable bottle, a *filter*- jug, -bottle or -straw can be a lifesaver. Especially on boats on during travels where portable refill options are rare. With a filtered water bottle, I can scoop water from the dirtiest river and drink it. I can drink water from any tap or source (except for salty water). Using a filter bottle has saved me from adding hundreds of plastic bottles to the trash pile, in just one month! The market has plenty of different filter bottles, jugs and straws available.

BAGS

In many western countries, you now have to pay 10 cents for a plastic bag. In the developing world, you have to say NO 10 times to avoid them. Bring a bag or two whenever you go shopping. If you do end up with a plastic bag in your hands, re-use it, for as long as you can.

STRAWS

The plastic straw is in the top six of single use plastics found in the ocean. It's a routine add-on in most of the world. By proactively showing up with your reusable straw you can say no to many plastic ones. This is especially great when you are in a coconut or cocktail country! Many options are out there: stainless steel, bamboo, glass and silicon. Heck, you can even use the branch of a papaya tree as a straw. Using my stainless steel straw has saved me hundreds of plastic ones. And have given me dozens of awareness raising conversations! Make it a habit.

BOTTOM UNITS

For the parents An average baby uses seven diapers a day. Assuming the little one is potty-trained by age two—that's over 5,000 diapers! After newspapers and packaging, diapers are the largest disposable item in our trash pile. Did you know that disposable diapers also have plastic in them? Every single disposable diaper ever used is still out there. The poo may be organic, but most diapers are not. Get some cool shark, dolphin, star or coconut printed cloth diapers, saving money, energy, toxins and waste. And your kid will look super cool in his unique outfit.

For the girls Women use an estimated 11,000 tampons or sanitary pads in a lifetime. The average pad contains as much plastic as four carrier bags. Most tampons contain plastic. Most tampons are bleached. We don't consciously eat plastic or bleach. Why would we want to put it in our bodies? And waterways? We can reduce plastic and chemicals in our ocean, and save a lot of money by choosing alternatives. What's a better solution? A reusable menstruation cup or pad. You can insert it like a tampon, you can still climb masts and dance like with a tampon—but you only need *one*. You can reuse it, over and over again. Try it! Please ditch the tampon—and if you really can't, at least use the organic tampons.

Recycle

Even if you dispose of your waste correctly, you never know where it will end up, so recycle where you can even before generating the waste! Compared to making a new plastic product, recycling uses less water, fossil fuel and resource extraction. But don't forget, plastic can only be down-cycled.

I'm talking a lot about plastic here, but another type of product with huge environmental impact is tech gear. It's called e-waste. Bring your old tech stuff to dealers that can use the parts. Or sell it. Apple has a recycling program, as well as most other tech brands. Please don't just throw it 'away.'

Products made from recycled-something are better than new. It helps to create awareness, *but,* it's not the solution! Eventually, it will still add to the trash pile. Rethink, refuse, reuse, reduce, recycle . . . and if no other option . . . waste.

16.9 CREATE CONTENT AND CAMPAIGN

*"Anyone who thinks people lack originality should
watch them folding road maps."*

– FRANKLIN P. JONES
(Engineer)

Create stories, photos, and videos and share your Atlantic Ocean experience with the world. The Atlantic Ocean crossing is a journey of inspiration, learning and gaining lots of new insights. Sharing the magic of the ocean will inspire, educate and increase awareness! For those living in the cities or far away from the sea, they don't see or realise the current state of the ocean, and will just keep going as they are. You can help to change attitudes and behaviour by sharing your experience!

Set up your online playground

You can spread the word via social media channels, an email newsletter, or you can even start a website. It can be set up in minutes. To help you get started with a website I have created a list of handy tools. Find them at *Oceannomad.co/resources.*

My online outlet is Oceanpreneur.co When WiFi allows, I share ocean adventure and conservation updates on my Instagram, Twitter, Facebook, and YouTube (@oceanpreneur). By doing all this, I hope to inspire for adventure and help people to take action!

Contribute content to apps and websites, and social media

More and more sailors navigate the seas through apps on their phones or tablets. Numerous sailor- platforms exist (for example Navionics, Noonsite, or ActiveCaptain) where you can add data about that ship-wreck, awesome viewpoint, happy hour or anchoring situation. Inform fellow sailors with relevant info, so they won't anchor right on a seagrass bed or disturb the **Marine Protected Area** with a noisy wake-boarding session. Write positive and negative reviews on anchorages to highlight good practices and discourage bad ones.

Learn more at *Navionics.com, ActiveCaptain.com,* and *Noonsite.com.*

Raise your voice & get involved

"The best way to predict the future
is to create it."

— PETER DRUCKER
(Author)

Think about what you can do with your skills and resources to make this world a better place. If you can read, write, talk and travel, you are blessed with a capacity to do great things for the people and the planet, not just for profit. Mingle and connect with individuals and organisations to make things happen. Get involved with an ocean organisation. Or why not start a project in your own town to ban the bottles, straws and bags?

We cannot wait for politicians to take the lead. They are too busy on a local scale instead of with the environmental problems on a greater scale.

Ideas to be heard

- Tell the restaurant owner why you choose not the have the bluefin tuna 'fish of the Day'. Perhaps he doesn't realise it's a bad thing.
- Fish can't speak. We must speak for them. The more we talk about the ocean, plastic, overfishing, all the ocean issues and its urgency, the more businesses and governments know we care, and the sooner they will act.
- Befriend and represent your favourite marine species. Let the world hear from them. Learn more on *TheTerramarProject.org/species*.
- Set up and sign petitions on *Change.org*. Signatures become victories!
- Write to your favourite brands to ask if they can provide the product in an alternative to plastic. Better yet, tell them on social media that you won't be buying the product any more until they do!
- Use your social media power to share what you learn, discover and explore. Encourage action and inspire your friends and followers to make good choices. Use local hashtags and location features on Instagram, Twitter or Facebook. You'll surely inspire someone.
- Share your ocean action and inspire the world via *1000oceanactions.org*.

16.10 SUPPORT OCEAN ADVOCATES & INITIATIVES

"Our problems are manmade—therefore, they can be solved by man. And man can be as big as he wants. No problem of human destiny is beyond human beings."

— JOHN F. KENNEDY
(35th U.S. President)

Support the politicians who take action on climate change. Use your right to vote. Many great things are done for the ocean. Support ocean conservation groups, influencers and their initiatives. Share their posts on social media, retweet, mention them. Instead of keeping the corporate world going, these advocates invest all their time for the benefit of the whole planet. Many of them are driven by dedication but are held back because of lack of funds. Donations and support from the public can help the change-makers to make more impact.

Discover and support innovative entrepreneurs on Kickstarter, Indiegogo, Patreon and Etsy. The most brilliant ideas show up that need support from the crowd, like Bakeys, who makes edible disposables, or Seabin, who created a bin that automatically cleans the sea. To raise funds for this book, I ran my own crowd funding campaign. To design the book cover, I ran a crowdsourcing contest. The support from the crowd has helped tremendously in making my own splash by getting this book out.

16.11 ORGANISE A HARBOUR CLEANUP

Organise a harbour clean-up with your **pontoon** or harbour. It will not only clean up the ocean, but it will also create awareness in the local community. In Las Palmas, pontoon L joined forces one day to clean up the marina. The wind had shifted, and the marina was full of trash.

Harbour Clean Up leaders Marjo & Edwin

16.12 CONNECT & TEAM UP

What has activated me the most to save the ocean is the inspiration from people around me. During the ocean adventure, you will have the opportunity to meet so many ocean-minded people with different backgrounds but a shared love for the ocean. This has given me so many insights about the ocean and our role in it as everyday citizens. Offline I've met the greatest people, but it has also become easier and easier to connect online, to follow and reach out to ocean scientists, ambassadors, athletes and anyone else that we can team up with to save the ocean.

16.13 BE AN INSPIRATION AND EXAMPLE

"Be the change you wish to see in the world."

– MAHATMA GANDHI
(champion of nonviolence and truth)

Perhaps the biggest challenge in ocean conservation is to win the hearts, minds and commitment of the people. We must not only focus on humanity but on every living being on our planet. We are all interconnected. We're all on a journey, and we all have our unique qualities when it comes to making a difference.

- Inspire your captain and community to make small lifestyle changes, by being a living example and taking small positive actions.
- Encourage marinas and yacht facility places to offer recycling facilities.
- Inspire fellow crew and captain, and your family and friends back home with what you see and learn.
- Encourage and educate people to make changes in their (single) plastic use by showing alternatives and setting the right example (re-usable bottles, canvas bags).
- Be an example in communities where awareness is low. Be mindful of your actions and purchases on the islands. Cruise ships, sailboats, (a lack of) local awareness on environmental problems, (a lack of) regulation and enforcement, and a lack of facilities and resources all takes its toll on the environment.

*Thoughtful travel take-away: Especially in Cape Verde and the Caribbean, local awareness about plastic and pollution is far behind the western world. Not everyone has access to education and the internet. Stuff we don't want in the western world or ingredients that are prohibited, now are shipped to more developing countries that don't have '**BPA**' or '**microplastic**' free regulations in place yet. Small Island Developing States (SIDS) with little resources and little waste management facilities in place have to manage the stuff that 'we' have thrown in there. The crappy plastic wrapped 'food' is often sold cheaper than the locally grown fruits, veggies, spices and nuts, because of (western-led) consumer demand. I hope to see more local people eating their 'oh so delicious' local produce, on a banana leaf, with a reusable fork. Wishful thinking? Maybe. But that's how it used to be. You can help to set the example by opting for local purchases, bring your own bag, and make a chat to increase awareness.*

- Be an ambassador for the ocean. Join forces with ocean conservation organisations.
- Increase your reach by participating in brand campaigns and using hashtags on your messages on Twitter and Instagram. Check: #awaveofchange #beneaththewaves #take3forthesea #5gyres #makeAsplash #Splash4theOcean #cleanswell #iamacarbonpirate.
- Practice what you preach.

Above all, love the ocean every day, and do the best you can to make it healthy again.

16.14 DIVE BELOW THE SURFACE

"The best way to observe a fish is to become a fish"

— JACQUES YVES COUSTEAU

An exciting part of sailing is dropping anchor in remote bays and to dive in! Learn how to snorkel, freedive or dive! Then spend as much time doing that as you can.

How can you contribute with diving?

- Reef—Help to collect data on the state of the reefs. Do a marine biology or science-based dive. Catch and learn about the invasive lionfish. Learn more at *Reef.org.*
- Help to survey and monitor the health of coral reefs. Nearly every destination worldwide has a reef check partner. Learn more at *ReefCheck.org.*
- Adopt a dive site and be an ocean steward for your local site. Learn more at Project AWARE, a conservation organisation that focuses on shark conservation and marine debris: *ProjectAware.org.*

Thoughtful take-away: Just look, don't touch or chase wildlife. Don't touch manta rays, shake hands with sea turtles, or pick up sea stars for the sake of a selfie. No one is picking you up while you sleep, right? They can get stressed and sick. Keep a minimum distance of one metre at all times to stay in the safe zone.

Mermaid time

16.15 GREEN YOUR DIET

One of the most impactful choices we can make every day for our own health and the ocean is what we put into our bodies. Our planet simply does not have the capacity to feed all of us the way we are consuming now. With estimates that 45% of all the land mass on Earth is used to raise animals for eating and milking, it's an understatement that we are putting pressure on the capacity of our planet (39). We've all been told since we were kids that we need meat, fish, and dairy. Now with more people and more knowledge, it has become evident that these foods are what we should not eat if we want to sustain the health of our ocean and our health (40).

Meat and dairy choice

Animal agriculture is a planet destructive and polluting industry. Eating just one meat dish has a bigger negative impact on the environment than your long-haul flight (41). One milk cow produces as much greenhouse gas in one day as a car that drives 70,000km (42). By not eating meat and dairy, you reduce your personal carbon footprint by at least 50% and even save over a thousand litres of water every single day (40).

I never liked meat. When I was a kid, I had to sit at the table until I finished my plate, but I just couldn't swallow it. Usually, I managed to sneak the meat away by putting it in my pocket or under my tongue and then going to the bathroom (until I was finally busted!). So cutting that one out was easy. Since, I sometimes ate it only because I assumed I needed it. The cheese was the tough part. As a Dutchy, cheese was all around me! Oh boy, and how I loved it. I was eating about a pound of cheese each week! I thought it would be impossible to cut that out—but knowing what I know now, not only the fact that it has a big impact on the environment but also how bad dairy is for our own health, it's a breeze to say no to that milk and cheese. It has made me discover so many other exciting food options. It's a journey, but a motivating one when you learn more about this oh-so-important topic.

Seafood choice

Should you still eat fish? The nutritional advice says to eat fish. It is a good protein with healthy omega-3 oils. Only our ocean doesn't have the capacity to deal with our hunger for fish anymore. We're simply fishing faster than the fish can rejuvenate. If you don't live on a small remote island or on an iceberg, you are most likely not dependent on fish for survival. In the long run, we are *all* dependent on the ocean for survival. Be compassionate and conscious about your choices for a healthy future for all. As consumers, we can shape the demand and supply for seafood by making the best choices we support ocean health.

But we do need the protein, healthy fats and irons, right? Today we have an abundance of food options available that offer the nutrition you need with little impact on the environment. Eating animals is no longer essential, it's a choice. And with each meal, the choice of what you eat is the number one factor contributing to climate change (40). Just start by learning more about the topics through books, studies and documentaries. With knowledge and awareness comes action. Make it about progress, not perfection.

Find book and documentary recommendations on *Oceannomad.co/resources* to educate yourself more about this topic.

Seamoss—a popular food in the Caribbean and a pure source of omegas and protein

16.16 OFFSET YOUR FOOTPRINT

The key is to reduce our carbon footprint. A carbon offset is a reduction in **CO2** emissions made, to compensate for the emissions we make by using the engine, flying into the harbour, or purchasing that eBook reader. It is not the solution, but it is a way to help address the imbalance that our daily lives have on our environment. You can compensate for the time you or a fellow boating buddy accidentally anchored in seagrass, not knowing that it's utterly important in the ecosystem.

Two offset ideas

- Adopt a coral with the Nature Conservancy (*Nature.org)* or Coral Restoration Foundation Bonaire (*crfbonaire.org*), or through a local initiative that isn't on the internet.

- Plant seagrass. Seagrasses occupy 0.1% of the seafloor, yet are responsible for absorbing 11% of the carbon buried in the ocean. Seagrass beds, mangroves, and coastal wetlands absorb carbon at a rate two to four times greater than tropical forests (43). Learn more at *SeagrassGrow.org*.

16.17   EDUCATE THE KIDDOS

Children are the future leaders and our biggest hope for change. Shifting behaviour patterns in adults who have created habits over many years can take generations, but the younger generations can create the right habits from the start. Take your kids, nephews, nieces, and friends out to the ocean. We protect what we love, and they will love it.

Suzanna, Turkish—English?" Nilsu, my 7-year-old neighbour, asks if I can open the Google translator. She speaks few words of English, and I speak few words of Turkish. But that's no problem! We have become good buddies via hand signals, facial expressions, and Google. She starts typing: "bugun icin tesekkur ederim. Denizin alti cok cok guzel yosunlar baliklar" Google says: "I thank you for today. Very, very beautiful golden algae fish in the sea." She smiles and gives me a hug. This week I helped Nilsu to get comfortable in the funderwaterzone. Where first she was afraid to go where she could not stand, she now happily takes off into the blue sea. Sometimes even without the inflatable crocodile! This is definitely the highlight of my week! She is discovering the magical world below the surface . . . As well as the trashed state the world is in. Nilsu, me and the crocodile have gone on some ocean exploration adventures. We discovered the 'golden fish' and . . . plastic! "Suzanne, plastic problem," and she points to an ice-cream wrapper floating by. She insists upon swimming there ASAP to get it out of there. Earlier, I showed her a few photos of my ocean explorations, including those of trashed beaches and fish nibbling plastic. It seems like this has triggered something. Not just her activism, but also her creativity. From one plastic bag, she makes a handle for the crocodile, haha! A future leader in the making!

~~~~~~

16.18 LEARN

> *"Knowing is the key to caring, and with caring, there is hope that people will be motivated to take positive actions."*

— SYLVIA EARLE

Never stop learning. The more we know, the better decisions we can make for our health and the oceans. Go on an expedition, watch films, Google, learn how to swim, dive, snorkel, or surf. Learn about places, cultures, environmental and social challenges. Take courses on sustainability, the galaxy, geography, food and oceans. Watch TEDx talks, listen to podcasts, read books, and watch documentaries (check the appendix for a complete list of ocean-related documentaries).

Look for MOOCs (Massive Open Online Courses). These are free, and it's pretty amazing to attend and to interact with dozens of other attendees from all over the world.

All sorts of MOOCs are out there on for example marine litter, sustainable living, climate change, ocean exploration, piracy, etc.

Find recommendations on courses and MOOC platforms on *Oceannomad.co/resources.*

16.19 EXPLORE MORE

> *"By replacing fear of the unknown with curiosity, we open ourselves up to an infinite stream of possibility. We can let fear rule our lives, or we can become childlike with curiosity, pushing our boundaries, leaping out of our comfort zones, and accepting what life puts before us."*

—ALAN WATTS
(Philosopher and motivational speaker)

We can do good and have fun at the same time. Enjoy every moment of being out there, connect with nature and realise how amazingly blessed we are to live on such a beautiful planet. This keeps us energised to keep going. Sometimes it can be a bit depressing to see, learn and experience the exploitation of people and our planet, but don't let this spoil your life now. We only have one life. Make it a good one! Not just for yourself, for everyone and every living being still to come on this planet.

16.20 CELEBRATE!

Celebrate your actions! Now is the time to act but now is also the time to live! Despite the challenges, there is so much beauty all around us. We don't know what will happen tomorrow so let's make the most out of every moment. Be present and mindful. By celebrating the little wins, we will stay energised to keep us going for the greater goal.

THANK YOU

I hope this book has excited and informed you for ocean adventure travel. I could put so much more information and ideas in here, but part of the adventure is the exploration into the unknown. So, whatever information you have not been able to find in here, explore and discover! Don't forget to check out more tips and goodies I've created and keep creating on *Oceannomad.co/resources*.

Thank YOU for having read Ocean Nomad.

I will revisit the information in the book and make updates over time. Your feedback will help to make more impact and make the next version better. I appreciate your honest review on Goodreads, Amazon, iTunes, or wherever else you bought the book, or you can email your book feedback to me directly at ahoy@oceannomad.co If you would like to recommend this book to a friend you can refer them to www.oceannomad.co, where they can purchase the book in their preferred format.

I'd love to connect with you as a fellow ocean nomad. You can find me on the socials at @Oceanpreneur. I'm on Facebook, Twitter, Pinterest, Instagram, YouTube, LinkedIn, and Patreon.

—Suzanne

OCEAN NOMAD COMMUNITY

Join the Ocean Nomad community to connect, receive support, interact and meet up with fellow nomadic ocean adventure seekers.

Find the tribe via Oceannomad.co/mmunity

APPENDIX & RESOURCES

MEASUREMENT CONVERSIONS

1 foot (ft) = 0.3048 metre (m)
1 metre (m) = 3.28084 feet (ft)
1 ton = 1,000 kilogram (kg)
1 gallon (gl) = 3.78541 liter (l)
1 knot (1kn) = 1 nautical mile (NM)
1 mile (on land) = 0.868976 nautical miles
1,000 metre = 0.539957 nautical miles
1 nautical mile = 1,852 metres or 1.15 land miles
1 nautical mile = 1 minute (' — or arcmin)
1 degree (°) = 60 minute.
60 minutes = 60 nautical miles
Celcius (°C) to Fahrenheit (°F): °F = (°C x 1.8) + 32
Fahrenheit (°F) to Celcius (°C): °C= (°F – 32) x 1.8

ABBREVIATIONS

AIS Automatic Identification System. Tracking system to avoid a collision at sea. AIS receiver is the minimum needed. Most boats also transmit signals.

ARC Atlantic Rally for Cruisers

ARC+ Atlantic Rally for Cruisers with a stop in Cape Verde (leaves earlier than the ARC)

CO2 "C" stands for carbon, "O" stands for oxygen, so carbon dioxide is often called "C-O-2, and written "CO2." CO2 is a gas. It is invisible and very important for the ecosystem.

COG Course Over Ground

EPIRB Emergency Position Indicating Radio Beacon. When this device is activated (either by sinking or manually) a signal will be send to rescue authorities with the distress location.

ETA Estimated Time of Arrival

FT Foot/feet 1 foot (ft) = 0.3048 metre.

GPS Global Positioning System. A navigational system using satellite signals to fix the location of a boat, or any other unit carrying a 'GPS.

MOB Man Over Board

MMSI Maritime Mobile Service Identity. A nine-digit unique number to a **VHF** radio.

MPA Marine Protected Area. The nature parks of the sea.

NM Nautical Miles. A nautical mile measures distance. Nautical miles are used for navigation. A nautical mile is equal to one minute of **latitude** on **longitude.** One nautical mile is equal to 1,852 metres or 1.15 land miles

NOAA National Oceanic and Atmospheric Administration. A resource for Atlantic weather reporting.

PCBs Poly Chlorinated Biphenyls. Toxic chemical. Banned a long time ago but still present in soil and waters.

PLB Personal Locator Beacon, a personal **EPIRB**—registered to the boat, you can carry in your pocket or hang around your neck.

SOG Speed Over Ground

STCW10 Standards of Training, Certification and Watch keeping for Seafarers. This is a basic safety certificate where you learn about personal safety and survival, firefighting, first aid/CPR, and personal safety and social responsibility.

TSS Traffic Separation Scheme

VHF radio Very High-Frequency radio used for communication between boats and ports in coastal zones. Maximum range usually about 20–25 miles maximum.

GLOSSARY

Anti-Cyclone A high-pressure weather system around which air slowly circulates clockwise. As opposed to cyclones, anticyclones are linked to calm and nice weather.

Beaufort Used to express wind speed in weather forecasting.

Beneteau A French boat builder that has a substantial worldwide market share in sailing yachts.

Berth A bed on a boat or the parking spot of a boat.

Bunk Bed on a boat. Also called berth.

Bilge The area at the bottom of the hull of a boat where water collects. This must be pumped out regularly.

Bimini Cover for the cockpit of a boat protecting from sun and wind.

Biofuel Fuel produced from an organic material including plant materials and animal waste. Palm oil is now becoming a popular source of **biofuel,** and it comes with all sorts of problems, such as deforestation, habitat destruction of the last orangutans, and indigenous rights violations.

Black water Waste water from the toilet.

Block A device used to change the angle of a line.

Bow The front of a boat.

Bowline The most useful knot on a boat (and in life). This knot won't go untied if there's no pull.

Callaloo A Caribbean 'spinach like' superfood brought from Africa.

Catamaran A boat with two hulls.

Charter An organised commercial sailing trip for which you pay to join.

Cleat hitch OXO To tie a line to a cleat.

Clove hitch This is a handy knot because it can be tied quickly and adjusted easily. It's used for securing fenders.

Cleat The unit used to secure a rope for a sail or when berthing Often from metal.

Coconut Tropical power drink and food. Number one reason to love the tropics.

Cockpit The seating area around / in front the steering wheel or tiller.

Crew Everyone on the boat except for the captain. As crew you help with whatever needs to be done to operate the boat.

Cruising Leisurely kind of sailing.

Cruising chute Big asymmetric light wind sail. Also called asymmetric **spinnaker** or gennaker.

Current A body of water moving in a definite direction, through a surrounding body of water in which there is less movement. A current in the ocean is generated by forces acting upon this flow, such as breaking waves, wind, the Coriolis effect, temperature and salinity differences. A current is different than tides, which are caused by the gravitational pull of the Sun and Moon.

DanBuoy   MOB pole = Man Over Board Pole. This is a pole that will float and drift with the person overboard. It makes it easy to locate the position of the man over board.

Dead zone   Zone in the ocean where no life exists at all anymore due to a lack of oxygen.

Deck   The flat top of the boat.

Delivery   Bringing a boat from A to B

Degrees N   Degrees North / Latitude

Degrees W   Degrees West / Longitude

Dinghy   Little inflatable boat to reach shore when on anchorage

Dock walking   Walking the docks in harbour and marinas with the aim to find a crew spot.

Down wind   With the wind coming from 'behind.'

Dry boat   A boat that does not allow alcohol when sailing.

Engine Room   The area where the engine is located.

Fenders   Boat bumpers. Usually air filled protectors you hang on the **guardrail** to protect the boat.

Figure-eight knot   Mostly used to make a stopper at the end of the line, preventing it from going out of a block.

Flares   An intense light or heat without an explosion. Flares are used for signalling, illumination in the event of an emergency or fog.

Forestay   A piece of standing rigging that keeps a mast from falling backwards.

Foul Weather Gear   Water and wind proof sailing apparel designed to keep seaman dry and warm from rain, spray, and wind.

Furling   Many boats have a roller furling **headsail.** It can 'furl' a sail by rolling it up.

Galley   The kitchen in a boat.

Ghost fishing   Lost fishing gear drifting in the ocean. Ghost fishing nets are one of the biggest killers of wildlife living in or near the ocean. Fish get tangled or trapped.

Genoa   A large **jib** sail at the front of the boat.

Goosewing   Sailing with two **headsails,** one on each side, often **poled** out. Figure out what that means!

Grab bag   The bag to grab in case of emergency disembarkation. It should be easily accessible and include communication tools, sun/wind protection, food, water and medical supplies.

Grey tank   The waste water tank from the sink and shower. Sometimes filtered. Sometimes not

Grib file   A free low kilobyte weather forecast you can download at sea with the **sat phone.**

Grog   Cape Verdean rum. It's the countries' national drink made from sugarcane, citrus and clove. It comes in all sorts of variations.

Guardrail   The railing around the boat that prevents from falling off.

Gust   A sudden peak in wind speed.

Headsail   A front sail.

Heading   The angle of the vessel to an object (e.g., true north). It is the direction in degrees that you are moving.

Heads   The toilet on the boat.

Helm   The steering tiller or wheel.

Hitch-sailing   Spontaneous crewing on a strangers' sailboat. Whether you have sailing experience or not, whether you contribute money or not, whether you found the boat in advance online or locally in the harbour, it's hitch-sailing.

Hoist   Verb used to bring the sails up.

Hurricane   Tropical Cyclonic storm with force 12 on the Beaufort Wind scale.

Island time   Being and doing at slow pace.

Jackstays   Lines from bow to **stern** on both port and **starboard** side where you can clip onto with your safety harness. A safety measure to prevent you from falling over board.

Jib   A triangular sail at the front of the boat.

Jibe   To shift from one side to the other when running before the wind—putting the **stern** of the boat through the wind (as opposed to a **tack** where the bow goes through the wind).

Ketch   A two-masted boat with the shorter mast, the mizzen, at the **stern** ahead of the wheel.

Knot   Wind, as well as boat speed, are indicated with 'knots.' A knot is one nautical mile per hour.

Latitude   Shows location north or south of the equator, measured in degrees (The horizontal lines on the chart)

Lee cloth   This is a net or cloth next to your bed to prevent you from falling out.

Leeward   The side sheltered or away from the wind

Leeward Islands   The islands that stretch from St. Maarten through Dominica.

Levante   Strong warm eastern wind coming from the Sahara.

Life jacket   A jacket that will keep you afloat in the unlikely event of falling over board. Life jackets should at least have a light, reflector and spray hood. It's an important personal safety measure.

Lime (to)   To chillax in the Caribbean.

Log(book)   A paper record of events in the management, operation, and navigation of a ship are written in the logbook.

Longitude   Shows location in the East or West Distance measured in degrees, relative to the Greenwich meridian. (The vertical lines on the chart)

MAYDAY   Distress alert to be made (only!) when immediate help is needed for the vessel you're on. And life is endangered.

Mainsail   The principal sail located behind the main mast of a sailing vessel.

Mercury   A heavy metal accumulating in fish and in high numbers dangerous to human health

Meridian   Any line of **longitude.**

Mess   The eating place below deck.

Microplastic   Particles of plastic smaller than 1mm in size.

Mizzen   The aft mast on a boat with two or more masts.

Minute   1 nautical mile on a chart. Degrees on charts (of which the earth has 360 degrees of **longitude**) are broken into 60 "minutes.

Monohull   Boat with one keel.

Navigation desk   The table with the charts and navigation tools. Also called chart table.

Mooring   A place to park the boat. Mooring is often referred to when attaching the boat to a mooring buoy.

Neptune   The god of the sea.

Northern hemisphere   The half of the planet earth north of the equator.

Not under command   Vessels not under command are unable to manoeuvre as required because of exceptional circumstance. They are granted special privileges, and other vessels must keep out of the way.

Ocean Acidification   The change of the pH (numeric indicator of alkalinity or acidity) in the ocean. When the ocean absorbs CO_2 from the atmosphere, a chemical reaction occurs that makes the water more acidic. This process is called ocean acidification.

Passage making   A voyage that requires navigation, planning, **seamanship,** sea-readiness, and competent seamanship.

PAN PAN   Emergency on the **VHF** radio, but no life-threatening situation.

Personal AIS Locator Beacon   This is a personal GPS tracking device that can locate you in the unlikely event that you fall over board.

Peso   Currency used in many Spanish speaking countries.

Phytoplankton   Tiny little sea weeds acting in the same way in the sea as tree leaves do on land.

Pilot   Sailors guide book usually has info on anchorages, marina's, sailing regions and passages.—Usually called a cruising guide. A pilot is a person who assists a commercial vessel into a harbour or port and charges a fortune to do so. Some vessels have to be guided in by a pilot usually if over 120' long.

Pole   Stick from the mast to sail to create a stronger rig.

Pontoon   A floating dock where boats are 'berthed'

Point of Sail   A term used to describe a sailing boats orientation in relation to the current wind direction.

Polymers   Plastic is made from processed oil and exists as a chain of molecules called polymers. The special property of the polymers is the large size of their molecules. These "super molecules" allow for bending, and for adding different types of chemicals.

Port side   The left-hand side on a boat when facing forward.

Rally   A sailing race, either competitive or leisurely.

Reef   1. Under water coral formation. 2. Reducing the size of the sails

Reusables   Items we can reuse to minimise waste (bottle, straw, plate, spork, cup)

Rig   'To rig the boat' is referred to as getting the boat ready. The rigging of a vessel is the system of masts and lines.

Rudder   The underwater attachment that controls the direction of the boat. The steering wheel or tiller **controls the rudder.**

Run   Going with the wind. Also called '**downwind**'. The wind comes from behind when 'running.'

Sargassum   A type of large brown seaweed

Satellite phone   A communication system using satellite that can send and receive data (calls, texts and sometimes email) when you're out of the coastal radio zone. A safety measure.

Seacocks   The valves which go through the holes in the hull (for waste water discharge and pumping up seawater).

Schooner   A sailing vessel with two or more masts, characteristically with the foremast smaller than the mainmast and no taller than the **mizzen** if there is one.

Seamanship   Weather, emergency, navigation, and technical aspects

Sécurité   Navigation warning on the **VHF** radio.

Sextant   Navigational instrument

Sheet   The control line for a sail.

Sock   The tube of a **spinnaker** or cruising chute sail.

Stern   The back of the boat.

Stay sail   A triangular sail between two masts.

Schengen Visa   Allows you to travel freely between 26 European countries that signed the treaty. These countries are Austria, Belgium, Czech Republic, Denmark, Estonia, Finland, France, Germany, Greece, Hungary, Iceland, Italy, Latvia, Liechtenstein, Lithuania, Luxembourg, Malta, Netherlands, Norway, Poland, Portugal, Romania, Slovakia, Slovenia, Spain, Sweden, and Switzerland.

SSB radio   Communication system that has large reach when out on the ocean.

Stern   The back of the boat.

Spinnaker   Big symmetric light wind sail used for downwind sailing.

Squall   A sudden, local **gust** or storm, travel 20–25 **knots,** and usually come with rain and sometimes thunder and lightning.

Starboard   The right-hand side on a boat when facing forward

Styrofoam   A type of plastic. Used a lot in the Caribbean for food take away. Today it's a common sight on the Caribbean beaches.

Sustainable   Maintaining a situation for the benefit of future generations. It's where social, economy and environment are in balance. A restorative and regenerative world is the ideal.

Swell   When the wind blows for a duration of time, it moves water, resulting in swell. Waves in the ocean are referred to as swell.

Tack   To shift from one side to the other when going upwind– putting the bow through the wind.

The Bounty   Alias name for boat #1 that a bunch of hitch-sailors left just before sailing out for the Atlantic.

Tropical Storm   Wind in a tropical depression reaches 35 knots (9 Beaufort). Tropical storms are named.

Yankee   A high-clew and small overlapped **headsail.**

Water maker   Machine on board to make water. About 30% of the ocean crossing boats have one.

Wet boat   A boat that allows booze while sailing.

Winch   The round block on which lines can be put to lock the lines and increase tension.

Winching   The action of putting tension on a line with a winch handle

Winch handle   The stick to put on a winch to put more tension on the **sheets** and halyards that hold the sails.

Windward   The side where the wind comes from.

Windward Islands   The Caribbean islands chain closest to the Atlantic, from Martinique through Grenada.

ACKNOWLEDGEMENTS

Similar to hitching a ride across the Atlantic, I had no idea what I was getting myself into when I decided 'let's write a book.' The 'writing' part appeared to be the easy part. Research, editing, structuring, analysing, editing and sorting out the wild wild west when it comes to self-publishing has been as adventurous as sailing across the Atlantic with strangers.

When I decide to do something, I find a way. I found the way to accomplish this book. But not without the support of so many. I could write a whole book of 'thank you's' expressing gratitude to everyone who has helped to make this book happen in one way or another.

An ocean of gratitude to all. Huge thanks to all who supported me in the crowdfunding campaign for this book. You didn't only provide me with the funds I needed to finish this book, you have motivated me to make it happen! Thank you for the patience in the slightly too ambitious timeline I initially created.

Thank you to everyone who supported with the surveys, beta-reading, proofing, feedback, and launch of this book. Special thanks to Jess, Dirk, Ludo, and José for editing, and Paul for your support in the graphic department. You all played an enormous part in improving the quality of this book.

Thank you, Captains, who dared to take me on board for the Atlantic crossing, and to my fellow crew members for making it such pleasant rides.

Heartfelt thanks to everyone I've encountered during the Ocean Nomad adventures, both at sea and on land during the writing process. Hosts, travellers and friends from all walks of life, places, and cultures. Thank you for your generosity, hospitality and companionship. You made the experience.

Thank you to all those I have never actually met but who have been following me and supporting me with their motivating words on social media.

Marjo & Edwin, my ocean mentors, for your support, inspiration, feedback, and friendship. I'm thrilled to have you as writers of the foreword for this book!

And most important, my mum and dad, for your continuous belief, love, support and encouragement.

Finally, to you my reader, without whom this book would not exist.

ABOUT THE AUTHOR

Suzanne in five words: explorer, mermaid, environmentalist, creator, and ocean nomad.

For over ten years, she has been slow travelling around the world, of which the last four have been mostly under sail, while living a minimalistic nomad lifestyle as a location independent entrepreneur. She was born and raised in The Netherlands but feels at home anywhere there's water. Her globetrotting has brought her to +45 countries on five continents, on +30 sailboats and travelling +14.000 nautical miles across the seas.

Suzanne has one calling; the ocean. She is most inspired when exploring the beauty of the sea and island destinations through play and outdoor action. She's a 'do it yourself' oceanographer learning about the ocean and nature through sailing, kitesurfing and freediving adventures. She creates ocean related sustainability projects and adventure (sports) content, experiences and expeditions to not just sustain her life but to restore life in the ocean. Her ocean adventures have opened her eyes to the beauty of nature, but also to the challenges the oceans are facing. Her experiences have made Suzanne a passionate ocean advocate and activist.

She occasionally works as a tourism sustainability consultant with specialisation in coastal & island sustainability and tourism destination adaptation to climate change. She completed a Bachelor in Commerce and a cum-laude master in Tourism Destination Management. She published a study on Tourism destinations' vulnerability to climate change: Nature-based tourism in Vava'u, the Kingdom of Tonga in the Sage Journal of Tourism and Hospitality Research. She's an AIDA freedive instructor. Her dream is to sail around the world in her own built green sailboat while making as much impact as possible for a healthier ocean. Her favourite colour is blue. She's obsessed with coconuts and frangipani flowers.

With the book Ocean Nomad, she aims to encourage, inspire, and inform for ocean adventure, action and conservation.

CONNECT WITH SUZANNE ON Oceanpreneur.co and @oceanpreneur on Social Media.

BIBLIOGRAPHY

1. Schinas, J.D. Catching a ride across the Atlantic. *Yacht Mollymawk*. [Online] march 2011. http://www.yachtmollymawk.com/2011/03/hitch-hiking-across-the-atlantic/.

2. Schinas, J.D. Sailing with hippies (Hitching a ride part II). *Yacht Mollymawk*. [Online] August 2014. http://www.yachtmollymawk.com/2014/08/hitch-hiking-across-the-atlantic-pt2/.

3. Division, NOAA Hurricane Research. *FAQ: How many hurricanes have there been in each month?* [Online] 2017. http://www.aoml.noaa.gov/hrd/tcfaq/E17.html.

4. FOE (Friends of the Earth). Cruise ships flushed more than 1 billion gallons of sewage into oceans last year. *Friends of the Earth*. [Online] 2013. http://www.foe.org/news/news-releases/2013-10-cruise-ships-flushed-more-than-1-billion-gallons-of-sewage-last-year.

5. Beaufort, Francis. NOAA. *Beaufort Windscale*. [Online] 1805. http://www.spc.noaa.gov/faq/tornado/beaufort.html.

6. *Evidence for ship noise impacts on humpback whale foraging behaviour.* Blair H. B., Merchant N. D., Friedlaender A. S., Wiley D. N. & Parks S. E. 7, 2016, Biol. Lett. , Vol. 12.

7. *Tobacco Product Waste: An Environmental Approach to Reduce Tobacco Consumption.* Novotny, T.E. & Slaughter, E. Curr Envir Health Rpt (2014) 1: 208. doi:10.1007/s40572-014-0016-x.

8. *One World, One Ocean, One Mission.* Anderson, T. L. 1, Canada : MacEwan University, 2013, Earth Common Journal, Vol. 3.

9. NASA. NOAA Data Show 2016 Warmest Year on Record Globally. *National Aeronautics and Space Administration Goddard Institute for Space Studies.* [Online] 2017. https://www.giss.nasa.gov/research/news/20170118/.

10. IPCC (Intergovernmental Panel on Climate Change). *Climate Change 2014: Mitigation of Climate Change. Contribution of Working Group III to the Fifth Assessment.* . New York : Cambridge University Press., 2014.

11. *Global phytoplankton decline over the past century.* Boyce, D. G., Lewis, M. R. & Worm, B. 2010, Nature, Vol. 466, pp. 591–596.

12. Spratt, D. What would 3 degrees mean? [Online] 2010. http://www.climate-codered.org/2010/09/what-would-3-degrees-mean.html.

13. Ellen MacArthur Foundation and McKinsey & Company. The New Plastics Economy: Rethinking the Future of Plastics. [Online] World Economic Forum, 2016.

14. World Economic Forum, Ellen MacArthur Foundation and McKinsey & Company. , *The New Plastics Economy — Rethinking the future of plastics*. [Online] 2016. http://www.ellenmacarthurfoundation.org/publications.

15. Eriksen M, Lebreton LCM, Carson HS, Thiel M, Moore CJ, Borerro JC, et al. Plastic Pollution in the World's Oceans: More than 5 Trillion Plastic Pieces Weighing over 250,000 Tons Afloat at Sea. [Online] 2014.

16. Sherrington, C. Plastics in the marine environment. *Eunomia*. [Online] 2016. http://www.eunomia.co.uk/reports-tools/plastics-in-the-marine-environment/.

17. Eriksen, M., Thiel, M., & Lebreton, L. Nature of Plastic Marine Pollution in the Subtropical Gyres. 2017.

18. IUCN. Primary Microplastics in the Oceans:. [Online] 2017. https://portals.iucn.org/library/sites/library/files/documents/2017-002.pdf.

19. Oceancleanwash. [Online] http://oceancleanwash.org/.

20. Chelsea M. Rochman, Eunha Hoh, Tomofumi Kurobe & Swee J. Teh. *Ingested plastic transfers hazardous chemicals to fish and induces hepatic stress*. Scientific Reports 3, Article number: 3263.

21. *Toxic Metals in Polyethylene Plastic Litter*. Nakashima, E., Isobe, A., Kako, S., Magome, S., Deki, N., Itai, T., & Takahashi, S. [ed.] X. Guo, N. Yoshie, N. Fujii, I I. C. Handoh, A. Isobe, & S. Tanabe (Eds.) In K. Omori. Tokyo : TERRAPUB, 2011, Interdisciplinary studies on environmental chemistry: Modeling and analysis of marine environmental problems. , Vol. 5.

22. Plymouth University. Plastics in the marine environment. [Online] https://www1.plymouth.ac.uk/research/mberc/Research/Marine%20pollution/Pages/ Plastics.aspx.

23. *Microplastics in bivalves cultured for human consumption*. Cauwenberghe (van), L., Janssen, C. 2014, Environmental Pollution, Vol. 193, pp. 65-70. DOI: 10.1016/j.envpol.2014.06.010.

24. *Plastic Degradation and Its Environmental Implications with Special Reference to Poly(ethylene terephthalate)* . Hayden K. Webb, Jaimys Arnott, Russell J. Crawford and Elena P. Ivanova *. 1, 2013, Polymers, Vol. 5. http://www.mdpi.com/2073-4360/5/1/1/htm.

25. Macfadyen, G., Huntington, T., & Cappell, R. *Abandoned, lost or otherwise discarded fishing gear*. Regional Seas Reports and Studies 185, FAO Fisheries and Aquaculture Technical Paper, UNEP. 2009. United Nations Environment Programme and Food and Agriculture Organization of the United Nations, "Abandoned, lost or otherwise discarded fishing gear", UNEP Regional Seas Reports and Studies, No. 185; FAO Fisheries and Aquaculture Technical

Paper, No. 523 (Rome, 2009). Available from www.unep.org/regionalseas/ marinelitter/publications/docs/Marine_Litter_Abandoned_Lost_Fishing_ Gear.pdf. 523.

26. *Tropical dead zones and mass mortalities on coral reefs.* Altieri, A. H., Harrison, S. B., Seemann, J., Collin, R., Diaz, R. J., & Knowlton, N. (2017). Tropical dead zones and mass mortalities on coral reefs. Proceedings of the National Academy of Sciences. 14, 2017, Proceedings of the National Academy of Sciences, Vol. 114, pp. 3660-3665.

27. Earle, Sylvia. A. *The world is Blue: How our fate and the ocean's are one.* Washington : National Geographic, 2009.

28. United Nations Food and Agriculture Organization (FAO). General situation of world fish stocks. [Online] http://www.fao.org/newsroom/common/ ecg/1000505/en/stocks.pdf.

29. Kaledjian, A., Brogan, G., Lowell, B., Warrenchuk, J., Enticknap, B., Shester, G., ... Cano- Stucco, D. *Wasted catch: Unsolved problems in U.S. fisheries.* s.l. : OCEANA, 2014.

30. Voedingscentrum. Voedingscentrum. *Vis.* [Online] 2017. http://www.voedingscentrum.nl/encyclopedie/vis.aspx.

31. *Impacts of Biodiversity Loss on Ocean Ecosystem Services.* Worm, Boris, et al. 5800, 2006, Science, Vol. 314, pp. 787-790.

32. Protect Planet Ocean. *Global facts about MPAs and marine reserves.* [Online] http://www.protectplanetocean.org/collections/introduction/introbox/ globalmpas/ introduction-item.html.

33. Atlas of Marine Protection. How much of our ocean is protected? *MPAtlas.* [Online] http://www.mpatlas.org/.

34. IUCN, & UNEP-WCMC. The official MPA map. *Protect Planet Ocean.* [Online] 2013. http://www.protectplanetocean.org/official_mpa_map.

35. Worldometer. World Population. *Worldometer.* [Online] http://www.worldometers.info/world-population/.

36. UN. *http://esa.un.org/unpd/wpp/Publications/Files/Key_Findings_ WPP_2015.pdf.* [Online]

37. *The climate mitigation gap: education and government recommendations miss the most effective individual actions.* Nicholas, Seth Wynes and Kimberly A. 7, 2017, Environmental Research Letters, Vol. 12. http://iopscience.iop.org/ article/10.1088/1748-9326/aa7541.

38. EWG. The Trouble With Ingredients in Sunscreens. [Online] http://www. ewg.org/sunscreen/report/the-trouble-with-sunscreen-chemicals/.

39. Oppenlander, Richard. Biodiversity and Food Choice: A Clarification. *Comfortably Unaware*. [Online] 2012. http://comfortablyunaware.com/blog/biodiversity-and-food-choice-a-clarification/.

40. Jusková, I. Thesis Study. What's in your carbon foodprint? *Isabela Jusko*. [Online] 2017. http://www.isabellajusko.ca/thesis#0.

41. Cowspiracy. *The Facts*. [Online] http://www.cowspiracy.com/facts/.

42. Everaert, C. (Executive producer), Soeters, K., & Zwanikken, G. (Directors). *Meat the truth [Documentary]*. Alalena Media Productions., 2008.

43. Seagrass Grow. [Online] http://www.SeagrassGrow.org.

44. Science World Report. Cigarette Filter Pollution Drastically Impacts the Environment with Leaching Chemicals. *Science World Report*. [Online] 2014. http://www.scienceworldreport.com/articles/14506/20140506/cigarette-filter-pollution-drastically-impacts-environment-leaching-chemicals.htm.

45. Dickens, Jill. Sailing with hippies (Hitching a ride part II). [Online] August 2014. http://www.yachtmollymawk.com/2014/08/hitch-hiking-across-the-atlantic-pt2/.

46. Rhein, M., S.R. Rintoul, S. Aoki, E. Campos, D. Chambers, R.A. Feely, S. Gulev, G.C. Johnson, S.A. Josey, A. Kostianoy, C. Mauritzen, D. Roemmich, L.D. Talley and F. Wang,. Observations: Ocean. *Climate Change 2013: The Physical Science Basis. Contribution of Working Group I to the Fifth Assessment Report of the Intergovernmental Panel on Climate Change*. Cambridge, United Kingdom and New York, NY, USA : Cambridge University Press, 2013, pp. 255-315. [Stocker, T.F., D. Qin, G.-K. Plattner, M. Tignor, S.K. Allen, J. Boschung, A. Nauels, Y. Xia, V. Bex and P.M. Midgley (eds.)]..

~ N O T E S ~

~ N O T E S ~

~ N O T E S ~

~ N O T E S ~

Printed in Great Britain
by Amazon